INTERPERSONAL

1010101010101010101010101010101010101010101010101010101010101

DIVIDE

INTERPERSONAL

1010101010101010101010101010101010101010101010101010101010101010101

DIVIDE

THE SEARCH FOR COMMUNITY IN A TECHNOLOGICAL AGE

MICHAEL BUGEJA
Iowa State University

New York   Oxford
OXFORD UNIVERSITY PRESS
2005

Oxford University Press

Oxford   New York
Auckland   Bangkok   Buenos Aires   Cape Town   Chennai
Dar es Salaam   Delhi   Hong Kong   Istanbul   Karachi   Kolkata
Kuala Lumpur   Madrid   Melbourne   Mexico City   Mumbai   Nairobi
São Paulo   Shanghai   Taipei   Tokyo   Toronto

Copyright © 2005 by Oxford University Press, Inc.

Published by Oxford University Press, Inc.
198 Madison Avenue, New York, New York 10016
www.oup.com

Oxford is a registered trademark of Oxford University Press

Library of Congress Cataloging-in-Publication Data
Bugeja, Michael J.
   Interpersonal divide : the search for community in a technological age / Michael
Bugeja.
      p. cm.
   Includes bibliographical references and index.
   ISBN 0-19-517340-6 (cloth) — ISBN 0-19-517339-2 (pbk.)
   1. Technology—Social aspects.   2. Mass media—Social aspects.   3. Social perception.
   4. Interpersonal relations.   5. Community.   I. Title.
   HM846.B84 2005
   303.48'33—dc22   2004049592

Printing number: 9 8 7 6 5 4 3 2 1

Printed in the United States of America
on acid-free paper

For Shane Michael

CONTENTS

       The Real and Virtually Real   81
       The Dawning of Mass Media   84
       The Advent of Marketing   88
       Vision and Values   91

5   Blurring of Identity and Place   98
       The Disembodied Self   98
       Mapping the Consumer Genome   104
       Moral and Social Upheaval   109
       Endangered Habitats   114

6   The Medium Is the Moral   122
       McLuhan, Revisited   122
       The New Generation Gap   129
       The Unnatural Order of Things   135

7   Icons and Caricatures   142
       Icons and Idols   142
       Icons and Advertising   148
       Mentors and Caricatures   153

8   Living Three-Dimensionally   161
       Virtues and Environments   161
       The Moral Importance of Place   163
       Dimensions of Community   171

9   Repatriation to the Village   179
       Ethical Inventories   179
       Foci of Our Discontent   183
       Mis-Mediated Messages   187
       A Place in the Village   191

       Notes   197
       Bibliography   215
       Index   219

PREFACE

The title of this book, *Interpersonal Divide*, alludes to the work of Pippa Norris, Harvard University political scientist, who defines the popular phrase "digital divide" as having three distinct components: the *global* divide associated with Internet access between industrialized and developing nations; the *social* divide between those with and without access in each nation; and the *democratic* divide between those who do and who do not use communication technology to participate in public life.[1] Those divides exist and deserve our attention; however, as governments and corporations collaborate to bridge those divides, for the common good and/or for profit, another more ominous void has developed, eroding relationships at home and at work. The phrase *interpersonal divide* concerns the social gap that develops when individuals misperceive reality because of media overconsumption and misinterpret others because of technology overuse. This book analyzes "the interpersonal divide" from different vantage points (ethical, pop cultural, historical, corporate, familial, and communal), detailing the overselling of media and technology and the impact on our behavior when we spend too much time in virtual rather than real habitats.

In documenting the void in our homes, workplaces, and communities, *Interpersonal Divide* traces media history to show how other generations coped with similar problems during great technological change. It also:

- Shows how each medium changes the message, resulting in misinterpretation of motives, causing deep rifts in personal and professional relationships.
- Discusses content from an applied ethics perspective, rather than from a self-help or theoretical one.
- Focuses on the importance of community in our lifelong quest for acceptance.

The approach here is general. As the sociologist Manuel Castells writes in *The Power of Identity*, a topic as broad and interdisciplinary as the topic of *Interpersonal Divide*, "*This is not a book about books.* Thus, I will not discuss existing theories on each topic, or cite every possible source on issues presented here."[2] Such an approach, writes Castells, would be pretentious and superficial. Indeed, the intent in any multidisciplinary work is to explain complex truths in plain language rather than to validate those truths via complex language. Journalist James Howard Kunstler emphasizes the importance of this in his watershed book on the erosion of community in our time, *Home from Nowhere*, arguing that "so many problems with our everyday environment are caused by the over-specialization of trained specialists unwilling to look at the bigger picture beyond the narrow purview of their specialty."[3] Also, concepts expressed here have been thoroughly researched but are presented without an abundance of statistics, tables, or numerical data that make universal ideas seem topical or obsolete. Jargon is eschewed for the same reason. Lexicons of media and technology change as rapidly as gadgets do. That is why, whenever possible, topics are defined generally rather than theoretically, engaging as many as possible in the conversation for as long a time as possible.

For instance, the phrase "media and technology" means different things to different people, depending on lifestyles and professions. Online gamers have their own views and vocabularies, as do consumer information advocates and information scientists. Thus, common meanings will be emphasized whenever possible in *Interpersonal Divide*. The word *media* means "the channels through which messages are delivered." *Technology* means "the mechanism delivering those messages." The focus is on the use and marketing of technology and media, rather than on the infrastructure of communication systems or computer networks. Those change rapidly to expand access, bridging the myriad digital divides. In sum, *Interpersonal Divide* discusses media and technology that will be with us for some time to come: mobile phones, television, personal computers, the Internet, and so on. The impact of those technologies will not change, even though the equipment that delivers them will.

Moreover, a broad, interdisciplinary approach allows for *synthesis*—the process of combining concepts usually not associated with each other, to envision deeper truths. That is why *Interpersonal Divide* brings together a number of intellectual strands that do not usually turn up in discussions of technology and media consumption. The objective is to assemble a new mosaic of the modern era that synthesizes such literatures as media studies, self-help and time management, character education and applied ethics, and science and technology studies. *Interpersonal Divide* postulates that media and technology are affecting millions in similar, negative ways. If so, those ways should be extant in a variety of activities and disciplines, primarily ones impacting communities. This methodology proved effective in Robert Putnam's best-selling book, *Bowling Alone: The Collapse and Revival of American Community*, in which he sought "as diverse a range of evidence as possible on continuities and change in American social life," theorizing that if "the transformation that I discern is as broad and deep as I believe it to be, it ought to show up in many different places, so I have cast a broad net."[4]

The "net" here also is broad, but the focus is narrow—an exploration of and response to our predicament of lost community in a mediated society. While other divides are closing in North America because of increased access, with multiple televisions and/or personal computers accumulating in households of every social bracket, as we shall see, the interpersonal impact of these devices has yet to be fully assessed, even though warnings surfaced as early as 1970. In his visionary book, *The Information Machines*, journalist and educator Ben Bagdikian wrote:

> It has taken two hundred years of the Industrial Revolution for men to realize that they are not very good at predicting the consequences of their inventions: to the surprise of almost everyone, automobiles changed sex habits. Information devices are no exception: machines for mass communications produce unexpected changes in the relationship of the individual to his society.[5]

This book documents and assesses changes resulting from the Technology Revolution of the 1990s. There was a similar assessment of television in the 1970s. In her popular 1977 book about TV's impact on society, *The Plug-In Drug*, Marie Winn asserts, "I am not an enemy of the medium nor do I believe it is devoid of value. My aim, instead, is to promote a new way of thinking about TV."[6] That is the aim here, too, concerning media and technology and their impact on community. Neither is this book a work of social panic, in which proponents of old media argue fervently against new media the way that newspaper publishers argued against the telegraph and later as telegraph companies argued against the telephone, as we shall learn in Chapter Four, recounting the historical impact of media and technology. The impulse of omnipresent proponents of technology reading *Interpersonal Divide* will be to dismiss it as a work of social panic, especially because the theme is "community" as found in physical place. "It is not surprising that the Internet is feared for its ability to remove individuals psychologically from their social settings (even though the phone, the television, the book and other media-based technocultures share this trait),"[7] writes educator Lelia Green in *Communication, Technology and Society.* What Green and other communication scholars routinely fail to assess, however, is the *cumulative* impact on society of media and technology proliferation and the escalating psychological impact of a technoculture that has identified digital gadgetry as the means to economic prosperity.

The philosophical analysis of that impact in *Interpersonal Divide* is an act of criticism and, as such, is covered by fair use standards of U.S. copyright law. Although the works of several scholars are cited here, only as much content as necessary has been used to make a point or clarify an issue. No book, for instance, is quoted beyond two hundred words and no article, beyond 5 percent of total content. On-line citations have been accessed during a period between 2001 and 2004, and copies of each site have been provided to the editors. Links associated with some citations may cease to work in the future because domains lapse or Web page formats change—issues associated with the very subject of this *book*, a medium that endures in libraries, once the intellectual hub of American communities. In her book *Cyberliteracy*, a rhetorical analysis of the Internet, Laura J. Gurak articulates a similar methodology. She quotes from books to make an observation or embellish an argument and cites works according to fair use.[8] "If anything," she writes, "examples used in this book bring positive value to the original by pointing readers to these sources."[9] (Books cited in *Interpersonal Divide* also are recommended as outside reading at the end of each chapter and in a complete bibliography at the end of the book.) Because hers also is an act of criticism, Gurak has not chosen to seek permissions, especially on use of Web material:

> For one, the Web pages contained herein are used for criticism. In addition, when a person or organization makes a Web site available to the world, that person or organization knows full well that the

resulting Web page will be uploaded onto thousands of computer screens, linked to by other Web sites, and printed out on desktop laser printers. None of these uses require written permission, and a book, especially an act of criticism, is hardly different.[10]

That is also the case in *Interpersonal Divide*.

Interpersonal Divide hopes to inspire dialogue and introspection with journal exercises, discussion and paper ideas, and suggested readings at the end of each chapter. The exercises, ideas, and selected readings are meant to develop awareness about the import of interpersonal communication in the high-tech media age. Certainly, the topic merits such attention, for media and technology are here to stay and will determine how we will live, interact, learn, and create in the future. Conversely, our search for community is universal and unique to our species. Face-to-face interaction—at home, work, and school and in public—remains a powerful mode of communication. As society examines the interpersonal divide, seeking resolutions, people will influence the future direction of media and technology as much as they will influence people. That relationship must be dual and beneficial, however. The Luddite's estrangement is as perilous as the marketer's spam or the guru's infomercial. Media and technology offer opportunities to enhance knowledge and establish global partnerships, disseminating data and information that can enhance human rights and participation. While it is true that media and technology also blur the line between home and work, with gadgets interrupting us at all hours every day, that phenomenon requires us to develop a common ethic and global outlook. Because media and technology are mobile, our ethical values must be, too, transcending geographic place. Our standards at home must apply as well at work. As we will learn in the Introduction, "The Need to Belong," not only must we discern what TV programming to consume and what PC programs to operate, and so on, we also must reaffirm the value of civic virtue and public life, revitalizing our families, workplaces, and communities. In that vein *Interpersonal Divide* assesses how, where, and when we use media and technology and what, why, and to whom we communicate instantaneously on demand, usually without a thought about the effect on conscience, consciousness, and core relationships.

ACKNOWLEDGMENTS

The author wishes to recognize colleagues who have deepened his conscience and expanded his consciousness during research and preparation of *Interpersonal Divide*, including Lady Borton, Daniela Dimitrova, Elizabeth Graham, Marilyn Greenwald, Heidi Nyland, Josep Rota, Shiwani Srivastava, Robert Stewart, and Guido Stempel. No book reaches its potential without constructive criticism. Comments and suggestions by external reviewers—Mark Kesselman (Columbia University), Bruce Umbaugh (Webster University), Patricia Raybon (University of Colorado at Boulder), Mary Helen Brown (Auburn University), Judith Sheppard (Auburn University), Nilanjana Bardhan (Southern Illinois University), Matthew Smith (Wittenberg University), and Wendy H. Papa (Central Michigan University)—and the copyediting and production assistance of Charles Naylor and Leslie Anglin are deeply appreciated. Finally, the author is especially grateful for the support of Niko Pfund, vice president and publisher at Oxford University Press, and the guidance of Peter Labella, senior editor, who helped focus the book on paramount issues of our high-tech media era.

The Need to Belong

> When Americans, depressed by the scary places where they work and dwell, contemplate some antidote, they often conjure up the image of the American small town. . . . For the idea of a small town represents a whole menu of human values that the gigantism of corporate enterprise has either obliterated or mocked.
>
> —JAMES HOWARD KUNSTLER, *The Geography of Nowhere*

Thought, Word, and Deed

We crave one thing, regardless of race, gender, culture, or social class: *acceptance*. The need to belong is powerful because, introvert or extrovert, we are social creatures with a conscience—the ethical inkblot upon which others and we ourselves make indelible marks. We etch more than outcomes and consequences of our actions there, involving others; we imprint our *thoughts* about actions before even taking them. From karma to Christ, this universal concept of conscience implores us to be mindful about our every *thought, word, and deed*. The conscience is the psyche's "inner ear" and vibrates with emotion—at times pleasant, at times horrifically unpleasant—in response to thoughts, words, and deeds before they are uttered or acted on and then afterward, so we can assess outcome, impact, and possible motive. When we concede, *We know in our hearts that we are right (or wrong)*, we refer to this inner compass. When we acknowledge, *We have lost our way*, we mean that we have not followed this compass. Although others may influence us, the way artists are influenced by masters (role models) or by dilettantes (idols), we are the primary sculptors of conscience; through it, we create magna opera or rock piles of our lives.

According to existential philosophy, we come into the world alone and we leave it alone. Birth and death are bookmarks of the human condition. While entrances and exits on earth may be solitary, our time

1

on the planet is social and physical, from the paths that we travel in our search for acceptance to the communities that we call home. Communities provide opportunities for acceptance, serving as "gathering place" or "proving ground." We meet friends, partners, merchants, and neighbors there. Through our interactions, we learn "people skills" and develop values and character.

We thrive in real habitats. Social activist Parker J. Palmer believes the most public place is the street, for there we meet strangers with whom we interact, even when nobody speaks. People send a message through the channel of their bodies in real place, acknowledging that "we occupy the same territory, belong to the same human community."[11] Throughout human history, children have played in neighborhoods, adults have interacted with others there, and entrepreneurs have done business nearby. True, suburban sprawl may have changed the nature of games, interactions, and commerce. Recreation centers may have replaced public parks; developments, homogenized housing; and mega malls, dislodged Main Streets. However, our relationships in these places for the most part remained social and genuine because we still had to communicate with strangers face-to-face. That fact remains pivotal when contemplating ramifications of the interpersonal divide. Even Palmer in his enlightened 1981 book, *The Company of Strangers,* could not foresee the erosion of community beyond the concourses of the mega mall which, he believed, had replaced public streets, deemed unsafe. When people perceive real habitat to be unsafe, Palmer warned, they withdraw from it, and it becomes unsafe. "Space is kept secure not primarily by good lighting or police power but by the presence of a healthy public life,"[12] he writes. The mall may not be the best public space in which to interact authentically with strangers, but it is better than doing so on-line, shopping the digital malls of Amazon.com and eBay. Increasingly in this manner, media and technology displace many of us from physical to virtual environs. Indeed, these days even in the public street a stranger seeking directions in a new city may have to wait patiently for a passerby without a cell phone, headset, or handheld device or risk interrupting another's virtual reality, the new social faux pas. The impact of living this way is cumulative, blurring boundaries and identities and occupying so much of our time that we have little left at day's end to devote to hometowns and each other.

Yet the need to belong is as urgent as ever, if not more so. According to Palmer, "More than ever we need the process of public life to renew our sense of belonging to one another," without which we pay a terrible price, losing "our sense of comfort and at-homeness in the world."[13] As a result, we yearn for acceptance and routinely look to media and technology to bridge the interpersonal void. Electronic communication promised to enhance relationships with family and friends, to increase productivity at work, and to provide us with more leisure time at home; instead, our personal and professional relationships often falter because communication systems alter *value* systems, with the primary emphasis on profit and entertainment; meanwhile, television viewing devours leisure time—a trend Palmer recognized in the early 1980s.[14] Consequently the search for acceptance is apt to be done sitting down in front of screens and monitors. That undermines the vitality of community where values—from civility to trustworthiness—are developed through face-to-face interaction, for even networks of virtuous individuals, when isolated, cannot advance civic virtue.[15] People deprived of interpersonal contact eventually suspect rather than trust others because their perception of reality has been skewed, prompting misinterpretation of messages and motives, thereby harming relationships.[16]

The term *community* in the Internet age is as likely to mean "network" as "hometown." Corporate communities also are "ecosystems," using a biological model based on mutual benefit—species that help each other, the way bees help flora, by pollinating them. Individual companies may not even compete with each other for turf but depend on each other according to the function of their infrastructures. Ecosystems change partners according to acquisition or corporate symbiosis, so existing systems may not remain intact for long. By way of example, at the end of the twentieth century, news magazine *Time* relied on entertainer Warner (and vice versa) and merged, attracting the interest of America Online. AOL needed content and relied on Time Warner to supply it in exchange for an electronic delivery platform for on-line users. The result? AOL Time Warner. This mega merger heralded "the dawn of a new media age in which former upstart companies of the Internet could dare to acquire powerful, traditional media companies,"[17] write the authors of *Media Debates: Great Issues for the Digital Age.* Everette E. Dennis and John C. Merrill also note other mergers establishing ecosystems which, in turn, have established the convention of such systems in society, including CBS/Westinghouse/Viacom and Disney/CapCities/ABC.

Media ecosystems as symbolized by AOL Time Warner have eroded constitutional freedoms in addition to basic tenets of the American entrepreneurial dream, especially as all this relates to community. We must remember that the blessings of liberty as articulated in the Bill of Rights were responsible for economic prosperity in America. Prosperity has not led to expansion of those freedoms in a so-called information society whose technologies, including the Internet, have been developed in large part by the U.S. military and intrude into our private affairs each day to such extent that most consumers either allow the invasion or purchase more technology to rid us of the pop-ups and spam of our screened and monitored lives.

Too many of us have traded the blessings of liberty founded in the community for the premiums of technology founded in the economy. As Dennis and Merrill remind us,

> For years media critics like Ben Bagdikian, former dean of journalism at the University of California–Berkeley, had warned about the negative effect of media concentration, especially on newspapers and broadcasting, where independent, family owned papers and broadcast stations fell in to the hands of big chains like Gannett, Thompson and Newhouse. Although these admonitions seem almost quaint compared to today's really big deals, as one critic called them, they nevertheless reflect deeply held American values that bigness is bad and diversity is good. People often equate freedom of expression and individualism with small-scale social institutions that are close to the people and accessible to all.[18]

Large-scale ecosystems symbolized by AOL Time Warner threaten our way of life. Because economic climates are volatile over time, AOL Time Warner may continue in its current formation or morph again into another ecosystem. But that is not the point. The problem with ecosystems has been priorities. Information technology has altered practices of American business, which prided itself on personalized customer service. That era is ending. Typically the focus is on serving interests of the high-tech corporate infrastructure rather than interests of the patron. "Customer service," at best, is usually digital and automated. As such, these ecosystems not only impede communication but also distort our sense of community—even the definition of that term. For instance, AOL Time Warner, like most such systems, promised in its on-line mission statement to "improve our communities—taking pride in serving the public interest as well as the interests of our share-holders."[19] Serving both interests seems like a "conflict of interest." As all corporations must answer to shareholders, the operative words here are "communities" and "public interest." What communities—our real or our virtual ones? What public interest, and where? AOL Time Warner also promised patrons to promote "an ethic of volun-teerism and civic engagement" so that "everyone can share in the bene-fits of the Internet Revolution." That seems like another conflict of interest. Volunteerism and civic engagement are rooted in physical place—not on the Internet. Microsoft, another such ecosystem, so vast at the start of the twenty-first century that the U.S. government filed an antitrust action, also waxed eloquently about the benefits of "community" in its 2001 on-line values statement: "Microsoft and its employees recognize that we have the responsibility, and opportu-nity, to contribute to the communities in which we live, in ways that make a meaningful difference to people's lives."[20] Who, precisely, is the "we" in that statement and where can we find them other than at Microsoft.com?

This book does not focus on Microsoft or AOL Time Warner. Those companies and their competitors may or may not remain intact or in business in the foreseeable future. Or they may continue to wield vast influence. The contention here is that they and other high-tech eco-systems have helped displace us at home and at work, intensifying our need to belong. As a consequence, most of us think of ourselves as consumers rather than as citizens of a great nation whose strength emanates from social, familial, and community bonds. How did we devalue our collective voice in our quest for acceptance?

The Search for Acceptance

The search for acceptance is intricately linked to the search for com-munity. "Acceptance" is the abstraction—an inner longing for some-thing greater than one's self. "Community" is the external source that provides fulfillment or reaffirmation. Acceptance is associated with the conscience; community, with consciousness. Both are part of the human condition. Past generations found acceptance in community because our interactions there, however challenging or intolerant, taught us essential interpersonal skills. We knew when to look someone in the eyes and "stand ground" and, equally as important, when *not* to do so. We knew how to read body language and tone of voice and adjust for them according to time, place, and occasion. We did this because we practiced. As children, we learned that we could stick out our tongues at playmates during recess but not during class. And it mattered at whom we wagged tongues on the school ground. Some would overlook the gesture and others, overreact. We refined our social skills growing up, along with our values—most of which concern treating others as we wish to be treated, that is, the Golden Rule. Schools reinforced that universal lesson. Extended families did, too. And if those families were dysfunctional, we could find mentors in the neighborhood. Now families, schools, neighborhoods, and workplaces are wired, and so are we, feeling displaced in homes and home offices, even though we communicate at ever faster processor speeds.

The first chapter of *Interpersonal Divide*, "Displacement in the Global Village," deals with this displacement. In attempting to resolve the various digital divides, society has unwittingly created an interpersonal one. That void warrants as much attention as the electronic *ones because each impacts the other.* A society with weak interpersonal skills cannot influence future innovations in media and technology so that they advance priorities of community, from access to education to civic participation. We will continue to spend too much time in virtual rather than real environments—e-mailing, chatting, browsing, computing, and consuming media—increasingly isolated from others, inundated with offers to buy products or services to sate the need to belong. The acquisition of things is a poor substitute for acceptance, just as cyberspace is a poor substitute for community. Such isolation complicates life, not because life has become complex in reality, but because we have forgotten how to cope with the rigors of the human condition.

Chapter Two, "The Human Condition," gauges the effect of this phenomenon on our conscience and consciousness. The conscience is our inner knowing of right and wrong involving others; consciousness, an awareness of our place in physical space, hometown to cosmos. The conscience demands that we love and be loved by others, that we share meaningful relationships with others, and that we contribute to community. Consciousness in part requires that we foresee the consequences of our thoughts, words, and deeds, enabling us to assess past actions and plan future ones. However, in many of us, overuse of technology and overconsumption of mass media have dulled conscience and deadened consciousness, forcing us to look for fulfillment in all the wrong cyber places. Instead of seeking acceptance in community with others, the psychologically disenfranchised seek self-help, only to encounter more media and technology—along with marketing ploys—associated with the most popular programs and seminars.

The hype of self-help is covered in Chapter Three, "Habits of a High-Tech Age." Marketing, rather than common sense, drives the multibillion dollar self-improvement industry that typically ignores the human condition. We all have the same life lessons. As gracefully as possible, we must accept the various beginnings and endings of biological existence: from childhood to childbirth, from middle age to maturity and beyond. People who spend too much time in virtual rather than real environments typically cannot cope with such a challenge. Instead they develop the "Seven Habits of Highly Mediated People," which include "listening for motive instead of for meaning" and "coveting what we lack and losing what we have." Add to these an accelerated biological clock, an ominous feeling, and—another product of the high-tech media age—that time is running out, even as our lifespans lengthen. That defies "common sense," another concept associated with community and one that defines the American psyche, beginning with Thomas Paine. Media and technology, billed as fonts of information, distort common sense.

Imagine traveling to a community and stopping at the visitors' information center, asking about sites of interest. Instead of reliable data, you get gossip and conjecture. When you complain, you are told that "information" is not necessary grounded in fact. "That doesn't make sense," you say. In virtual domains, it *does*. According to historian Theodore Roszak, "In the past, the word (information) has always denoted a sensible statement that conveyed a recognizable, verbal meaning, usually what we would call a fact."[21] In the high-tech media age, information has lost its common-sense definition, Roszak notes, and has come to mean electronic messages that can be counted, catalogued, encoded, and decoded. The depreciation of information not only impacts education as Internet use expands, especially in schools, but also the reliability of journalism, with the audience typically unable to decipher fact from factoid and factoid from fiction. Worse, some do not recognize those distinctions. Many more do not care.

Society has faced similar challenges in earlier times of great technological change. Chapter Four documents the impact of media and tech-

nology during the nineteenth century, when mass media and marketing were conceived, along with the telegraph, telephone, and radio. The
telegraph has been called "the Victorian Internet." More important,
perhaps, for a basis of comparison, Western Union owned the telegraph
wires upon which the Associated Press relied to communicate the
news—an ecosystem prototype. Brand marketing also evolved, along
with chain newspapers, whose owners bought out competitors and
created magazines out of them, including the *Ladies Home Journal* and
the *Saturday Evening Post*—not necessarily to serve the public, but to
provide a forum for national brand merchandise. From this perspective, readers can fathom the foci of their discontent.

The blurring of identity and place has also resulted in social and
moral upheavals. Because of media and technology, work now intrudes
on family life to such extent that we literally have lost touch with our
boundaries, roles, and identities. The phenomenon of access via communication devices is unprecedented in human history, according to a
report in the *Sacramento Bee* newspaper, which states:

> The ubiquitous nature of access made possible by these devices blurs
> the lines between personal and work time. When electronic com-
> munications become a substitute for face-to-face connections, valued
> relationships can suffer.[22]

The experience has become so widespread that a new, primarily tech-
nology-based self-help industry emerged in the early twenty-first century, called "life-balance training," to help people distinguish between
work and play and thereby control stress. Chapter Five deals with this
social upheaval and documents the impact of the Internet revolution
on the family, the educational system, the health care industry, and
crime. When we hurt, we shop—pursuing acceptance through possessions rather than through principles. Marketing facilitates that, using
high-tech, invasive methods that promise to infiltrate our homes with
more precision and alacrity as technologies converge with mass media. In the recent past, marketers mapped "the consumer genome,"
violating privacy and other values to sell product in the name of the
bottom line. That may be the only "line" whose meaning has not
blurred in the wake of new technologies.

The medium is the message, social critic Marshall McLuhan proclaimed in the 1960s, envisioning a global village. Instead we have in-
herited a *global mall.* McLuhan is still viewed as an "Internet

Nostradamus" who prophesied worldwide civic engagement, thanks to technology. McLuhan never foresaw the Web but based his idealism on TV, believing that patterns of low-density lines and dots forced the human brain to interact with the picture tube, to make sense of moving images. His biological model, upon which so much scholarship is based, is flawed scientifically and metaphorically; Chapter Six advances a physics paradigm to explain and explore cyberspace, assessing the impact of virtual habitat, which puts a person in two places simultaneously so that consciousness is split and content of messages, altered.

McLuhan embraced technology, in part because of the antiestablishment baby boomer generation. In the 1960s activists deplored capitalism and demanded reliable information about the Vietnam War in particular and the government in general. Many of those baby boomers would become dot.com moguls in the 1990s and still believe that technology enhances the "information economy." That phrase is used so often that few question its generic meaning. Historian Roszak notes the emptiness of "exuberant talk" about "the information economy" or "the information society."[23] However, he and other social critics fail to assess the gap between baby boomers who associate media and technology with *information* and their children ("X-ers") and/or grandchildren ("Web-sters") who associate media and technology with *entertainment*. Likewise, entertainment is now associated with media and technology, from equipment and upgrades required to download everything from digital movies (removing patrons from public theaters) to on-line gaming (removing enthusiasts from public arcades). "This is all very good news for the elites controlling enterprises involved in the supply of new ICT products and services, as the message neatly complements the sales and promotional efforts of their own marketing divisions,"[24] writes Paschal Preston in *Reshaping Communications*, which also criticizes the prevailing ideas of the so-called "Information Society." One such idea advanced by members of the baby boomer generation is that their children utilize media and technology to access education, thereby achieving social mobility. That generational fallacy is another digital divide, eroding relationships at home and work along with the interpersonal skills needed to sustain community.

The emphasis on entertainment has given us icons and caricatures, rather than role models and mentors. Media and technology tend to flatten perception of community, prodding us to believe that every person and issue has two sides rather than many. Such oversimplification affects the conscience because we no longer can intuit ethics—whose values emanate from community, based on the social norms of our species. When community is displaced, so are our morals. We may yearn for reliable mentors, readily found in real rather than virtual domains, but interact with them and adopt their values so infrequently that we no longer know how to live "three-dimensionally."

"Living Three-Dimensionally" is the title and focus of the next-to-last chapter. People pursue acceptance to be at peace with and to feel empowered among others. Peace is not the absence of conflict but the inner knowing that one can meet any challenge. Empowerment is the realization of priorities and the recognition of options to realize goals. Those who live three-dimensionally measure the quality of their world:

- *linearly*, in the time spent interacting meaningfully with others in community, from clerks at the checkout counter to VIPs at the country club.
- *horizontally*, in valued relationships that transcend race, sex, and class, acknowledging the insights of others across a broad social spectrum.
- *deeply*, in contributions made to community through those interactions and relationships.

Interpersonal contact is three-dimensional, subject to time, participants, and place. Such contact is a basic component of community for the vast majority of world cultures. In our culture, it can convey ethical values to future generations—values, incidentally, that can shape media and technology in a dual, beneficial association with society. Communication scholars have long noted that "orality," or unmediated discourse, "creates and sustains cultural values, concretizes the unique understandings embedded within those values, and transmits those values from one generation to the next."[25]

To live otherwise is to allow media and technology to alter perception of the world and our place in it. People who consume too much media and use technology too often may develop a myopic outlook on life, viewing issues and events:

- *flatly*, characterizing people as worthy or unworthy, based on their race, class, religion, culture, politic, or belief.

- *episodically*, measuring happiness on outcomes of incidents over which we have little control.

We do have control over ethics and actions. The last chapter of *Interpersonal Divide* addresses that. To repatriate to the village—to families, workplaces, and hometowns—we must analyze the role of technology and media in our lives. We need to temper use. But we also need to use technology and media, astonishing tools, to advance priorities and contribute to the common good. As philosopher Andrew Feenberg writes in *Questioning Technology*, demands for technology that enhances "humane, democratic, and safe work" can influence the future development of electronic communication.[26] Before that can happen, however, we must reacquaint ourselves with the mediated effects of electronic communication, from e-mail to mobile phone, ascertaining how each medium alters content and obscures motives, adjusting for that in our interactions. Finally we must ask why we bought a particular device and then determine if we are using it for that purpose. If we do not answer that question, *marketing will*.

The need to belong is a lifelong quest. Although each individual travels a different path to the oracle, each path must wend through real rather than virtual community. Assignments at the end of each chapter emphasize that point through

- *Journal Exercises*, featuring assignments that test key points through firsthand analysis. Exercises assess the impact of media and mediated communication in everyday activities and build on each other, preparing for the next chapter.
- *Discussion/Paper Ideas*, applying insights from readings and exercises and encouraging collaborative learning in a format that requires interpersonal dialogue—the point of *Interpersonal Divide*. This section has three other features:
  1. *It reemphasizes central theses and themes on each chapter topic.*
  2. *It reaffirms journal observations in a shared setting.*
  3. *It tests the validity of assertions in the text, fostering reflection and debate.*
- *Suggested Readings*, featuring books that affirm or present a different viewpoint on the chapter topic. Several works, published in past decades, were included because their insights have not become obsolete like yesterday's software. Enduring ideas and ideals shape perception and sharpen debate.

Assignments are meant to remind readers about what they know in the depth of their conscience and breadth of their consciousness—the significance of interpersonal skills, the social consequences when we neglect them, and the benefits when we utilize them in our high-tech media world.

Displacement in the Global Village

The evolution of media has decreased the significance of physical presence in the experience of people and events. One can now be an audience to a social performance without being physically present; one can communicate "directly" with others without meeting in the same place. As a result, the physical structures that once divided our society into many distinct spatial settings for interaction have been greatly reduced in social significance.

—JOSHUA MEYROWITZ, *No Sense of Place*

High-Tech and Original Habitats

We are living in an era of rapid population growth and community displacement. That combination will spawn many challenges in the twenty-first century—chief among them, the ability to communicate clearly and resolve differences in a high-tech media age. Interpersonal skills are needed now more than ever. As population in the United States expands from 275 million to 375 million by 2025, we must develop effective means to cope face-to-face with neighbors, strangers, employers, coworkers, relatives, and friends. That prospect, however, appears unlikely unless we come to terms with displacement—an unfathomable feeling of isolation not only in our hometowns but also in our *homes*—connected, wired, and cabled to the outside world.

Displacement used to occur in real habitat. Developers would build subdivisions or engineers would construct highways or dams, destroying community infrastructures and causing property values to rise or fall. Displacement happened in the aftermath of natural disasters, too—hurricanes and floods, for instance—or manmade ones, including chemical spills, toxic dumps, gangland racketeering, and rural or urban flight. Historically, technology (in all its mechanical forms) precipitates displacement. Following World War II, mass production of cars altered municipal planning, resulting in a mosaic of interstates, highways, and roads replete with strip and mega malls, truck and rest stations, chain restaurants, and billboards. Journalist James Howard Kunstler has documented that transformation which powered our economy until communication technology took hold in the 1990s. Kunstler dubs physical displacement "the process of destruction," which obliterated distinctions between "city life" and "country life" and which has led to "a landscape of scary places, the geography of nowhere, that has simply ceased to be a credible human habitat."[27]

Having ravaged physical habitat, corporate ecosystems are sullying virtual habitat. Kunstler's premise, "the geography of nowhere," the title of his bestselling 1994 book, was metaphoric. He contended that displacement to accommodate automobiles homogenized the U.S. landscape, so that every place looked like no place in particular. What was metaphoric in 1994 has become factual in our time. We who live in the silicon valleys of the interpersonal divide travel the same interstates in our automobiles, whizzing by billboards and eating at the same chain restaurants while speaking on mobile phones, oblivious of the displaced countryside. We open garage doors by remote to enter houses without stepping outside, retreat to solitary computer rooms with high-speed access, and download messages and spam from Internet highways with televisions providing background noise like the automobile hum of yore.

Media appliances and computer technology displace us in confines of our homes. The typical middle-class house contains a television set for each family member and computers for the parents and children. To put this into perspective, the total number of television sets at the start of the twenty-first century was 267 million, according to the National Association of Broadcasters—approaching the benchmark of nearly one TV set for each man, woman, and child in the United States.[28] That figure will continue to grow as high-definition television sets and other innovations take hold, remaindering traditional sets to the electronic dump yard. All segments of society are gaining in computer access, too, even members of low-income wired households. In 2001, writes Sonia Arrison, director of the Center for Technology Studies at the Pacific Research Institute, "25 percent of lower income people were online, and if things continue at this rate, it won't be long before virtually everyone who wants to connect can."[29] Computer use has grown so rapidly—with 60 percent of homes having access—that discarded units have become a major environmental concern. Studies show that more than 55 million PCs are to be buried as solid waste, with lead-based monitors and CPUs contaminating landfills.[30]

Other gadgets keep members of households homebound and apart from each other. Add to TV and PC use telephones with separate lines and caller identifications, "family" cell phones with myriad media functions, answering machines, laptops, Web and video cameras, Internet stations, security and video monitors, motion detectors, handheld devices, gaming consoles, DVD and digital audio players, CD stereo systems, wave radios, cable and satellite access, and more. People who use these gadgets and consume these services in their homes are spending more time apart from each other and their friends and neighbors. Then they go to work and use the same gadgets again. Then they become depressed because of work-related stress or family-related dysfunction and seek self-improvement . . . again using the same appliances and services that are the source of their problems, listening to inspirational videos or visiting Web sites instead of resolving issues interpersonally, face-to-face.

The African proverb embraced by Hillary Clinton—"It takes a village to raise a child"—nevertheless acknowledges the vitality of community, which provides basic human needs, from child and health care to education and employment. In essence the maxim emphasizes the communal ethic of cooperation and engagement. We should take note. It will take more than a *digital* global village to raise a child in the twenty-first century. Technology can surveil children at day care but not care for them. It can visit houses virtually through telemedicine but not make house calls interpersonally. It can facilitate distance learning but not engage learners without physical facilities. It can host neighborhood associations at a Web site address without "neighbors" ever associating on-site at a real address.

Howard Rheingold overlooks these points in his influential 1993 book, *The Virtual Community: Homesteading on the Electronic Frontier*, which carries a retraction in 2000, noting "nostalgia" for genuine community and asking questions like this in hindsight: "To what extent are strong, intimate relationships possible on the Net?"[31] Rheingold begins his book with an anecdote about his daughter:

"Daddy is saying 'Holy moly!' to his computer again!"

Those words have become a family code for the way my virtual community has infiltrated our real world. My seven-year-old daughter knows that her father congregates with a family of invisible friends who seem to gather in his computer. Sometimes he talks to them, even if nobody else can see them. And she knows that these invisible friends sometimes show up in the flesh, materializing from the next block or the other side of the planet.

Rheingold's anecdote was cute in 1993. By 2000 it was obsolete. The typical seven-year-old daughter in the author's income bracket already would have learned from parental example and would no longer hover gleefully around Daddy's enchanted PC. She would be on-line in her room with her own computer. The "magic" of cyber-friends, naively depicted as "invisible friends," would already have become her social norm. Between 1993 and 2000 many children went from playing in parks in front of neighbors . . . to playing in mall arcades in front of parents . . . to playing in living-rooms on consoles in front of each other . . . to playing online in their rooms in front of no one in a place that is actually not there. "No matter how much we work and play in cyberspace, we don't really live there, and we can't eat there either,"[32] writes Laura J. Gurak in *Cyberliteracy: Navigating the Internet with Awareness*. While acknowledging cyberspace as a virtual place, Gurak emphasizes that users are material beings with physical needs and desires. Awareness, rather than community, is her dominant theme. Fair enough. But we also need to be aware of the loss of community and the impact on our well-being. "Consequences of what we do on the Internet resound in our physical world," she adds, "and as the world becomes more and more wired, it will be increasingly critical for people to step back and recognize how the virtual affects the physical."[33]

Far from making life more convenient and work easier, media and technology have blurred the boundaries between home and work so that work intrudes on family and family on work to such extent that many of us no longer know where we are—literally. Employers use e-mail, voice mail, and mobile phones to interrupt activities from sex to camping on weekdays and holidays, in the name of productivity. Conversely, children and spouses interrupt business meetings with inquiries about when to order pizza and what to put on it, in the name of convenience. Productivity and convenience are banes, not benefits, for typical consumers. Machines that promise them obscure interpersonal boundaries, placing individuals in virtual habitats at odds with physical circumstances. That defines displacement. That creates the interpersonal divide. Each habitat, virtual or physical, necessitates different roles, voice tones, gestures, diction, and interactions. Moreover each medium—from e-mail to mobile phone, from chat room to Web cam—changes the message so that misinterpretation of motive abounds, complicating relationships and increasing stress. Although the circumstances of displacement vary, all such scenarios will have in common:

- Clash of environments, virtual and real.
- Blurring of work-home boundaries.
- Blurring of role and identity.
- Influence on values and priorities.
- Impact of all of the above on relationships.

Increasingly, work displaces family life and vice versa. Americans on average work more than almost any other people in the industrialized world and with fewer holidays, a trend likely to continue because of electronic communication. Studies show that Americans enjoy only 16.5 hours of leisure per week, adding almost an extra month of work since the early 1980s—a number predicted to grow in the digital years ahead.[34] More time at work means more interaction with technology. In her watershed book on the topic, *The Overworked American*, Juliet B. Schor not only points to the computer as a factor in the decline of leisure but also in the decline of interpersonal skills. "Once people become acclimated to the speed of the computer," she writes, "normal human intercourse becomes laborious."[35] Intrusions and interruptions are the norm, from pop-up Web pages to instant messages. The technology entertains and advertises as much as it educates or informs. At home we compute and consume media in separate rooms in the same dwelling. Leisure time traditionally devoted to family life is increasingly spent mainly watching television, with more than 75 percent of U.S. twelve-year-olds with a set in their bedrooms.[36] Family members require separate televisions, computers, telephones, and other gadgets and services because programming—from cable to software—is pegged to a person's perceived needs and desires, according to marketing research. So parents and children typically are alone consuming media and using technology, clicking here and there via mouse, button, or remote, seeking community in an elusive, never-ending browse.

The search for community in the Judeo-Christian culture is biblical, literally and metaphorically. It is the dominant theme in Genesis. Eden is the "original" habitat. Adam and Eve feel no shame "naked" in paradise before God. They seek neither approval nor acceptance. However, after eating fruit from the tree of the knowledge of good and evil, they feel shame and wear clothes, trying to hide their betrayal from God. He casts them out of paradise, and the search for community begins, becoming more pronounced with Cain and Abel. God favors Abel but appeals to Cain: "If you do what is right, will you not be accepted?" (Genesis 4:7). Doing right by God is the lesson of Adam and Eve. Doing right by *others* is the lesson of Cain and Abel. The first lesson appeals to the conscience, our inner knowledge of right and wrong. The second lesson appeals to consciousness, an instinctual awareness of how our actions affect others. When Cain ignores the lesson and slays his brother, he is forced to spend the rest of his life as "a restless wanderer on earth" (Genesis 4:12). The Adam and Eve narrative is as intricately linked to the Cain and Abel narrative as the conscience is to consciousness. The lesson is universal. Conscience and consciousness must work in tandem harmoniously for us to meet everyday challenges—and enjoy the abundant rewards—of life in community with others.

That consummate rule transcends culture, region, and religion. The Genesis story, like so many other parables and tracts, foreshadows the Golden Rule: *Do unto others what you would have them do unto you.* Confucius believed that "reciprocity" was the highest principle of conduct: *Do not do to others what you do not want them to do to you* (Analects 15.23). Similar truths also can be found in Hinduism, Islam, and Buddhism and appeal to conscience and consciousness, constructs of the human condition, covered in the next chapter. A rudimentary knowledge of these concepts is useful at this point, however, to illustrate the search for community.

Conscience and consciousness are metaphysical, or beyond scientific measurement. Nevertheless, they determine as much as our genome whether we will lead fulfilling and productive lives or empty, painful ones. Philosophers have debated the essence of conscience and consciousness for centuries because those aspects of human existence influence the well-being of nations as well as individuals. Although philosophers may use different terminologies or advance various theories, too esoteric or speculative to enumerate here, many would agree that the conscience demands:

- That we love and be loved by others.
- That we have meaningful relationships with others.
- That we contribute to community.

Consciousness demands:

- That we see the world as it actually is rather than how we would like it to be.
- That we foresee the impact of our actions before taking them.
- That we assess consequences of past actions to make informed choices in the future.

When we live by those tenets, we experience acceptance. We feel balanced, whole. We can empathize with others but also take action when necessary, employing as much power as needed to address a situation without creating greater problems or causing harm to innocent others. We not only contribute to community; we derive joy from it. Others praise our character, adopt our values, and seek us as role models or mentors—the highest honor that neighbors can bestow. We lead by example rather than decree. That is the age-old standard. Before the self-help guru and the celebrity psychologist, before the televangelist and motivational speaker, role models and mentors inspired us to interact honorably among others in community and to leave a situation or place in better condition than we found it. When we did that, we found something else: *acceptance flows from within.*

The Interpersonal Divide

Lacking acceptance, we feel unloved. Lacking love, we feel afraid. Maybe we should. When we lose a sense of place, we also lose a sense of occasion—how to behave in real time and place in the company of others. We are forgetting how to resolve problems without creating greater ones because we are more apt to use electronic communication to mediate our disputes, instead of resolving them face-to-face. We may misinterpret motives because the messages we send and receive do not convey the subtle but vital voice tones, body movements, and other guiding interpersonal cues of physical place. We cannot "get along" with each other because we don't know how to "get on" with each other, showing grace and forgiveness in the wake of grievance or transgression. While most pundits and educators debate the digital divide, bemoaning the underclass of people without computer access, a wider fault line has been eroding communities: the *interpersonal* divide.

Road rage. School shootings. Race riots. Workplace violence. Domestic violence. Media thrive on such stories because they showcase the elements of sensational news, especially compelling video. Real news is inherently sensational, as the world witnessed during the September 11, 2001, terrorist attacks in New York City, Washington D.C., and western Pennsylvania. The medium united Americans across the country, but for many international viewers, the vast United States seemed at the edge of collapse, along with the Twin Towers of the World Trade Center. (That, of course, was a built-in aspect of the terrorists' goal.) Relatives and friends watching CNN around the globe e-mailed or phoned residents thousands of miles from the attack to see if they were all right. Alas, as the hijackers also knew, flying planes into the Trade Center and Pentagon, television news increases fear as it decreases geographical boundaries.

The terrorist attacks caught the news media by surprise. In the preceding months, reporters were engrossed in a sordid affair involving Congressman Gary Condit and intern Chandra Levy, still missing in September 2001 (and later discovered murdered). The media hyped speculation that Condit may have had a role in Levy's disappearance, which law enforcement could not substantiate. Death by foul play is tragic, of course; but in this case the media embellished conjecture until the coverage became trite. Juxtaposition of the tragic and trite exposed the overconsumption of rehashed news, televised seven days a week, twenty-four hours a day—the same seven minutes around the clock. That warps our sense of place. The medium of choice—television—narrows perception as it increases apprehension of the world. As a result we often interact reluctantly with those who share our space, believing the world to be more dangerous than it actually is, a self-fulfilling prophecy.

This is more than cultivation theory—the notion that we tend to view reality in the manner that television depicts it. This is a simple fact of hours in the day. If we spend them consuming media, we lose them interacting with others in real environments. That enhances any cultivation effect compounded by commercial messages that sponsor media and target our fears even more than the news. The focus on fear is longstanding, dating back to the early twentieth century, when emerging corporations began marketing national brands and feeding the consumerism still running rampant in today's high-tech media world. As social economist Juliet B. Schor explains, revisiting the history of advertising in the 1920s, "For the first time, business began to use advertising as a psychological weapon against consumers. 'Scare copy' was invented. Without Listerine, Postum, or a Buick, the consumer would be left a spinster, fall victim to a crippling disease, or be passed over for a promotion."[37]

Fear is the fuel of marketing. That is not a play on words. The phrase *optimum level of fear* is a marketing concept. Marketers compile statistics on potential customers, identifying perceived needs, often associated with acceptance. Advertisers utilize data to create commercials—about a hair- or weight-loss product, say. Data might indicate that people in a certain age or income bracket worry about aging, confusing loss of hair with loss of love (or loss of weight with gain thereof). Advertisements exploit that fear, using before-and-after testimonials of bald or obese partners who once yearned for intimacy and found it, thanks to an over-the-counter elixir endorsed by an actor or clinician. The "before" testimonial generates the fear and the "after" testimonial, the persuasion, affirmed by the endorsement and "money-back" guarantee, so that customers actually have "nothing to lose." Commercials can generate too much fear, embellishing testimonials; or persuasion can be weak, with unlikely or unenthusiastic endorsements. But when fear and persuasion combine, the optimum—or prime motivator—has been achieved.

Buying habits emanate out of *epistemic* emotions—or knowledge of consequences—chief among them, fear and hope. "To put people in a state of fear," write professors John and Nicholas Jackson O'Shaughnessy, authors of *The Marketing of Emotion*, "advertisers need to dramatize the unpleasant consequences and stress the high probability of their occurring."[38] In other words, if men in middle age believe that women dislike baldness (Condition A), and deduce that baldness will deprive them of romantic opportunities (Consequence B), then fear of that scenario will prompt them to purchase a hair-loss product in the hope that it will break the link between Condition A and Consequence B. In describing the power of emotion, the O'Shaughnessys note that empirical studies show that the more fear is aroused in consumers, the more likely they will take preventive measures. "This being so," they write, "advertising would find it advantageous to give the target audience information on some or all of the following: (1) the severity and nearness of the threat; (2) the probability of its occurrence;

(3) the effectiveness of certain coping strategies; and (4) the speed and ease with which the coping response can be implemented."[39] When those components align harmoniously, the optimal level of fear will have been achieved, causing consumers to reach for their credit cards (a font of marketing data in the first place).

Methods promise to become more invasive. As computer and television networks fuse with "interactive TV" (the ultimate oxymoron) marketers can target fear more precisely and direct it into specific homes and even into specific *rooms* in such homes. The father in his home office will learn more about Viagra, the mother in the exercise room about Metabolite, the son in the family room about End-Zit, and the daughter in the bedroom about WonderBreast. Fear of rejection will be the common denominator in this household, displacing family members. As journalist James Howard Kunstler notes, when television becomes the focal point of family life, the entire house is sealed off from the outside world, which family members view as "an abstraction filtered through television, just as the weather is an abstraction filtered through air conditioning."[40] Marketers help create the abstraction by emphasizing optimum levels of fear, undermining perception of community.

Marketing has become so influential because techniques are powered by technology. For instance, marketers do not have to invest as much anymore in expensive direct mail campaigns with supervisors assessing cost versus effectiveness. Expenses have shifted from company to consumer. Companies send bulk e-mail "spam" or place "cookies"—files inserted into home computers that chart purchasing patterns—with cost assessed to the customer who pays for Internet access. Apart from questions about privacy, refinement of target audiences can lead to deceptive practices, writes Herbert Rotfeld, professor of marketing at Auburn University and author of the aptly named book, *Adventures in Misplaced Marketing*. Rotfeld believes that marketers with access to computerized data could direct deceptive television commercials via cable to susceptible audiences. "Infomercials could use cable networks to prey upon the worries and fears of selected groups. And also in theory, various vulnerable individuals could be specifically targeted for deceptive messages they are prone to believe via the Internet. Children, elderly or more gullible people would have tailor-made deceptive messages sent directly to their computer screens."[41] In sum, the optimal level of fear has become easier to achieve, thanks to converging technologies.

The search for acceptance used to be conducted in community. Now it is conducted as much in virtual as physical place. That widens the interpersonal divide and, in part, addresses why the venerable task of deepening conscience and expanding consciousness has become so difficult in our time. People intuit this and seek self-help, to be covered later. The self-improvement industry also utilizes media and technology which, in turn, must answer to marketing. People answer to the human condition, learning to hear conscience and heed consciousness and eventually balancing the two—or else they suffer consequences of community. That has been the norm until recently. What changed is reliance on technology to mediate discourse, hindering conscience, and on media to inform consciousness, hindering our vision of and place in the world. Self-help programs usually cannot correct that view when they rely on the same electronic devices and marketing ploys—from motivational videos on leadership habits (with spam offers, direct mail catalogues, and on-line boutiques), to virtual psychotherapy (with consultations via e-mail)—targeting likely consumers and treating them according to credit card balance rather than emotional balance.

The human condition brooks no shortcuts to wellness. The ancients understood this, from Moses to Mohammad, from Socrates to Siddhartha. Living ethically requires lifelong commitment and regular assessment. Then as now communication was key. Without communication, we lack the ability to share ideas, explain intent, express love, enjoy relationships, and contribute substantially to society. Without communication, consciousness is equally misinformed. We cannot perceive reality or evaluate the true impact of our thoughts, words, and deeds. Until recently, however, communication was mostly interpersonal, or face-to-face. People spoke plainly to each other—sometimes appropriately and sometimes, inappropriately—but usually authentically because of facial gestures, tone of voice, time of day, occasion of place, possibility of witnesses, and so on. We could read expressions of love, hate, or indifference in body language and could interpret ill intent or goodwill first hand, without needing media analysts to construe the situation or technology to process that information at ever-faster speeds.

We live now in cabled enclaves. Too many of us feel anxious not because we fail to communicate—for we *do* communicate too frequently with each other electronically—but because of fundamental high-tech fallacies. Many consumers buy technology because they believe it saves time and improves communication, not only with friends and associates, but also with corporations and organizations—enhancing relationships. Such beliefs are suspect. Consider these fallacies about technology and the interpersonal lessons required to overcome them:

1. *Widespread availability of electronic devices assures swift communication with others.* The availability sets up false expectations that others with e-mail, mobile phones, and Internet access should be contacting us or replying quickly to our messages. When they don't, perhaps because they are inundated with spam or interacting with others, we feel emotionally displaced. The fallacy is associated with time and place. Our biological clocks, as we shall learn, have been reset by computers and our sense of occasion—the appropriateness of a message based on content, timing, and relationship—hopelessly distorted. Many of us bought technology because it promised to bring us closer to others or help us work more efficiently. Because technology is instantaneous we anticipate speedy replies to messages, regardless of our relationships with others—from family in the next town to strangers in the next hemisphere—and grow testy when experiencing delays. Often we feel betrayed when e-mail addresses or phone numbers are blocked out so that we cannot communicate whenever, wherever, and to whomever we wish. Lesson: *Technology may function "on demand" but people usually do not.*

2. *Communication tools ensure access to companies.* Companies require consumers to use computer technology to access accounts or partake in promotions or other benefits, charging fees if people want personal treatment. The fallacy here is that access to companies would benefit the consumer, providing service on demand. We may assume that we can access such treatment with a Touch-Tone telephone, as long as we are willing to wade through complex dial systems. We wait, listening to promotional audio, growing impatient, often only to get an operator who lacks authority to answer questions or make decisions. When that happens, people feel displaced and manipulated on three levels: they pay fees to contact someone who lacks interpersonal skills or information; they are denied computer access or are forced to use it; they must communicate with machines. Lesson: *Access to companies is apt to benefit companies rather than consumers.*

3. *Communication technology enhances personal and professional relationships.* This fallacy involves advertising best-case scenarios. That

works with depictions of hamburgers because ground beef on a bun is basically ground beef on a pun. True, the burger that you order at the counter may not be perfectly cooked and presented appealingly with ultra-crisp lettuce and juicy red tomato. But this quality burger is possible occasionally if not often. In the end, ground beef is ground beef and lettuce, lettuce. Best-case scenarios about communication technology—such as gleeful America Online users proclaiming, *We have mail!*—convey an inherently deceptive notion that engaging in e-mail fosters acceptance. E-mail is just as likely to deprive users of that feeling. As media critics warned us in the 1960s, content and intent of our messages change when we communicate them to others through machines. Simple questions—"Where have you been? When are you coming home?"—mean one thing when uttered face to face, depending on place, voice tone, circumstance, and occasion; and another thing when mediated by computer, answering machine, or telephone. In the first instance, the person asking the questions conveys subtleties of motive; however, in the second instance, the medium deletes those subtleties, forcing the listener to figure it all out. That is difficult, without customary interpersonal cues, and may prompt users to misinterpret content and intent. Lesson: *Electronic communication is as apt to complicate as enhance relationships, displacing us at home and at work.*

Displacement, at the epicenter of the interpersonal divide, impacts the economy, too. In a sequel to *The Geography of Nowhere*, titled *Home from Nowhere*, James Howard Kunstler observes that healthy communities were also supported by local economies. Those economies, Kunstler asserts, have been "extirpated by an insidious corporate colonialism that doesn't care about the places from which it extracts its profits or the people subject to its operations. Without the underpinning of genuine community and its institutions, family life has predictably disintegrated, because the family alone cannot bear all the burdens and perform all the functions of itself and the community."[42] The stress on families is exacerbated when wage earners are displaced by computers.

Big Box Displacement

An issue in many communities concerns debate about so-called "big box" retailers like Wal-Mart displacing local entrepreneurs. Ironically, anti-sprawl activists voicing concern about local economies have created hundreds of Web sites combating big box displacement. One such top site at the turn of the century was sprawl-busters.com, which heralded Al Norman as the guru of the anti-Wal-Mart movement. Sprawl-busters, a prototypical site influenced by Internet marketing techniques, states that:

> Al Norman achieved national attention in October of 1993 when he successfully stopped Wal-Mart from locating in his hometown of Greenfield, Massachusetts. Since then he has appeared on 60 Minutes, and gained widespread media attention from the Wall Street Journal to *Fortune* magazine.[43]

Sprawl-busters also reported that Norman was editor of the monthly publication *Sprawl-Busters Alert* and author of *Slam-Dunking Wal-Mart!: How You Can Stop Superstore Sprawl in Your Hometown*, with checks for the book payable to Raphel Marketing in Atlantic City.[44] Nonetheless, anti-sprawl activists like Norman make good arguments about local businesses being displaced by big box merchants. Unfortunately, activists often rely on media coverage and computer technology to advance their viewpoint. Doing so, they overlook a far more menacing "big box" displacement in front of them—the PC monitor and TV screen.

Digital displacement erodes civic rights, guaranteed by the First Amendment. Whatever you think about Wal-Mart—or anti-megastore activists, for that matter—digital displacement deletes physical place, and with it, rights of assembly and petition. Assembly, in the traditional sense, not only requires locale but also symbol to deepen awareness of abusive power or social injustices. For instance, Dr. Martin Luther King's "I Have a Dream" speech was delivered in 1963 on the steps of the Lincoln Memorial, an apt symbol etched in collective conscience. How effective would that speech have been without that representative backdrop? Because symbol is associated with place, activists and media alike tend to target the Wal-Marts of commerce and government rather than digital counterparts that promulgate virtual rather than real access.

John Seigenthaler, chairman emeritus of *The Tennessean* and founder of the First Amendment Center at Vanderbilt University, sees a parallel between perceptions of nuclear energy in the 1960s and Internet in the current one. As a young Tennessean, Seigenthaler was schooled about the economic potential of atomic power. "It was only after being a journalist and an editor that I realized that all those editorials we had written about safety of nuclear power and the equation of Tennessee Valley Autho̲ ̲ ̲ as motherhood was flawed,"[45] he said. Seigenthaler believes that t̲h̲e public has been conditioned to think of anything on the Internet in the same way that he in another time thought about the TVA and nuclear power. "Whenever I meet technologists who are caught up in the sweep and miracle of Internet I am reminded of TVA and atomic power. It shouldn't take a Chernobyl to alert us to the fact that there is a gnawing at th̲e̲ commercial Internet concerning some practices that are not only bawdy but also cheap."

In actuality, Amazon.com and eBay also damage local businesses and sustainable econo̲m̲ies. However, activists lodge relatively few protests against these e-commerce megastores, mainly because there is no place to assemble in cyberspace. In other words, there is no "there" there without which activists cannot disrupt Chamber of Commerce meetings, make speeches at City Council, display signs at building sites, and position themselves in front of bulldozers and authorities. Paul McMasters, First Amendment ombudsman for the Freedom Forum and former associate editorial director of *USA Today*, notes that assembly— "one of the orphan freedoms along with petition"[46]—doesn't get sufficient attention in First Amendment debates, especially ones addressing new technologies. "Freedom of expression doesn't mean much without assembly and petition because those two things are the best ways to galvanize and organize public support and get the attention of the people in power." Meanwhile, activists targeting Wal-Mart will share and vend their protest techniques on-line while digital mega malls like Amazon.com and eBay displace businesses on Main Street without anyone knowing it because of the absence of place.

The more we bridge the digital divide, the more likely consumers will buy on-line. According to Arbitron, a media and marketing research firm, seven out of ten U.S. households had Internet access as of 2002, one out of four people used Internet at work, and four in ten purchased goods on-line, with those figures apt to burgeon each year with increasing broadband access.[47] Anti-sprawl activists and supportive neighborhood groups may want to refocus their attention on the technology in their own domains. Chances are, they already have been assimilated with the rest of us into the ranks of marketing and technology, sharing similar social psychographics:

- Wasting too much time in the nothingness of cyberspace.
- Spending too much money accessing that nothingness.
- Feeling that nothingness instinctively because there literally is no "there" there.

Worse, we have forgotten how to locate the "there"—through meaningful interaction with others in the community or through meaningful contributions to the community. This is a relatively recent phenomenon. Civic engagement involving face-to-face interaction had been steadily rising in the twentieth century (except during the Depression); since the 1960s, however, such involvement has plummeted, even though mailing list membership, facilitated by technology, shows expanding membership lists.[48] In part, this is only natural, because society is suffering symptoms associated with mediated communication, undermining any momentary impulse to participate in community: lying, deceiving, being uncivil, overreacting to perceived slights, simplifying problems to place blame, listening for motive instead of for meaning and, worst of all, coveting what we lack and losing what we have. These "7 Habits of Highly Mediated People" are covered in Chapter Three.

Such behaviors endanger the American dream. Owning a business is part of that dream. In the past entrepreneurs attracted patrons by interacting with customers, creating jobs in neighborhoods, and sponsoring community events. Big box merchants, particularly Wal-Mart, are poor substitutes for general stores on Main Street whose surviving shopkeepers are being displaced again, this time by media and technology.

This, too, was predictable. The easy dot.com days of the latter 1990s created fortunes out of thin air, inflating market values of untested companies touting high-tech services. Several such companies were phantom, luring investors with illusory accounting and slick Web design techniques to conjure notions of unlimited growth. People poured life savings into tech stocks and mutual funds. But many novice investors failed to realize that markets trade in a *symbolic* rather than a real world, from the icons that identify corporations on the digital tickertape to the estimates that determine their worth. Symbolic and virtual worlds have much in common. As Berkeley physicist and political scientist Gene Rochlin writes in his award-winning commentary on technology, *Trapped in the Net: The Unanticipated Consequences of Computerization,*

Because markets trade in wealth rather than creating it, because what they deal in are symbols and promises rather than tangible goods, they have been able to exploit the new opportunities of computers, the computerized databases and information systems, and computerized networks almost as quickly as the technical means have progressed. In the process, they have transformed the structure of the financial world in ways that were never anticipated.[49]

One unanticipated consequence of computerization has been the transformation of public libraries and local bookstores. They have lost patrons because of Internet access. As Scott Carlson writes in "The Deserted Library" in *The Chronicle of Higher Education*, "Clearly, the burgeoning use of electronic databases has sent the buzz of library activity onto the Internet. The shift leaves many librarians and scholars wondering and worrying about the future of what has traditionally been the social and intellectual heart of campus. . . ."[50] Similarly, local bookstores have been the social and intellectual heart of communities. They contributed to the economy too. Owner-managers, even ones of national chains, hired assistant managers, sales associates, and customer service and maintenance staff. In the 1980s several stores opened cafés so that customers could relax with latté and a good read. For all purposes, that predominant milieu changed after Amazon.com entered the market.

Amazon poses as a national chain but circumvents the added costs of erecting or leasing community outlets across the country. Neither does it need a huge national sales force the way Wal-Mart does to sell product interpersonally, face-to-face, or maintenance crews to keep up stores. Customer service is via e-mail, requiring less interaction and fewer representatives. Central addresses must be maintained, of course, but they are full of computers that communicate with the computers of distributors. That kind of automation supposedly cuts costs, along with the work force. With all this cost-cutting, and with 30 million cumulative customers at the start of the twenty-first century—with roughly one Amazon employee serving every 4,000 patrons—the corporation, founded in 1995, still struggled to post a net profit into the twenty-first century. As Lee Barney, writing for *TheStreet.com*, quipped, "When is $1 billion in quarterly online sales just not good enough? When you're Amazon.com, and you spend more than that in the same time frame."[51] Perhaps in the future Amazon will succeed, falter, or merge with a nurturing ecosystem. Concerning displacement, however, the issue at hand is "growth" versus profit. That is the eco-system conundrum, and Amazon has become the standard. When the company halted plans in 2001 to add a $40 million addition to its ex-isting building in Seattle, a company spokesperson observed that Amazon is "getting healthy by slowing down growth and spending and adjusting supply to better suit demand, which is far lower than what every dot-com anticipated."[52] Predictably Amazon planned to achieve "health" by laying off 1,300 workers, a move that augured more tech-nology and automated customer service. Amazon may rehire those workers or provide more personalized service in the future. But these scenarios are superfluous. Their impact on local business is the point.

Increasingly companies operating in physical place must compete with rivals in virtual place. Media ecosystems do this effortlessly. Local en-trepreneurs do so at risk. Consider local bookstore owners. Sooner or later they contend with Amazon and spend part of their operating bud-gets on technology and domain names—aboutmybookstore.com or simi-lar concoctions. Then they dole out for domain services, including notices for renewal or listings in databases. In cyberspace, everyone pays.[53] In addition to physical costs, entrepreneurs start paying virtual costs to do business on Main Street *and* on the Internet, creating and updating Web sites and buying software, computer access, and accessories. Following Amazon's lead, many downsize staff, automate customer service, and measure quarterly earnings rather than net profits, inflating the technol-ogy sector of a service economy that, oxymoronically, *lacks* service. As Herbert Rotfeld quips in *Adventures in Misplaced Marketing*, "With-out bad service, there wouldn't be any service at all."[54]

Historian Theodore Roszak observes that the current so-called "in-formation economy" is overpopulated by "service companies," includ-ing credit bureaus, data managers, and marketing experts. According to Roszak, "These enterprises, in turn, have helped to create a thrust-ing new profession of computer systems specialists whose assignment is to brainstorm more and more applications for information technol-ogy and to sell those applications to every business on the scene."[55]

Computer-assisted marketing, in particular, has exacerbated the interpersonal divide. Why should customers feel valued when routine service is denied them? Why should they feel important in their homes when customer service representatives require that they voice com-plaints via e-mail, only to be answered by computers decoding com-mon scripts via "artificial intelligence," another on-line oxymoron along with "tech support"? Technology was supposed to offer the consumer more choices. Because of marketing, each choice comes with a fee. Spam pop-up offers continually interrupt word processing and Web browsing, forcing users to endure the ubiquitous hourly onslaught unless, of course, they purchase pop-up killer software. In this, they have a choice. Telephone companies and other utilities inform consumers that they will be charged monthly fees if they keep paying bills with checks rather than with credit cards on-line. The choice is in the credit card, not in the method of payment. Consumers pay similar fees associated with cable access; computer and software support; electronic banking; video and audio feeds, Internet memberships, subscriptions, library access and more, with services sliced up and apportioned out to anyone willing to pay them without companies honoring the most basic component of customer service: *loyalty*.

Loyalty is a value associated with time and trust. Companies used to build loyalty over time through dependable service. That generates trust, a powerful motivator associated with "brand loyalty." The authors of *The Marketing of Emotion* define trust as an occasional unequal exchange between consumer and merchant, noting: "We may accept the higher price, the delay in service, and so on because we trust the supplier will make amends in the longer term."[56] That may no longer apply with on-line purchases because of technology, which routinely overlooks the longer term, operating in an instantaneous environment with little, if any, follow-up by customer representatives, once a product has been ordered. Representatives who do follow up are usually only interested in selling additional accessories or services, using the original purchase as an excuse to contact the consumer. The result is an emphasis on selling at all costs, eroding standards of trust, which many merchants placed in technology rather than in people. In essence the tool meant to help us at the workplace, to make life simpler or efficient, has metamorphosed into something ominous when we were looking at economic indicators rather than ourselves. "[W]e have become the objects of our own technology. The toolmaker has become the tool,"[57] writes Dinesh D'Souza, policy analyst and John M. Olin Research Fellow. That sums up the situation. Technology has reversed the natural order of things.

Much of this book is common sense. The adage—*If something seems too good to be true, it probably is*—pertains to the overselling of technology as a way to keep in touch. Communication technology is too good to be true, and nothing—even holography technology that simulates depth and dimension—can substitute for the real thing. Many of us understand this on some level. But few of us are acting on that knowledge. Fact is, emotional breakdowns are usually preceded by communication breakdowns. We e-mail, browse, fax, pixel, and cell-phone every waking hour of the day, misinterpreting as much as we communicate because the medium changes meaning and masks motive and intent. We have lost touch with our own motivations as well. The more we communicate electronically, the more we misinterpret, deepening levels of displacement and amplifying our desire for acceptance. Many of us take offense or take the offensive, complicating our lives because we have forgotten basic consumerism: Why did we buy the technology? Does it suit our needs? Does it advance or undermine our priorities? How are we using it at home and work and what is that use displacing? How has computer access altered our primary relationships and community activities? How much are we spending annually for access fees, computer equipment, software, upgrades and repairs, credit card debt, and more for the convenience of on-line shopping so that we do not have to leave our homes?

If we fail to answer these questions, marketing will.

Loss of Perspective

To feel accepted rather than displaced, we must repatriate to our communities, where most of our transactions and interactions should occur. However, to participate productively in community, we must develop interpersonal skills and ethical habits. When we do, perception becomes keen. We ascertain goals and priorities, emphasizing the essentials of life:

- *Unconditional Acceptance.* Partners and/or children to love and be loved by.
- *Meaningful Relationships.* Significant networks of friends and colleagues who work with us toward common goals that benefit partners, children, and shared living space.
- *Civic Engagement.* Contributions that enhance the well-being of others or the vitality of community.
- *Insight.* Clear vision of challenges that undermine love, friendship, well-being, and community.

- *Discretion*. Experience or knowledge to accept what we can change and what we cannot, living in the moment rather than reacting to it.
- *Mindfulness*. Leaving relationships and environments in better shape than we found them.
- *Gratitude*. Appreciating the blessings of each phase of biological life, from childhood to having children, from respecting the elderly to becoming the elderly, reflecting on the love, friends, and contributions of mortal life.

These principles shaped the values of past generations that knew the importance of community. That standard can exist again when individuals address consequences of the interpersonal divide and influence the future directions of media and technology. Otherwise marketing will continue to oversell information as an essential commodity. Internet users are drowning in information—much of it unreliable, deceptive, or downright fraudulent. So much information is available that the most important data—possessing economic and proprietary value—are routinely withheld from public view. According to educator Lelia Green, author of *Communication, Technology and Society*, "Although our economy is an information economy and information continues to proliferate and accumulate, it is often the withholding of information that has the capacity to generate the greatest value."[58] In that sense, digital-divide arguments about access for the social underclasses really do not address the fundamental problem, debated in the United States since Frederick Douglass in the nineteenth century, of *access to education* as an overriding principle of social equity in the Republic. Access to Internet without equitable educational opportunity further disenfranchises the underclasses. As Green aptly states, "[T]he information poor often don't know where to start looking."[59] Worse, when they do gain access, they not only are buried in information but also in marketing pop-ups, promotions, and spam that often target the information poor, precisely because they lack the discernment required to navigate the corrupted Web.

Even the most privileged, educated sectors of society—including academia—routinely fall prey to viruses, scams, and marketing ploys, as evidenced by the millions pumped annually into technology support, the digital janitors of the Information Age. We are living as much in the "Age of Information *About* Information" as we are living in the Information Age. There is a critical difference. Information is educational because it transforms data into knowledge and, as such, enhances life and shapes character. Information usually sells once or sells the same thing repeatedly, the way that a book sells, or a seminar. Information *about* information sells as often as marketers can devise ways to mete out access to the databank, search engine, or electronic device, from monthly fees for Internet-based software use to annual ones for data search privileges. As Nicholas Negroponte, founder of MIT's Media Lab, muses in an intriguing but nevertheless shortsighted book, *Being Digital*, "*TV Guide* has been known to make larger profits than all four networks combined," suggesting "that the value of information about information can be greater than the value of information itself."[60] Negroponte's book, published in 1996 about emerging technologies, is a good but outdated read, not because his prophesies about the digital world are flawed fundamentally; they aren't. But because, like most scientist-professors, he failed to factor into his vision of a brave new electronic world, marketing's role in overselling information.

With so much emphasis on information, addressing the various digital divides, citizens ought to be well-informed. That is not the case. Relatively few technophiles, even ones who are college-educated or college educators, apprehend the import of scientific discoveries. These discoveries, especially in physics and molecular biology, occurred because of computer networks, databanks, and technology, splendid tools when used properly. Instead of informing the public about discoveries, the news media, largely ignorant about science, missed or hyped these stories, focusing on entertainment coverage or celebrity news, as prescribed by their own marketing reports. According to Haynes Johnson, Knight Chair at the University of Maryland's Philip Merrill College of Journalism, the public needs more news on such topics as environmental degradation, global warming, and "revolutions of science, health and technology that are changing life as never before, presenting grave risks as well as great promise."[61] He adds, "This is what news is made of, the *real* stuff of journalism, far more significant than anyone's 15 minutes of scandal, celebrity or fame."[62]

The news media have yet to embrace that standard. Case in point: Between 1992 and 1994, NASA's Cosmic Background Explorer Satellite Program had been processing data that affirmed the Big Bang. Physicist Stephen Hawking, usually understated, proclaimed this "the discovery of the century, if not of all time."[63] However, when COBE's project leader George Smoot published his findings in *Wrinkles in Time*, released in 1994, he had to compete with "the trial of the century" involving O.J. Simpson's purported slayings of his wife and companion. Hence the public was not adequately informed about a cosmological model that rivaled that of Copernicus. Breakthroughs in molecular biology were equally significant. Coverage, however, was often sensationalized, beginning with the first cloned sheep "Dolly" (invoking her Dolly Parton mammary namesake) and continuing with genetic therapies and stem cell research, all of which was covered theatrically, politically, or not at all.

Then there are issues of privacy—routinely violated by marketing and technology—in return for access to the databank or service or in return for the promotional free gift. Even virtual homesteader Howard Rheingold acknowledges that risk, noting that individual dossiers are gold mines for "professional privacy brokers" who are beginning to discover that the masses "would freely allow someone else to collect and use and even sell personal information, in return for payment or subsidies."[64]

Profit notwithstanding, data collection and public access to online information can heal us in the right hands or harm us in the wrong ones. Medical technology saves lives. However, improper access to digital dossiers may breach privacy as never before. Richard Smith, chief technology officer for the Privacy Foundation, has warned that most people believe that personal information about them is intensely private; marketers view such information as just another commodity. As example, Smith notes that patients using the antidepressant Zoloft may fill prescriptions at pharmacies that record every purchase in a computer network operated by a management firm, which processes benefits and insurance information. Writes Smith:

> This information is then provided to drug companies for marketing purposes. Doctors typically receive phone calls from drug company sales persons that go something like this: "We see that last year you only prescribed our drug 15 percent of the time to treat a particular condition, yet the national average is 30 percent. What can we do to get this percentage raised?"[65]

That kind of casual marketing use, Smith adds, violates a person's privacy to such extent that he or she may have difficulty obtaining health insurance or even a job. Worse, some supermarket and pharmacy chains create a two-tier system of clientele—those with store-issued savings cards and those without. Cards provide discounts, which companies recoup by selling marketing data tracking consumers' purchases, even prescriptions. So no discount actually is given, even though we perceive that it is. Finally, the emphasis on marketing creates a two-class system: *those who can afford to pay more and keep their privacy . . . and those who cannot.*

Tim Berners-Lee, inventor of the World Wide Web, believes that misuse of private information is the paramount concern for most consumers. "With consequences ranging from the threat of junk mail to the denial of health insurance, the problem is serious, and two aspects of the Web make the worry worse. One is that information can be collected much more easily, and the other is that it can be used very easily to tailor what a person experiences."[66] Berners-Lee is alluding to the influence of technology on perception, which has become so pervasive that we no longer even acknowledge it—even when failing to do so results in fraud and unfairness.

Cyber crime has risen with proliferation of home computers in typical households. Offenses in virtual environs are complicated by the absence of physical place, an issue to be analyzed later. People are stalked, defrauded, and victimized through networks so that the authorities do not know whom to charge: the person who owns the server but not the specific computer, the person who owns the specific computer but may not have used it to commit a crime, the person who may have used it from another computer and server, and so on, a situation compounded by jurisdiction, because all this can happen from any point on the globe. The consequence of that is appalling. When law enforcement cannot enforce the law, victims are dehumanized twice—by crime and lack of redress—resulting in the obliteration of rights, along with place and identity.

Without interpersonal intelligence, we are never really sure of our roles, responses, and emotions. That causes stress and undermines perception, too. How can we discern challenge or seize opportunity when we are apt to mistake opportunity for challenge and vice versa? No self-help manual will help, despite the testimonials of marketing, because what one person sees as an opportunity—a change in career or marital status—another may see as a challenge, based on how each individual perceives the situation. And perception varies from person to person based on development of conscience and consciousness, both of which suffer when people lack time to interact meaningfully with others or to reflect on actions affecting others. Technology was supposed to help. Computers, meant to simplify tasks and reduce workload, have done just the opposite. According to Jill Andresky Fraser, finance editor of *Inc.* magazine, "The overwork, stress, and insecurity of today's workplaces has been exacerbated, not relieved, by the proliferation of high-tech equipment—laptop computers, cell phones, electronic desk calendars, beepers, portable fax machines, Palm Pilots, and more—that help people try to keep up with growing workloads while also making it impossible for them to fully escape their jobs and relax."[67] Without relaxation, we cannot appreciate the life journey of the human condition, which all of us share.

A Lifelong Quest

It bears repeating. This book is not a self-help manual with steps to attain acceptance. The subtitle of this book, *The Search for Community*, is a lifelong quest driven by our collective need for acceptance. The journey has spiritual and Darwinian ramifications, depending on one's religion or worldview. Arguments can be made that humans are social creatures whose survival relies on how they treat others in community or that humans are spiritual creatures whose salvation relies on the same criterion. Accordingly our hunger for acceptance has meaning because it brings us into contact with others and educates us by pang of conscience or pain of consciousness. In the end no one escapes consequences of the human condition. The search for community begins and ends with acceptance of that condition upon which biology and theology rely, requiring us:

- To be aware that life is short and so must be enjoyed, forcing us to relish each moment of beauty, grace, or compassion and learn from each moment of loss, pain, or betrayal.
- To feel alive when childhood ends and responsibility begins, when reproduction ends and middle age begins, when wisdom begins in old age only to end with the obliteration of consciousness . . . or the eternal metamorphosis thereof.

Media and technology, when used properly, can aid us in the search for community. They are potent tools that require more than installation manuals or programming guides. We need to appreciate how they affect our lives at home and at work and how we can use them wisely to preserve our perception, priorities, and, above all, *principles*. In that respect there is hope in the high-tech media world.

In past eras, people had two sets of values—one at work and one at home. The work ethic usually was influenced by specific professions and the personal ethic, by family. Increasingly, people of conscience advocate one set of values to serve in both places. *That makes sense*. Because media and technology transcend place, so must our values. Naturally those values differ from person to person but rely on conscience and consciousness working in tandem to enrich community, to which all paths lead, according to dictates of the human condition. As we shall see in the next chapter, understanding that condition emphasizes common bonds and can help us feel at peace and empowered.

Journal Exercise

Take an inventory of media appliances and technology devices in your home and workplace/school. Make observations about each appliance and device, concerning:

- *Utility*. Which ones are efficient and why? Which ones are intrusive and why? Which ones are used primarily for (a) entertainment, (b) information, (c) communication?
- *Time*. Which ones save time and which waste time? How, if at all, is time saved and how do you spend that spare time—in real or in virtual environments?
- *Impact*. Which ones influence relationships at home and at work/ school, for better or worse? Which ones blur boundaries between home and work/school? How much money do you spend each month operating or using these appliances and devices, including estimated electrical costs, monthly fees or service charges, upgrades and accessories, and so on?

Discussion/Paper Ideas for Chapter One

- Discuss observations from the Journal Exercise above.
- Discuss the validity of these assertions:

1. Technological displacement occurs when we experience:
   ✓ Clash of environments, virtual and real.
   ✓ Blurring of work-home boundaries.
   ✓ Blurring of role and identity.
   ✓ Influence on values and priorities.
   ✓ Impact of all of the above on relationships.
2. We are living as much in the "Age of Information About Information" as we are living in the Information Age.
3. Without interpersonal intelligence, we are never really sure of our roles, responses, and emotions, especially when we spend significant time each day consuming media and using technology.

- Discuss central theses and themes on displacement from Suggested Readings below.

Suggested Readings from Chapter One

Green, Lelia. *Communication, Technology and Society*. Thousand Oaks, CA: Sage, 2002.

Gurak, Laura J. *Cyberliteracy: Navigating the Internet with Awareness*. New Haven, CT: Yale University Press, 2001.

Kunstler, James Howard. *The Geography of Nowhere*. New York: Simon & Schuster, 1994.

Kunstler, James Howard. *Home from Nowhere: Remaking Our Everyday World for the 21st Century*. New York: Simon & Schuster, 1996.

Putnam, Robert D. *Bowling Alone: The Collapse and Revival of American Community*. New York: Simon & Schuster, 2000.

Schor, Juliet B. *The Overworked American: The Unexpected Decline of Leisure*. New York: Basic Books, 1992.

The Human Condition

All moral philosophy may as well be applied to a common and private life, as to one of richer composition: every man carries the entire form of human condition.

—MICHEL DE MONTAIGNE, *Essays*

Peace and Empowerment

When we feel accepted, a temporary state, we feel at peace and empowered, able to cope with rigors of the human condition: from the daily disappointments and minuscule arguments to the long-term illnesses and sudden losses that accumulate as we grow old. The path to peace and empowerment intersects with conscience and consciousness. Peace involves the conscience; empowerment, consciousness. The conscience is associated with ethics, an inner knowledge of right and wrong, based on how we treat others and ourselves. Consciousness is associated with awareness, the ability to foresee consequences of our actions on others and ourselves. We need both conscience and consciousness to experience emotional and intellectual balance. To be sure, many of our problems at home and work stem from stress and feelings of ineffectiveness—by-products of a high-tech age. We spend too many hours each day in front of television and computer screens, clicking a remote or a mouse. Media and technology are mobile and have followed us outdoors. Cell phones and handheld computers are ubiquitous reminders that humans in the twenty-first century dwell in more than one place at any time, splitting consciousness to multitask in parks, cars, schools, restaurants, and malls. Using these devices we become less mindful of surroundings and our own behavior, blurring consciousness and dulling the conscience. We may not intuit right or wrong, looking inward for answers, when our attention is interrupted regularly and diverted

40

from physical to virtual environments. Our vision of community becomes myopic, too, because we must rely on skewed perception the few hours each day that we venture outdoors. And when we do, we tend to navigate physical terrain by motor vehicle which, contends journalist James Howard Kunstler in *The Geography of Nowhere*, "connects the inhabitants to the inside of their car" with the outside world a mere "element for moving through, as submarines move through water."[68] For many users of mobile technology, community metamorphoses into elevator music. We know it is out there but are not really paying attention.

We are seldom out of touch with anyone anywhere anymore. An electronic gadget or portable computer is usually within reach. Many individuals enjoy instantaneous access to family, friends, and colleagues and yet, despite such contact, feel a void in their lives. Slowly, almost imperceptibly, some of us are losing the ability to interact meaningfully with others, face-to-face, because we opt for on-demand rather than physical contact, relying on technology to mediate our thoughts, words, and deeds. And we pay a price, not only in access fees but in feelings.

Ironically, people so "in touch" via electronic communication often are out of touch emotionally with themselves and each other. Technology is not to blame, of course, because we choose how to use it; but there is no excuse for ignorance of interpersonal communication. Human beings are meant to interact with each other face-to-face in physical habitat, developing language and social skills. From childhood to adulthood we learn the importance of timing and articulation, which consciousness provides, along with mindfulness, which the conscience provides. Those aptitudes are waning. The convenience and availability of high-tech gadgets entice us to interact on impulse. Communication suffers when

- *Contact is untimely rather than opportune.* We cause interruptions at work or disruptions at home, forgetting that the "occasion" of a conversation—the hour, date, and place—usually is as important as content itself. A message worth sharing should be conveyed at a propitious moment in the appropriate setting.
- *Content is capricious rather than cogent.* We lack time to collect our thoughts, failing to articulate them lucidly. We ramble or react, omit details or divulge too many. Effective exchanges require foresight and insight.

• *Dialogue is mediated rather than meaningful.* No matter how contemplative the speaker, or cogent the message, electronic communication filters out aspects of content and motive, modifying meaning. Senders and receivers of mediated messages may not compensate for missing components—lack of voice tone in e-mail and facial expression in voice mail, and so on.

• *Consciousness is divided rather than directed.* People must contend with intrusions of real on virtual habitat (or vice versa) and sometimes cannot concentrate adequately on the topic at hand. Intrusions are the norm when we communicate on impulse without a sense of occasion or an inkling of forethought, relying on machines to convey content and intent.

We are inundated with electronic messages each day—untimely, capricious, mediated, and unfocused—from any number of devices at home, work, or within reach. Each incident, in and of itself, may seem minor. We may shrug off the rudeness of occasional e-mail or the intrusion of cell phone chat. But the cumulative effect is chilling. Life becomes less happy and more complex because we often spend part of our day perpetuating or mending disagreements, justifying viewpoints, or clarifying ourselves. The convenience of technology is offset by the fritter of follow-up. The more messages we send or receive, the greater the volume of follow-up and frustration. It takes a toll. Eventually we become less mindful of others and doubt their word when they give it, because we get it electronically through various media replete with advertisements, spam, viruses, and other virtual vexations. Worse, we suffer the onslaught isolated from others in private or oblivious of them in public. Preoccupied with our issues or agendas, we distrust or ignore others and physical habitat in general. As the Dalai Lama puts it, lamenting the loss of community, "This in turn encourages us to suppose that because others are not important for my happiness, their happiness is not important for me."[69] That symbiosis violates vital elements of emotional well-being. We give only to those who give to us and rely only on those who promise reciprocal levels of security, love, and materialism. We end up treating a few select individuals as we wish to be treated. *Everyone else is expendable.*

That may seem practical and efficient, according to the dictates of time management. The philosophy of self-centeredness may work for years. Until something goes wrong, and something always goes wrong, according to the dictates of the human condition. We may lose our jobs or possessions, fall ill or out of love. We may be deceived, harmed, or manipulated by strangers or by those in whom we have placed great trust. Or the people we care about may suffer those tribulations, overlooking our needs while they focus on their own. To whom shall we turn in such moments if we hitherto have failed to treat others *according to the occasion or the task at hand*—thanking the store clerk; listening to a child; advising a colleague; helping a friend; showing grace in the wake of incivility and forgiveness in the wake of affront? Doing so we appreciate the ordinary aspects of life, learning mindfulness and coping skills. Day by day, gesture by gesture, the cumulative effect is ennobling. We may rely on it during times of loss or challenge. Otherwise when personal worlds collapse, as they surely shall, we collapse with them. And when we do, we seek self-help.

Self-help has become a multibillion-dollar multimedia industry. Psychologists and "spiritual" guides inundate us with infomercials, videos, software, Web sites, and more, promising wholeness if only we purchase their product or subscribe to their service. Millions of consumers buy into the idea, lured by testimonials offering peace of mind or empowerment, and attempt to attain them electronically, estranged from community. The search for acceptance becomes ever more desperate. We click through life aimlessly as in a desert, coming to an occasional oasis but never reaching our true "destination"—the root word of which, fittingly, means "purpose," or *destiny*.

The conscience grants us peace when we realize that how we treat others determines our own well-being and fulfillment. Community, in fact, is founded on that principle, from secular laws to religious morals. Several theologians have attempted to define conscience, including Dietrich Bonhoeffer, who resisted Hitler and was executed, acting on his beliefs. He writes:

> Conscience comes from a depth which lies beyond a man's own will and his own reason and it makes itself heard as the call of human existence with itself. Conscience comes as an indictment of the loss of this unity and as a warning against the loss of one's self. Primarily it is directed not toward a particular kind of doing but toward a particular mode of being.[70]

Bonhoeffer's 1937 book, *The Cost of Discipleship*, ultimately cost him his life. Imprisoned, however, his conscience blossomed. Bonhoeffer eventually found meaning in "a thorough preparation for a new start and a new task when peace comes,"[71] he wrote shortly before his death in April 1944. He was referring to peace of mind, content that his captivity was a meaningful experience that would safeguard Germany's future. Bonhoeffer, like all great masters of conscience, including Mahatma Gandhi, Mother Teresa, and Martin Luther King, realized that peace emanates out of community and is inspired by commitment. In modern times, the word "peace" harkens the media stereotype of a cabin surrounded by evergreens at a tranquil lake. That may be leisure, not peace: *the wherewithal to meet challenges effectively by interacting with others according to a set of firmly held beliefs.* As Bonhoeffer's beliefs indicate, peace usually entails action. That is why activists stage "peace" marches. The *belief* behind a march unites and motivates participants. Peace also involves working with others to contribute to the community or future generations. In a word, peace concerns *others*, not you. That is why mediated self-improvement programs frequently fail, unable to alter habits or behavior, because techniques focus on the person instead of on his or her relationship with others in *physical* habitat, without which the conscience continually founders.

Likewise "empowerment" has little to do with leverage in relationships or business. That may involve assertiveness or authority, not empowerment: *an expansive knowing of how thoughts, words, and deeds affect others and ourselves.* That knowledge empowers us. We perceive consequences of actions before taking them and a wider range of choices before making them. Ironically empowerment requires a modicum of tranquility so that we can reflect on past choices and foresee the likely result of future ones. In time we learn that our decisions ripple through other people, the way a pebble ripples a pond. That pond is community. We are ripples of the same substance. Acknowledging that, we become more mindful of others and ourselves.

Ideally, conscience and consciousness work in tandem as effortlessly as hand-eye coordination. They inform us about how we should regard our own and others' actions and choices. They tell us how to interpret the world emotionally and intellectually, putting events into perspective and establishing priorities so we can live fulfilling lives. When that happens, we experience stability and social acceptance. We are actualized, and our lives become as authentic as our surroundings. As a result, we develop *character.*

Character is a moral tattoo. The Greek word for it, *charakter*, stands for "a graving tool" as if others may come to know us through the values we have engraved on our person. Only the community can bestow character. Virtual environments cannot because they change rapidly, lack social structure, cater to demand, and delete aspects of interpersonal engagement—from physical sensation to metaphysical transformation. Neither can we claim to possess character, for that would come across as self-righteous; others in society deem whether we have or lack character. They also call "character into question" or determine if we act "out of character." When character is found lacking, conscience and consciousness have been misinforming each other, generating false feelings of offense, guilt, urgency, abandonment, entitlement, or distress. We alienate those who normally would share information, conversation, or companionship; perform kind or reciprocal deeds; affirm viewpoints, talents, or worthiness; or generally be helpful or available.

Community plays an integral role in our moral development. Simply put, *community* is a place for "communion"—the true habitat for humanity—where people share lives, rear children, and partake in the essentials of healthy and productive living. Communities include native countries, hometowns, homes, workplaces, churches, schools, and neighborhoods. The conditions of community necessitate face-to-face interaction in physical places. Each of those locales, where we spend most our days, instills in us a "standard of living"—an *ethical* as well as economical living standard—and influences character.

Survival in Virtual Environments

Because of media and technology, community has gone virtual. Virtual reality is, literally, another dimension with its own addresses, highways, domains, languages, cultures, protocols, policies, laws, mores, conventions, and more. The ecosystems that created this habitat promote product over principle and consumption over conscience. We took our ethics into this artificial environment, believing they would remain intact. In fact, our civic virtues—love of family, hometown, and country; respect for others; concern about future generations and the common good—are undergoing great change to accommodate the environs of cyberspace and airwave, where we dwell for a good part of most days. We need others. But when we reach out to touch them, we are apt to touch keyboards or remotes as often as each other.

We are social creatures who rely on the company of others. According to zoologist and science writer Matt Ridley, "original virtue" is based on this biological precept. "We live in towns, work in teams, and our lives are spiders' webs of connections—linking us to relatives, colleagues, companions, friends, superiors, inferiors. We are, misanthropes notwithstanding, unable to live without each other."[72] Our virtues and principles are pegged to survival as a group rather than as individuals. Writes Ridley, "Even on a practical level, it is probably a million years since any human being was entirely and convincingly self-sufficient: able to survive without trading his skills for those of his fellow humans."[73] We are programmed genetically for community more than any other primate. Similar arguments can be made from a spiritual perspective, encompassing Moses and the Ten Commandments, essentially a set of community laws. Biologically, spiritually, and ethically, we are obligated to partake of, to participate in, and to nurture community by elevating standards and inspiring social and/or spiritual development. Such development is associated with the search for acceptance. According to distinguished philosopher Simon Blackburn of the University of Cambridge, the environment in which "we human beings flourish is largely a social environment. We succeed in the eyes of each other."[74] Author, teacher, and spiritualist Ram Dass, who once researched human consciousness at Harvard during the turbulent 1960s, concluded that community helps reorient ourselves spiritually. "It helps to have fellow seekers in your life who can help you to stay on-track," he writes, "and who remind you gently when you seem to have lost your way."[75]

Many of us fail to appreciate our reliance on community and the welfare of others. Instead we focus almost exclusively on our own needs or wishes for wealth, security, authority, romance, and physical and emotional well-being. Mass media reinforces such desires by manipulating our emotions to sell products or services based on perceived rather than real need. With the right market data, advertisers can appeal to perceived need so powerfully that feelings interfere with rational behavior. As professors John and Nicholas Jackson O'Shaughnessy write in *The Marketing Power of Emotion*,

> Thoughts about buying are not listless mental acts. They can be exciting and can involve strong likes and dislikes, anxieties, and aspirations. Just think about the emotional component of buying a new

car. Emotions intensify wants and desires and intensify motivation. Even ethical behavior can be suppressed because of a failure to generate the emotion needed to motivate moral action.[76]

Because media and technology have saturated our lives, we have grown accustomed or desensitized to such manipulation. Concentrating on our needs, rather than on our habitats—from home to hometown—we may no longer feel the "tug" of conscience that informs us when we are being misled. The tug that most of us feel on an everyday basis is a leash, directing us to this product or that service. Like canines, we either resist or acquiesce.

We endure hundreds of media messages each day. They tell us what we require or lack to make life easier, less painful, quicker, more connected, and convenient. And yet, if anything, our lives have become more painful and complicated and less convenient. The more time we save via technology, the more we squander using *other* technology— or, just as likely—multitasking, watching television and using a laptop computer, say. Bombarded with junk mail, e-mail, spam, direct marketing, advertising, sales pitches, and premiums, we ignore the written and spoken word out of distrust or cynicism, because we have become desensitized to language. Many of us have built up such resistance to advertising messages—*buy this car, get the girl; use this lotion, get the guy*—that we neglect authentic needs, unable to distinguish between real or perceived ones. Without keen perception, we deceive ourselves, pulling false alarms when life is fine or silencing real alarms when life is deficient. Lacking the wherewithal to perceive others and ourselves objectively, we slowly lose the ability to face the daily challenges of life.

The Marketing of Self-Help

When we succumb to self-help, what do we encounter? More media and technology. Even authors of insightful books addressing the overuse of media and technology err in this regard. Case in point: Jill Andresky Fraser's *White-Collar Sweatshop: The Deterioration of Work and Its Rewards in Corporate America*, cited in this book, discusses the blurring of boundaries between home and work caused by communication technology, especially computers. In documenting that problem, she discloses:

The course of my research coincided with the growing involvement of more people (and more *different* kinds of people) with the Internet, and I expanded my activities accordingly. Besides regularly visiting a host of websites and chat rooms that focus on work-related issues, I posted descriptions of my project in a variety of Internet sites, complete with "hyperlinks" that could connect interested people directly to my e-mail address.[77]

It does not occur to Fraser that the very people complaining about technology lengthening their workday are visiting Internet sites for self-help advice rather than interacting meaningfully with their partners, friends, neighbors, and children. Granted, Fraser, finance editor of *Inc.* magazine, knows where to locate technology-exploited white-collar workers as sources for her book; however, she seems to miss the point that their perceptions concerning their situation may, in fact, be skewed because they are looking for answers in cyberspace instead of physical place, seeking self-help from the medium that has deprived them of it.

That symptom, unfortunately, is the norm in the computerized self-help industry. Self-help companies use electronic devices to reach clientele and sell their product lines. Merchandise includes popular magazines; trade books; e-books; audio and video tapes; CD and DVD recordings; computer software; electronic schedulers and pocket devices; and other home office digital gadgets—to name but a few. Products are sold on-line or through infomercial and direct mail catalogue or at retreats and professional seminars. Self-help topics literally span the alphabet from A to Z—*abuse* to *Zen*—and cover just about everything else in between: *anger, anxiety, aromatherapy, biofeedback, body language, business opportunities, career development, codependency, communication, continuing education, corporate training, creativity, dating, death, depression, dieting, divorce, eating disorders, empowerment, family, fitness, friendship, happiness, herbal medicine, leadership, love, management training, massage therapy, meditation, motivation, natural health, nutrition, parenting, positive thinking, public speaking, religion, relaxation, sexuality, stress management, teenagers, therapy/counseling, time management, women's issues,* and more.

Marketers make use of such categories to target new users and expand client lists. Self-help publishers, corporations, product manufacturers, and seminar developers compile mailing lists—files of names, e-mail addresses, etc.—of those who inquire about or use their products or services. These lists are rented to direct marketing and research companies. In turn these firms compile and rent out new lists. For instance, those who enroll in career development seminars might have an interest in enhancing their public speaking skills, while those who have purchased divorce videos might have an interest in assertiveness training or financial planning. Some lists keep expanding—such as dieting, fitness, happiness, parenting, stress management, and positive thinking (to name a few)—because they are associated with symptoms of media overexposure. Some lists keep spinning off like television sitcoms. Dieting feeds nutrition which feeds herbal medicine which feeds therapy and counseling. Thus, self-help never ends. Clientele merely "cross over."

For the most part, the components of consumerism and morality do not mix well. Problems concern:

• *Real versus perceived needs.* Marketing touts perceived needs, rather than real ones, from instant prosperity to easy popularity, with products and services that promise these rewards. The short-term objective is to sell. Authentic self-help is inherently ethical and so touts real rather than perceived needs, emphasizing priorities, from physical wellness to civic participation. The long-term objective is to live well.

• *Exclusion versus inclusion.* Individuals in front of computer screens are physically isolated because of the nature of technology and/ or the content of programming. As such, marketers track and target users, compiling data on perceived needs and promoting programming that appeals to those needs. People who participate with others in community are harder to compartmentalize. They interact in physical habitat with humanity while their mediated counterparts interact through digital devices that lord over their daily lives. Civic-minded individuals devote time to community to derive a sense of inclusion. Those who rely on technology often squander time seeking inclusion electronically, only to end up excluded from the company of others.

• *Marketing versus moral development.* Marketing targets people with messages that indirectly reaffirm or directly play off feelings, especially fear and inadequacy. The goal is to influence consumer spending habits. Moral development seeks to ease fears and reaffirm self-worth so that people can experience genuine feelings, free of manipulation, with the singular goal of nurturing lifelong learning habits to help us cope and come to terms with the human condition.

Individuals who resist moral development seek to circumvent the human condition, in one aspect or another, whether they realize it or not.

The Ethics of Our Condition

Because we have consciousness, the human condition is humanity's main concern. We know that we will die and, in dying, lose everything material and ethereal, including loved ones. That has been the lesson of history, from which no one is exempt, from peripatetic saint to bunkered despot. According to journalist James Howard Kunstler,

> History doesn't believe anybody's advertising. History doesn't care whether nations rise or fall. History is merciless and life is tragic. Human consciousness begins with the notion that there is a beginning, a middle, and an end to all things.[78]

We do not know if consciousness remains intact at the moment of death and beyond. There are also clues that consciousness is shared and universal. Even some agnostic scientists intuit that conscious awareness of the human condition is a fundamental fact of reality. The conscience supports that belief by instilling in each individual a collective (if uneven) awareness of right and wrong. Perhaps, then, the only genuine self-help emanates out of the conscience, bestowing life with purpose and death with meaning. Great intellects have grappled with this mystifying duality, concluding, as did Albert Einstein, that without ethical culture—or *collective conscience*—"there is no salvation for humanity."[79]

Moral development requires service to and interaction with members of community. Good Samaritans are found in every great religion, from the Judeo-Christian to Confucian-Jen traditions. Confucius, in fact, makes the "perfect kindness" of *jen* the core of his philosophy. The word is difficult to translate into English but basically means "humanity and benevolence."[80] Habitat, of course, is the core concept of Darwinism, the care of which ultimately determines survival. When we take our communities for granted, or worse—take without giving to others—we pollute the moral atmosphere, lower the ethical standard of living, and create unhealthy habitats, including elitist neighborhoods and bigoted hometowns, dysfunctional families and uncivil workplaces, and/or dogmatic churches and doctrinaire schools. In sum, the universal conundrum has deepened within us, for without communal feeling—the notion that all of us must face the potential obliteration of identity—we are condemned to ponder that prospect alone, believing our problems are individual when they are, by nature, collective.

Some of us, initially at least, had no choice with respect to emotional well-being, being born into dysfunctional families or encountering troubled individuals innocently or unknowingly. Over time, however, for the majority of people that is no excuse. The conscience should tweak our emotions and consciousness, our intellect, informing us that something has gone wrong with our lives. When love becomes conditional and social acceptance exploitative we have to prove our worth repeatedly by violating values and limiting perception. But if we rebel against manipulative or controlling conditions on principle, cleaving to ethical doctrines, we strike a universal chord—in ourselves and others—even in those who might otherwise reproach us. They may acknowledge, however begrudgingly, that we possess character. If we succumb to unjust conditions, going along to get along—*no matter how ignoble that might feel to us*—we yield moral ground and betray our values. Thereafter our world seems as flat as ancient myth.

When we fail to perceive the world as it actually is, our moral dexterity falters. Instead of partaking in abundance, which communities potentially offer us, we live from one crisis to the next and soon face *real* emergencies, confrontations, and stress. Moreover, because of impaired perception, we lack the wherewithal to meet challenges; thus, we are deprived of peace. If anything, our hunger for acceptance is heightened. That remains a constant. Now we begin the agonizing process of self-deception, depression, addiction, and degradation, alienating us from those we desire (partners), need (employers), serve (clients), love (family), enjoy (friends), and rely on (ourselves). Cut off from the essentials of life, we lack empowerment. We watch more media or indulge in mindless technology. We pursue self-help from the source of the affliction. We have literally lost *our way*.

Our life path begins in early childhood. For the first seven or so years of life, the ego develops and, according to Ram Dass, resembles an actor preparing for a performance. "[The ego] selects its costumes, learns its lines, its timing, its gestures, its way of movement, even the choices of roles it may play when it leaves the dressing room and stands before an audience of other Egos across the footlights."[81] Then, without warning, we attain consciousness. Although levels thereof may vary, many of us awake one day and intuit Descartes' famous dictate: *I think, therefore I am.* As soon as we realize that truth, the conscience, like a radio station, turns on and transmits to the self: *I am, therefore I feel.*

Scientists generally acknowledge the existence of consciousness, a universal awareness linked to the human condition. A leading proponent of the consciousness view is Paul Davies, professor of mathematical physics at the University of Adelaide, who writes:

> I belong to the group of scientists who do not subscribe to a conventional religion but nevertheless deny that the universe is a purposeless accident. Through my scientific work I have come to believe more and more strongly that the physical universe is put together with an ingenuity so astonishing that I cannot accept it merely as a brute fact. There must, it seems to me, be a deeper level of explanation. Whether one wishes to call that deeper level "God" is a matter of taste and definition. Furthermore, I have come to the point of view that mind—i.e., conscious awareness of the world—is not a meaningless and incidental quirk of nature, but an absolutely fundamental facet of reality.[82]

Few scientists make such a case for the conscience, perhaps because it flies in the face of Darwinism. Practicing the Golden Rule, treating others as one wishes to be treated, does not necessarily ensure one's rung in the food chain. Without acknowledging conscience as biological fact, zoologist Matt Ridley tries valiantly in his *Origins of Virtue* to link Darwinism to the origins of ethics, stating, "Our minds have been built by selfish genes, but they have been built to be social, trustworthy, and cooperative. That is the paradox this book has tried to explain." Alas, however, he might have found a quicker path to the oracle in his 300-page book by honoring the golden rule of science, otherwise known as Occam's razor: *Scientific truth must be both elegant and simple.* That notion comes down to us in part from William of Occam, a thirteenth century English cleric and philosopher, who believed "plurality should not be assumed without necessity." Or in modern lingo, "Keep it simple." Ridley's pluralities, however eloquent, to explain away conscience violate that tenet. Evidence of the conscience exists in every corner of the globe. *Its source cannot be known.* That, too, is part of the human condition.

The conscience is a universal precept, appropriately found in Article 1 of the United Nations' Universal Declaration of Human Rights: "All human beings are born free and equal in dignity and rights. They are endowed with reason and *conscience* [emphasis added] and should act towards one another in a spirit of brotherhood."[83] We understand that spirit regardless of culture or upbringing as soon as we reason that we have consciousness. Up until that time, the ego demanded unconditional devotion, yearning instinctively for a state of innocence which we, upon entry into the world, began to lose. Before consciousness and conscience, our notion of right and wrong was governed primarily by punishment and reward, a parent's spank or hug. Our senses were ruled, by and large, by physical pain: a hunger pang, for instance, or a flesh wound. Suddenly we felt *psychic* pain and perceived a broader spectrum of emotions: guilt, deceit, betrayal, temptation, manipulation, and more, but also honor, fairness, courage, kindness, and compassion. We also began to feel (or fear) death, at first the death of others—from pets to parents—and eventually that of ourselves.

Death accompanies consciousness. We become aware that all things end, even us. Such a notion is implied in Descartes' dictate: *I think, therefore I am, will be, and was.* Consciousness ties us to others because we all must come to terms with the same physical fate: *the imminent obliteration of individual identity.* Paradoxically, the conscience unites us collectively because we all must come to terms with the same spiritual fate: *What is in the other also is in me.* These universal truths encompass and counterbalance the human condition, reminding us about the insignificance of personhood and the importance of neighborhood. To love one's neighbors as oneself is not a religious tenet, a metaphysical concept, or a lifestyle choice but a core prerequisite of life on earth. Believing otherwise, the search for acceptance becomes elusive or shallow.

The degree to which we accept or deny these universal truths governs our actions. *There is no other ethic but the human condition. There is no other choice but unconditional love.* We confront these paradoxical, incontrovertible truths every day. We experience mortality and intuit morality. Life on earth comes with instructions—not only in the genome—but also in the conscience. Thus, we feel "sparks of recognition" when we do right by others and "pangs of regret" when we do wrong. The Greeks called this phenomenon *synderesis*, a divine spark that ignites an innate understanding of ethics. The biblical symbol for synderesis is an eagle (Ezekiel 1: 4–14), one of the four faces of a mythi-cal creature emerging from clouds as we must emerge from ignorance into mindfulness. The other faces are decidedly earthbound: man (rea-son), lion (anger), and ox (appetite). Only the transcendent eagle can perceive the panorama of worldly things; its vision is not only sharp but *steady*. Unlike the owl, the eagle can gaze into the sun—the font of soul-felt enlightenment. For our purposes, this eagle represents con-science by virtue of its unwavering gaze and consciousness by virtue of its vision.

To enhance conscience and consciousness, we need to assess at what we have gazed in an electronic age and how, if at all, that has affected our vision. In other eras, people gazed mostly at stars and each other. Our collective vision was governed by culture and community—some-times brutally, sometimes benevolently—but always *authentically* so. Social problems from slavery to tyranny, and the courage required to address them, were readily apparent. However slowly or sorrowfully, society rose to the challenge. That may cease to be the case. Because of media and technology, our perception is at risk along with our view of reality, altering notions of the self as well as of the real, explaining why so many seekers of self-help suffer from "identity problems." Why not? In less than a half-century, human beings have acquired the capacity to end life atomically and to live life virtually.

As a result we glorify technology, believing media hype about the social benefits of computerization. Those benefits exist, but not exclu-sively at the expense of community. Community must influence tech-nology, and vice versa, to advance the collective good. Glorification impedes that process. In truth, Murphy's Law (if something can go wrong, *it will*) has melded with Moore's Law (computer power doubles every 18 months or so). Surprisingly, many scientists do not recognize that prospect, prophesying that computers will be more intelligent than humans by 2020—the age of "post humanity"—quips Selmer Brings-jord, professor of logic and cognitive science and director of the Minds & Machines Lab at Rensselaer Polytechnic Institute. Bringsjord be-lieves that computers and robots will remain inferior to human beings precisely because they "don't have feelings; they have inner lives on a par with those of rocks. No amount of processing speed is ever going to surmount that obstacle."[84] That obstacle is lack of conscience and consciousness, distinctly human characteristics.

Convenience over Conscience

Technology cannot ease aspects of the human condition. However, when combined with media, technology can wield great influence on conscience and consciousness and, in turn, on moral and spiritual development. Specifically, media and technology have altered the meaning of community to include airwave and cyberspace which, of course, are not physical but virtual habitats. Yet some of us spend most of our days there—although there is no "there *there*"—watching television passively or computing interactively and idly, letting both media and technology set the pace and standard of living in our *real* habitats.

Because of television, we generally wear the same style of clothes, speak the same slang, eat the same fast foods, and adopt the same social values, with variation occurring according to brand or generation labels (baby boomer, gen X, gen Y, etc.). For instance baby boomers buy Land's End; gen Xers, The Gap; gen Yers, Old Navy. *All buy jeans.* There is also variety in buns, hamburgers, toppings, and condiments. Commercials for Pepsi and Coca-Cola have greater variety than the drinks themselves. MTV lingo and culture are as narrow as but differ from ESPN lingo and culture. True, cable television may have given viewers hundreds more channels from which to choose, along with hundreds more infomercials masquerading as programming; however, the producers and celebrities are stylistically uniform, for the most part, because New York and Los Angeles remain the premiere marketing hubs. In fact, although the average TV viewer has access to sixty-plus channels—a number that continues to grow with each survey—the number of channels actually viewed has not grown beyond thirteen in recent years.[85] If anything, the plethora of channels appealing to distinct markets helps generate sales of more TV sets, with 3.36 sets per home and 29 percent of families owning four or more units.[86] With sets in living and bedrooms, kitchens, dens, home offices, and basements, family members are separated not only by walls but by different demographics and interests. Chasms widen the longer we dare to watch. We may share the same genome with parents and siblings, but not the same consumer habits. Alone in our rooms, marketing strategies target our perceived "character traits" and programming reinforces them. As a result, family members lose touch with each other even though they live under one roof.

By some estimates, more than two-thirds of all U.S. homes now have computer access, a number sure to skyrocket in the future.[87] Educators had long hoped that personal computers would lure more people away from passive TV-watching into the interactive Web; but that has not happened. "There is currently almost no indication that Internet access cannibalizes television usage,"[88] states Nielsen Media Research in an annual report, "TV Viewing in Internet Households." Internet users are influenced by television viewing habits. For instance, even though such users have access to thousands of sites, they typically only visit with any regularly a mere handful of sites. As the Nielsen report also observes, "The power of portals is evident from the fact that despite thousands of sites available, 90 percent of the online audience visits at least one of the top 10 sites in a given month."[89]

Computer use has added hours to the time we spend looking at screens instead of each other. That weighs heavily on our ability to interact effectively with family, friends, colleagues, and supervisors during challenging times at home or crises at work. We are squandering more of our lives chatting, surfing, or interacting idly with others, all of which tends to homogenize important relationships and shorten attention spans. We visit home pages rather than homes but convince ourselves that we are interacting responsibly with family and friends simply because we are keeping up with their lives. We marvel at the convenience of digital technology, remembering how time-consuming it was to pen letters, develop snapshots, or see relatives during holidays and vacations. And yet, in scrapbooks and holy books of baby boomers, are yellowed letters with black-and-white photographs of grandparents and ancestors—precious as time itself—marked not only by the passage of time but also by the authenticity of handwriting and stationery. The children of baby boomers will have e-mail and pixels, a karmic fate, for they have been taught to elevate convenience, which technology can provide, over substance, which it cannot. They will have lived in an information age in which the medium of the message was deemed more important than the sender or contents of the message itself.

Few scholars saw this more clearly than Howard Gardner, MacArthur fellow and professor of education at Harvard University. In his best-selling book *Leading Minds*, Gardner argues that an increase in the quantity of information does not necessarily mean an increase in the quality of information. He observes:

With every passing year, it becomes easier for individuals not only to learn almost instantaneously what is happening around the world but also to participate in the "global information super-highway." . . . Indeed, more channels often mean more low-grade, spurious, and specious information; and the ubiquitous temptation to transmit easily digested sound bites will come as no surprise to anyone who has explored the powers of the unschooled mind. Such a barrage of undigested and often simplistic information may make it even more difficult to have an uncluttered mind that can discern the big picture.[90]

We no longer see the *interpersonal* big picture. When we use powerful information tools like home computers and mobile phones, we may believe that we are tending to key relationships. In actuality what we are doing, more often than not, requires no more of a commitment than reading a newspaper or leaving a sticky note on the refrigerator. E-mailing, in fact, is easier than sticky notes because we can leave them at multiple addresses in virtual reality. Sticky notes require more energy, focus, and commitment. Colleagues at work realize this when we communicate electronically across cubicles rather than discuss issues face-to-face. Experts on anger at the workplace encourage employees to "be direct,"[91] which often translates to "react via electronic messages." Colleagues and supervisors need to open fewer laptops and more office doors. Again, technology offers incredible convenience—enabling workers to finish reports efficiently and supervisors to communicate via e-mail with all manner of clients and employees—but it cannot sustain substance or build teamwork for long. Face-to-face interactions provide substance because messages and exchanges are less apt to be diluted, misinterpreted, or otherwise transformed by technology. Face-to-face interactions build teamwork for the same reasons. Corporations pay millions of dollars hiring consultants to help them retain experienced managers and then communicate with those managers electronically and superficially. The word *network* used to involve people; now it involves servers. That, as much as the economy, may be why employees have become so "mobile," flitting from job to job, seeking recognition at work because they cannot find it at home, in part because media and technology have blurred those boundaries. Yet some of us wonder nostalgically why we cannot always rely on families and friends during personal upheaval and on colleagues and supervisors during professional crises. The answer may be that media and technology have altered those relationships without our even noticing it.

Many of us overlook the impact because:

- We have invested heavily in media and technology at home and at the office, incorporating entertainment centers and computer work stations into our daily activities to such extent that these tools now *define* rather than enhance such activities.
- We do not understand the marketing strategies of media and technology because they are interwoven now into technical or operational structures, targeting and influencing us as never before.
- We seek self-help quickly and effortlessly, hoping to make a few lifestyle changes, as we would with diet, to overcome life-threatening behaviors that deprive us of joy and fulfillment.

The typical reader has to be deprogrammed from the cult of media and technology, miraculous tools which, if used properly, can expand conscience and consciousness. However if these electronic tools are used improperly, no self-improvement method (even the most popular) can ensure lasting social acceptance or career effectiveness. Over-consumption of media and overuse of technology have shortened attention spans, along with tempers. The hard fact is that enhancing consciousness so that we foresee the impact of our actions on others—part of that "big picture"—requires practice and steadfastness of purpose. Mihaly Csikszentmihalyi, psychologist and author, asserts that methods to free consciousness have eluded humankind for millennia. We cannot condense such wisdom into a formula as self-help books often attempt to do. Like art and other complex forms of expertise, Csikszentmihalyi notes, such wisdom "must be earned through trial-and-error experience by each individual, generation after generation."[92] That experience, which all of us share, is part of the human condition. That condition, which many of us resist, is the font of such wisdom. That font is found in community, from which many of us have been displaced, developing distinct habits which, as we shall learn, are being shaped by media and technology.

Journal Exercise

During the course of a week, analyze the impact of technology in your electronic exchanges at home or at school/work. Note the following:

- *Was contact untimely rather than opportune?* Be sure to catalogue interruptions at school/work and disruptions at home. Jot down the medium used to make contact, along with the time of and the reason for the contact. Determine whether the message:
  1. Was timely for the medium, given the reason for contact.
  2. Was untimely for the medium, given the reason for contact.
  3. Could have been conveyed at a more propitious moment.
  4. Probably should have been conveyed face-to-face at a different time or date.
  5. Probably would not have been conveyed face-to-face at the particular time of day that the message was sent.
- *Was content capricious rather than cogent?* Determine the import of each message, noting whether:
  1. *Language* was (a) clear, (b) somewhat clear, (c) unclear.
  2. *Content* was (a) important, (b) somewhat important, (c) unimportant.
- *What components of face-to-face dialogue were filtered by the particular medium?* Examine how sight, sound, touch, and so on would have enhanced content. Determine how the medium may have modified meaning.

Discussion/Paper Ideas for Chapter Two

- Discuss observations from the Journal Exercise above.
- Discuss the validity of these assertions:
  1. Many of us are losing the ability to interact meaningfully with others, face to face, because we opt for on-demand rather than physical contact, relying on technology to mediate our thoughts, words, and deeds.
  2. Bombarded with junk mail, e-mail, spam, direct marketing, advertising, sales pitches, and premiums, we may ignore the written and spoken word out of distrust or cynicism, because we have become desensitized to language.
  3. When combined with media, technology can wield great influence on conscience and consciousness and, in turn, on moral and spiritual development.
- Discuss central theses and themes on ethics, conscience, and/or consciousness from Suggested Readings below.

Suggested Readings from Chapter Two

Fraser, Jill Andresky. *White-Collar Sweatshop: The Deterioration of Work and Its Rewards in Corporate America.* New York: Norton, 2001.

O'Shaughnessy, John, and O'Shaughnessy, Nicholas Jackson. *The Marketing Power of Emotion.* New York: Oxford University Press, 2003.

Ridley, Matt. *The Origins of Virtue: Human Instincts and the Evolution of Cooperation.* New York: Penguin, 1996.

Habits of a High-Tech Age

Exactly how, and on what terms, are we renegotiating the boundaries between our selves and our technologized environment? What kind of multiple distributed system do I become when I live part of the day as a teenage girl in a chatroom, part of the day as a serious professional in a webconference, part of the day slaying enemies as Zaxxon, the steel-eyed assassin of an online gaming tribe?

—HOWARD RHEINGOLD, *The Virtual Community: Homesteading on the Electronic Frontier*

The Hype of Self-Help

Self-help is complex. In a word, it involves the "self," which varies from person to person, according to experience, encounters, education, generation, culture, family, and other influences. Because of the above variables, psychologists, therapists, trainers, dieticians, attorneys, and other counselors usually treat their clients' situations personally and exclusively. Seeking solutions to persistent problems, expert and client alike devote time, share commitment, and interact face-to face to foster trust, overcoming individual challenges.

The self-help industry generalizes the "self" to sell help using media and technology. Potential consumers are profiled by race, class, region, gender, shopping habits, credit card purchases, financial records, lifestyle and census statistics, and other database traits so as to target individuals as inexpensively as possible and to sell to those targets as much and as often as possible. Computer-assisted marketing relies on technology to accumulate data on each person, using that information to profile individuals—a privacy concern, as we shall learn; nonetheless, such personal data itself is a general commodity to be captured, combined in lists of like profiles, stored, packaged, and sold. The self-help industry relies on that data because it leans heavily on marketing for clients. In addition to manuals and books, creators of the most admired self-improvement programs use media and technology to define users' daily activities via electronic schedules, videos, cassettes, CD-ROMS, and more; weave marketing strategies to sell product seamlessly into their lesson plans and seminars; and offer as quick reward simple lifestyle changes that eventually leave users craving more self-help or worse, believing that something is wrong with them morally or spiritually that cannot be corrected because, Lord knows, they tried and failed.

Typically people in crisis or transition need useful advice from an expert who knows or has come to know intimately their *individual* situations. People victimized by violence, for instance, may exhibit similar behaviors as found in diagnostic manuals; however, the unique constellation of facts surrounding a particular incident may contain the key to effective treatment. In probing those facts cautiously over time, a therapist may learn about a client's personal experiences associated with social class, ethnicity, religion, present and past partners, familial and cultural histories, and more. This is very private stuff. People usually only share such details with experts in whom they have placed great trust, knowing personal information enhances therapy or advice. Marketing is interested in the same data on a broader social scale for monetary reasons. Trust plays little role in the process of pooling one person's information with others of like profile in the databank. When information is generalized in such a manner, so must the advice, from abuse to Zen.

Good advice requires trust on several levels:

- *Track record.* A trustworthy expert with a history of helping others with similar problems and who also possesses proper education and training.
- *Personal referrals.* Client(s) who investigate that expert's reputation based on word-of-mouth, or referrals from sources and people whose judgment they trust.
- *Compatibility.* A mutual trust between client(s) and expert based on:
  1. a willingness to change lifestyle or habits, on the part of client(s).
  2. a customized protocol to accomplish those goals, on the part of expert.
- *Confidentiality.* Trust in the client-expert relationship in which people seeking advice can be open about hopes, fears, and transgressions, without the risk of privacy invasion.

Local experts who provide effective self-help typically enjoy good reputation in the community. They rely on community to establish track records and garner referrals. They serve clients in suites located within the community, and those places symbolize the partnerships and mutual trust created there.

Media and technology may inspire many things but not trust. Community should do that. The two words are often combined—"community trust"—involving public, charitable, or financial institutions that provide funds or grants to improve services or to foster development in hometowns. For instance, the New York Community Trust manages almost $2 billion in charitable assets generated by citizens, businesses, and families.[93] Similar community organizations often use media and technology to establish or generate funds, but they do not depend on such tools to establish or generate "trust," which requires volunteerism and interpersonal communication skills. As Robert D. Putnam observes in his work about the collapse and revival of American communities,

> The poverty of social cues in computer-mediated communication inhibits interpersonal collaboration and trust, especially when the interaction is anonymous and not nested in a wider social context. Experiments that compare face-to-face and computer-mediated communication confirm that the richer the medium of communication the more sociable, personal, trusting and friendly the encounter.[94]

Those values are also important at the computer-mediated workplace, the source of stress and unhappiness for many individuals seeking self-help and mental wellness. Gerry Lange and Todd Domke, authors of *Cain & Abel at Work*, note that psychiatrists and psychologists help countless people in face-to-face sessions, treating individual disorders, family crises, or personal dilemmas. "But," they add, "some TV and radio shrinks who psychoanalyze the whole of society and give out generic advice ... have helped create a never-never land where people who do not know themselves are sharing their anguish with people they barely know and/or should not trust."[95]

Trust is essential in such counseling because the self is as individual as a fingerprint. The self not only includes the sum of a person's conscience and consciousness but also how those entities work in tandem with each other—harmoniously or dysfunctionally. No two people, even

twins, can have identical levels of moral development and social awareness at any one point in time. Life is far too random for that, exposing
each of us to unique sets of feelings, thoughts, experiences, and encounters—along with responses to those stimuli, in turn generating *more* feelings, thoughts, experiences, and encounters—all of which affect, impair,
or enlighten our conscience and consciousness. Each second of life introduces us to moral variation, based at least in part on the company we
keep. Which is why, in addition to *love thy neighbor as thyself*, the sages
from Black Elk to Buddha to Christ advise: *judge not, that ye be not
judged*. That universal precept generally is lost on people who overuse
technology and overconsume media. As discussed earlier, overuse of
technology leads to impatience, impulse, and poor interpersonal skills.
Overconsumption of media leads to easy stereotypes and knee-jerk reactions. In the end those tendencies lead to bad habits that complicate
our lives and relationships.

Creators of self-improvement methods typically overlook bad interpersonal habits of the high-tech media age. Marketers also avoid the
complexities of life, which vary from person to person, because they use
private data to make broad generalizations. Psychological symptoms as
generalized in diagnostic manuals are easily adapted to marketing manuals. While symptoms may be general, uniqueness of experience is not.
Some people are more sensitive to situations or events; others, less so;
and a few, oblivious. That is why effective counseling takes time, face-
to-face sessions, follow-up, medication and/or behavior modification as
prescribed by accountable practitioners. Marketing methods cannot take
into account our individuality and so, are likely to fail, especially when
self-help programs use promotional strategies to target users and violate their own doctrines to sell products. For example, do people coping
with time management really need slick catalogues of merchandise and
high-end boutiques to plan their weeks in detail for the remainder of their
days? If so, how do they adapt to the chaos at work and the uproar at
home—facts of modern life—when schedules give a false sense of order
in a disordered world? Do couples struggling with relationship problems really require soul mate infomercials that peddle videos to prevent
divorce? If so, will they watch these videos alone, adapting to the constraints of their schedules, instead of making time to interact lovingly
with each other? Do families struggling with money management really
require pricey multimedia software promising effortless prosperity? If
so, will they come to equate spiritual with economic growth? Market-

ers believe so. What we are seeing now in the booming self-help industry mirrors, to some extent, what we saw in the 1970s with televangelism. Marketing does not complement faith, either; it eventually must dominate faith, amending Scripture to augment sales, because that's what salesmanship does: it skews truth to align it with the target market.

To be sure, a few such self-help books and methods are based on long-standing pedagogies and philosophies. For better or worse, values education has been an integral aspect of the American dream and work ethic, beginning with the Puritan philosophy—God will make known through wealth and abundance the chosen "Elect" in society—and continuing with Benjamin Franklin's thrift- and self-reliance–based philosophy. These should be topics of reference books, not self-help. To make matters worse, many modern-day self-help gurus pollute pedagogy with product and, more important, overlook the impact of media and technology on conscience and consciousness. When they do, they indirectly ignore the role of community in our lives, promising to help people build and use buckets but neglecting to tell them where to find the well.

Even the most evolved patrons of self-help seminars thirst increasingly for guidance. This has resulted in religion being incorporated into many character-building programs. As media and marketing analysts note, spiritual self-improvement is the fastest growing segment of the industry, featuring such self-help stars as Iyanla Vanzant, whose message of love-based empowerment is sound but whose media influence occasionally escapes her. In fact, the introduction of her bestseller *Yesterday I Cried* opens with her awaiting a film crew:

> I had no idea what I would be asked during the interview. This was, after all, the award-winning CBS *Sunday Morning*. They could ask me anything about anything, and I would be obliged to respond. What if I was asked about something that I had not yet healed? Suppose I couldn't get my mouth open to respond? What would people think if I were asked a question on national television about the little challenge I was now facing in my own life?[96]

Of course, Vanzant overcomes this and many more life obstacles, including sexual abuse, teen pregnancy, and divorce. She earns a law degree and founds a ministry. Vanzant's drive, if not her methods, obviously have worked for her and, by extension, may work for a select portion of her target audience. Media and faith also work for her.

She is not alone, of course, as self-help methods—from the low-key Mormon influence of Stephen Covey to the high-profile Inner Peace influence of Marianne Williamson—rely in varying degrees on faith to achieve peace and empowerment. That is natural because moral and spiritual growth may be linked to development of conscience and consciousness. But to overlook or gloss over the influence of media and technology, using them to deliver product with self-help, also has profound moral and spiritual implications, especially when methods and merchandise fail to live up to their billing. Without community, people long for acceptance and, finding little in the confines of their homes and home offices, entertain themselves with media and delude themselves with technology. That has led to an epidemic of dubious behaviors.

Seven Habits of Highly Mediated People

When society overemphasizes any philosophy or innovation, a corresponding psychosis will emerge. According to literary critic and rhetorician Kenneth Burke, "[T]here will be a particular recipe of overstressings and understressings peculiar to the given institutional structure," with a cultural tendency to "see everything in terms of this particular recipe of emphases."[97] Modern culture has so overemphasized media and technology that their overuse and consumption are bound to engender certain attitudes. By way of example, Burke notes that an advocate for "free market freedom"—overemphasized in the twentieth century—would believe freedom itself would be lost if society abandoned laissez-faire capitalism. That is a kind of psychosis, for a society can foster freedom without a prescribed set of market considerations. In sum, Burke warns, it is the overemphasis that generates the dysfunction, not the individual components.

Likewise media and technology, mere tools, are not responsible for dubious behaviors in our society. However, the overuse and overconsumption of media and technology may be root causes for several antisocial behaviors because the gadgetry wields subtle but continuous influence in typical homes and workplaces, undermining essential interpersonal skills necessary for well-being and/or leadership.

"The essence of leadership is the ability to influence others,"[98] according to authors of *Interpersonal Communication: Relating to Others*, which references Stephen Covey's immensely successful *Seven Habits of Highly Effective People*—tenets that have inspired leadership proficiency in thousands. Those habits include being proactive, thinking win/win, and putting first things first, among other concepts, all of which emanate out of interpersonal intelligence and which are undermined by overuse and overconsumption of media and technology. Simply put, people who rely on mediated information and communication often misunderstand life and each other to such extent that they routinely commit a host of ethical errors countermanding Covey's tried-and-true techniques. These errors include:

- **No. 1.** *Assuming you own a lie after you tell it.* People who lack perception believe that they can easily deceive others. After all, that is what happens on television with simple plot lines manipulating characters in complex settings. Because liars want to control others, they also believe that they own psychological copyrights to their lies. Typically they underestimate the consequences of their untruths and envision happier endings—as pat and nifty as on TV—than what usually happens in real life. Fact is, as soon as you tell a falsehood, those who hear it also own it. That is the lesson of community. Others can challenge the initial lie or test and investigate it, causing the liar to tell more untruths or commit more serious ethical errors in defense of the original lie. That ruins relationships and causes more social isolation, in addition to that associated with media consumption and technology use. To lie once is to lie repeatedly, risking alienation. As Aristotle espoused, *The least initial deviation from the truth is multiplied later a thousandfold.*
- **No. 2.** *Assuming you have two options: to lie or tell the truth.* People who lack perception also lack discretion. Media exposure, as we have said, erodes both. When challenged at home or at work, people with poor perception usually cannot ascertain the range of apt responses. In some part this is a result of living in an era of talking heads that stick to their party lines and sound bites even when confronted with contradictory evidence. Worse, opposing viewpoints in news and politics often promote simple solutions to complex problems with media personalities leaking sensitive or private information. Discreet people realize that truth can be untimely, confidential, or inappropriate for the occasion. *Truth heard through filters of self-interest can be more damaging than no truth at all.* Conversely, indiscreet people tend to lie in tense situations believing the truth will negate their interests. Lies temporarily ease tension but also require continual shoring up (see

No. 1 above). Actually we enjoy a wide range of choices. For example, we do not have to discuss the issue at hand until able to deal with it effectively. We can also change the subject matter to better suit the time, place, and occasion. Or we can tell the *real* truth: that we find the discussion untimely or inappropriate. Truth will set us free, but only if we respect it enough to share with the right people at the right time and place so that it has maximum, positive impact. Otherwise keep your own counsel according to Shakespeare's maxim: *The better part of valor is discretion.*

• **No. 3.** *Not counting or cutting your losses.* We witness this flaw of Shakespearean tragedies every day on the evening news. We experience it in our public and private lives, obsessed with everyday dramas of dysfunction. A relatively minor problem, misjudgment, miscommunication, or momentary lapse in character is denied or ignored. A timely apology is withheld. Criticism mounts, as do denials, precipitating more ethical errors and lapses and even triggering cover-ups that eventually jeopardize relationships at home and at work. When the smoke clears, as it inevitably does, all that is left is the ego of an otherwise decent person who should have counted a loss as a loss and gone on with life. Everyone suffers setbacks or acts unconscionably. Successful people count and cut their losses and find closure so they can refocus again on well-being or prosperity. This is ancient advice. As the Roman poet Catullus advised, *Count your losses as losses* . . . or risk losing everything (see No. 4 below).

• **No. 4.** *Coveting what you lack and losing what you have.* The grass is always greener on the other side of the street, subdivision, campus, or workplace; and so is the money. Or so it may seem, especially when we see countless commercials and infomercials that reaffirm that fallacy, promising easy riches or lavish lifestyles when we buy their elixirs or subscribe to their miracles. Envy not only involves salary, lifestyle, or luxury but also power and people, from job titles to sexual partners. When you obsess over what you lack or cannot have, you devalue what you *do* have, cease to nurture or protect it and, eventually, jeopardize or lose it. Envy and undue ambition undermine perception, keeping focus on the future so we do not appreciate the present and come to resent the past. We lose a sense of proportion and priorities, taking offense too easily at real or perceived slights and putting our desires ahead of our contributions. True ambition seeks to make contributions by focusing on what you can do in the present and what you learned in the past. The future will take care of itself. *Subdue your desire for things*, as Horace, another Roman poet suggests, *or it will subdue you.*

- **No. 5.** *Defending your motives as pure and damning others' motives as self-serving.* Even if our motives are well-intentioned—which frequently is the case—we cannot fully know the motives of others because we cannot read their minds; we only guess at motives, based on our perception. Conversely, newsmakers and celebrity lawyers routinely justify their actions or assertions as appropriate, condemning opponents or damning the motives of others, including victims. They perceive this as strategy rather than as immorality. When we do similarly, we harm relationships at home and at work and further damage perception, which varies from person to person because of the uniqueness of encounters and everyday interactions; however, as perception grows, all of us come to realize, as the sages realized before us, that our own viewpoint is exceedingly narrow. Hence: *Give others the benefit of the doubt.*

- **No. 6.** *Guessing at motive but acting on it as if it were truth.* Even if one can guess another person's motive accurately—in itself, an extremely difficult task—truth like a rainbow contains many colors and hues. Also like a rainbow, truth varies or may be invisible, depending on where you stand in relation to the light. Media simplify and manipulate messages, so we never truly perceive the complexities of issues and agendas, even ones that may have great bearing on our lives. Because awareness by nature is limited, the motives we assign others usually are incorrect and, as such, tend to complicate situations and compound problems. Thus, Albert Einstein's famous quotation: *Problems cannot be solved at the same level of awareness that created them.*

- **No. 7.** *Simplifying the cause of problems so as to place blame.* Journalists and newsmakers tend to simplify truths with complex language instead of conveying complex truths in simple language. That influences behavior in mediated classrooms and livingrooms. Even when we pinpoint root causes of a problem, issues of truth—and rainbows, for that matter—contain many hues and fonts. That is why problem-solving requires conscientious analysis. Otherwise we may create a bevy of new problems for each one we try to solve by oversimplification. People react to such tactics and often strike back angrily, justifying their actions, not because they were right or wrong but because an adversary has accused them of something that the adversary cannot assuredly know: *motive and cause*. Problems deepen and multiply when we misperceive others in this manner. Those who judge others will themselves be judged. That returns us to No. 1 above, restarting the cycle of errors: *What goes around comes around*.

That last saying alludes to the consequences of "free will" in community. We can assert our will out of self-interest or in the community interest. If the goal is acceptance, the former likely will fail and the latter, bring rewards. Ethical behavior also is based on free will and community. We learn to make choices that enhance our relationships, treating others as we wish to be treated and foreseeing the consequences of our actions. Over time, living ethically sharpens perception so that we can alter our behaviors, combining ethics with interpersonal communication. Because of media and technology, however, our perception of time has been skewed; we may feel that time is running out, a habit so prevalent in our time that it demands special attention.

The Accelerated Biological Clock

The influence of media and technology on our lives may seem subtle on the surface. However, that influence permeates nearly everything we do to such degree that we no longer even intuit it and so cannot adjust for it. Technology warps time, accelerating it, and place, transcending it. Media, based on marketing, targets and prescribes lifestyle. We align our everyday clocks to the processor speed of computers and our lifestyle clocks to the storylines of media, all of which are out of synch with reality. That affects our "biological clock," a concept typically associated with women and reproduction. That clock ticks for everyone and involves men and women growing gracefully into each stage of biological life. When we do not, we feel empty, out of step with nature's lifecycle—not because we really are, but because *we misread the time*. We divorce or leave partners after reproductive years, confronting "biological death." We confront "parental death" when we cannot have children or when our children graduate from high school or college and leave home. We come face-to-face with our own demise in midlife with maturity or menopause, trying to recapture the excitement of our mating years or the traditions of familial ones. These biological bookmarks are in place for a good reason, concerning the conscience; we must grow into them agreeably because they free us to contribute to community, without which our lives lose meaning, according to the moral programming of our species.

The search for community in a high-tech media age is directly associated with acceptance, a hallmark of human beings and rooted in physical place. As James Howard Kunstler observes,

> There is a reason that human beings long for a sense of permanence. This longing is not limited to children, for it touches the profoundest aspects of our existence: that life is short, fraught with uncertainty, and sometimes tragic. We know not where we come from, still less where we are going, and to keep from going crazy while we are here, we want to feel that we truly belong to a specific part of the world.[99]

In the above excerpt, Kunstler associates community with the human condition, noting the importance of time. Instead of appreciating the blessings and beauties of each phase of life, mediated people displaced from community tend to focus on the loss rather than the gain and try to rewind their inner clocks that have fixed settings, honoring the calendar of the human condition.

Our clocks are set in synch with real time, allowing us to interact meaningfully with others in physical environs. When we resist that, interacting electronically or uncivilly, we feel angry and hassled in the very places meant for us to feel secure or to provide for that security: *home and work*. Those unsettling symptoms are likely to worsen because the high-tech media revolution has yet to peak and likely will grow and infect us throughout our extended lifespans. From home shopping to home office, from distance learning to long-distance love affairs, we remain at the mercy of media and technology. We must incorporate these powerful tools conscientiously into our lives, acknowledging the effect on our biological clocks and synchronizing them with real time and lifespan. Otherwise we may recognize life's moral and spiritual dimensions, but nevertheless repeat the same life-altering errors. We may blame each other or ourselves for the flatness of existence, the everyday angers at work, and shallow relationships at home, searching for answers or soul mates—anything to alleviate stress and emptiness—when we might just reevaluate the techno-media environment that targets and amuses us around the clock.

When media and technology accelerate time, the search for acceptance becomes desperate. Many of us feel so because we incorrectly believe that time is running out—*incorrectly*, because lifespans in the industrialized world will continue to lengthen, with projections as high as age ninety in the twenty-first century, requiring several changes in career. Still we react to job disappointment—loss of position, title, transfer or promotion—not as a temporary setback which all people experience and which we, too, shall overcome; but as definitive proof of our worth (or lack thereof) at the workplace. We feel similarly when rebuffed by a romantic interest or when plans fall through to have children, to see them through college on adequate savings, to have grandchildren, and to retire on IRAs to Florida, and so on, as media tell us that normal people do. Past generations had time to reflect on such matters after-hours on weekdays and on weekends. They may have kept up with the Joneses, their neighbors, as social norm; but the current middle class keeps up with the Dow Joneses and the mediated accouterments of financial planning. In a word, past generations interacted more than we do in community, with half of all Americans in the 1960s spending time in clubs and local groups, compared to less than one quarter in the 1990s,[100] and witnessed cases of personal defeat and triumph, setback and comeback. For people of conscience, that experience helped shape their character and priorities. There was a time for home, a time for work, and a time for community. Time was associated with place, and both were valued. Now many of us believe we lack time because electronic communication allows home to intrude on work and vice versa, blurring boundaries. Work is a chief source of stress, with one in four workers chronically angry on the job.[101] Supervisors can contact us at any hour or at any location, and they *do*, trespassing on interpersonal boundaries.

Many of us sense that basic relationships are slipping away from us because we lack time to nurture them. We seek self-help. And experts advise us "to do more with less." That is the mantra of the digital era that celebrates multitasking because it cuts costs. Computers multitask efficiently. *People do not.* They need time, attention, and support. "In our complex world it is almost a cultural issue as we try to do more and more in less time," says Joshua Rubinstein, a researcher with the Federal Aviation Administration, where the impact of multitasking is studied as a life-death matter, because pilots and controllers must work efficiently *and* effectively. Rubinstein believes the computerized workplace tempts people to use "spare moments" to perform additional tasks, noting, "multitasking could actually be less efficient if you are doing rapid switches back and forth."[102] When we give up our spare

moments to multitask rather than reflect on or enjoy life, we accelerate our inner clocks, causing stress.

Stress levels rise when we perform too many tasks under real or
imagined deadlines. That also generates ill will and undermines colle-
giality—so much so that persistent anger dominates at the typical
American workplace, according to a CBS News report.[103] An ABC
News poll shows that society has become more uncivil, with more than
one in three Americans claiming that someone gestured obscenely at
them while driving recently and 73 percent believing that manners are
worse today than two or three decades ago.[104] The latter revelation is
surprising on one level because America in the 1970s was involved in
the Vietnam War with its turbulent protests and tragic aftermath.
However, on another level, it is predictable because media and technology had not yet infected every aspect of life at home and at work,
accelerating our clocks and tempers.

Now even neighbors feud on-line, venting their anger on the
Internet for all to see. Describing such an incident in a Maryland town,
Bryan Burrough writes in *Vanity Fair*:

> Ever gotten into an argument with a neighbor and remarked, "hey,
> what's the worst they could do? Make us move?" Unfortunately, it
> turns out there *is* worse. Nothing here has ever been the same. It
> might have all died down, hurt feelings healed, tempers cooled—
> except for the Internet. Now every last scrap of village gossip is on-
> line for the global village to read and may remain there for eternity.
> Smarty alecks from all over the world chime in with comments and
> criticisms, which naturally has only fanned the flames of neighbor-
> hood strife in the once peaceful community of Fishing Creek Farm.[105]

The particulars of that feud are media-related and too complicated
to delve into here. Admittedly, most neighborhood squabbles are resolved in court rather than on the Internet. Still, the Fishing Creek Farm
example above shows lengths that neighbors go using technology as
weaponry. Unfortunately we can relate to that. After all, we have received flaming e-mails in CAPS at work and anonymous hang-up calls
at home. We have gone on virus alert when told that "worms" will
infect our PCs. We have watched talking heads shout at each other on
news shows and guests assault each other on talk shows. The cumulative effect on our psyches is significant. Many of us feel in perpetual
crisis because technology is mobile and omnipresent, interrupting us

at any moment and accelerating time in the process. Time, actually, is not running out. Patience, however, *is*.

Wondering What Is Real

People in crisis or transition often wonder what is real in their lives: *Is my marriage real or a farce? Am I really being harassed at work, or am I just imagining that I am? Is this career my true calling, or am I kidding myself? Do I really want a baby, or am I trying to save my relationship?* At some point in our lives, all of us ask such telling questions. We do so because the stakes have become so high that we want to take a personal inventory, mustering the courage to accept the real—no matter how disappointing or distasteful—and to shed the artificial. Again this innate, universal impulse is associated with conscience and consciousness.

Reality, as we said, is linked to *consciousness*, an awareness of the world as it really is, rather than as we would like it to be. Self-image is associated with *conscience*, informing us how to interpret our own and other people's thoughts, words, and deeds. As such, reality and self-image are woven into the fabric of community upon which we rely in our search for acceptance, from the places that we inhabit to the people that we meet. Moreover, community—however we choose to define that term, as hometown, state, nation, or world—also has a conscience and consciousness. Humanity is the ultimate community. It possesses a *collective* conscience, or an awareness of common virtues and vices, in addition to a *collective* consciousness, or an awareness of common behaviors. When we react with disgust to a bulletin of another mass murder at a high school, for instance, we know that millions more share that same inner gnawing at the gut. That is the collective conscience. When we foresee more such shootings, because tragedies involving youth have become commonplace in our time—in part, because of media—that is the collective consciousness. In other eras, the collective consciousness and conscience were influenced by real events that happened in our geographical habitats. In modern times, collective awareness and social mores are as likely to be shaped by virtual events, brought to us by media and technology, as by real events in our midst. That phenomenon also affects perception and desensitizes humanity more than many of us realize. Without perception, consciousness is dulled; without sensitivity, conscience is, too.

Too often, writes journalist Judith Marlane, technology determines content of media: "It has been said with poignancy that what we do not know can kill us. The abundance of time and space devoted to the coverage of violence and crime creates a misperception of reality, desensitizes viewers, and provides a critical disservice to the public."[106] Marlane notes that such coverage replaces topics of greater import to the community, including education and race relations. A Knight Foundation study verifies her claim, stating that newspapers are adopting the techniques of advertising and entertainment by using market research focus groups to deliver what readers want rather than what they need to make intelligent choices in their communities. Authors of the report write, "When the world is more closely linked than ever, when 'globalization' means not a slogan but a reality, when economic, social and political events abroad directly and powerfully affect those at home, foreign correspondence is sharply cut back, if not entirely eliminated by most daily newspapers and TV networks."[107] In a global era, international news has hometown political impact. However, news executives are shaping politics more than voters, a distinct phenomenon afflicting our social identity. As sociologist Manuel Castells observes in *The Power of Identity*, political projects and politicians have entered "electronic space," programming community agendas according to "*the overarching principles governing news media: the race for audience ratings, in competition with entertainment; the necessary detachment from politics, to induce credibility.*"[108]

In sum, a desensitized, narrow view of reality not only afflicts individual conscience and consciousness, but collective ones as well. Worse, because we suffer similar symptoms and because media and technology, which trigger those symptoms, infiltrate every aspect of our lives, the world and our geographic place in it are blurred so routinely that we have become accustomed to tunnel vision. Consider this prospect: If consciousness bestows the gift of *vision* so we can see how our choices affect others, and if conscience bestows the gift of *intuition* so we can access that vision, shouldn't we inquire whether our vision is colored in some part by technology rather than by reality and our interpretation by media rather than by experience? And if it is, about the world at large—if we believe, however fleetingly for instance, that African-American men are either athletes or criminals, as programming often depicts them, or blond women either buxom or daft—why should notions about our private world be any more reliable?

The world according to media may not mirror our own. But they influence perception. Many of us make life-altering decisions without questioning whether what we see or interpret in our private world is accurate enough to act upon. Spouses fighting or filing for divorce or child custody need clear vision and strong intuition—in this period perhaps more than any other in their lives. So do others quitting good jobs or remaining in dead-end ones or jeopardizing their health with bad habits. More likely than not, though, people in these and similar situations fear potential outcomes so much that their perception and sensitivity, at this critical juncture, are both unreliable. They may seek legal or medical help to fend off those outcomes or to restore a sense of wellness; but they may not question habits of a high-tech media age that caused or contributed to their problems in the first place. When we are in crisis or transition, our first priority should be to deepen vision and embrace values. Otherwise any solution, no matter how enticing in the short term, may disappoint us in the future.

To deepen vision and values, our habitats must be *actual* for the self to be *actualized* or whole psychologically. When we feel whole, we are at peace and empowered, confident that we can cope with or resolve the challenges or confrontations that await us each day at home and at work. We may desire long-term success or solutions. However, we also realize that we can live with any outcome because we have acted conscientiously or have foreseen the consequences of our words, actions, and choices. The ability to achieve goals or resolve problems bestows a sense of empowerment. Feeling empowered, we enjoy peace of mind. Better still, the ability to foresee outcomes or accept consequences bestows a deeper state of being, the sensation of *wholeness*. Spiritual people call that state "atonement"—or "at *one*ness." Another phrase is "I am together" or "I have gotten it together." The word *together* implies community as much as completion, because those who achieve atonement or wholeness have done so in their interactions with others as much as in their acceptance of themselves. Accordingly, whole people are less concerned about themselves and more mindful about others and aware of their environs, from the beauty of nature to the diversity of human nature. They usually enjoy abundant lives.

In the present age, media and technology saturate our lives. They dictate schedules, program activities, and otherwise occupy time. Wholeness is more difficult to achieve. Partly, this is due to where we spend our days: in a real or a virtual habitat. A real one has three physical dimensions—up, down, and breadth—and intricate human sensations: a mix of ground, sound, wind, smell, texture, and so on. Interpersonal skills are based on those dimensions and influenced by such physical formats as touch, eye contact, smell, space (seating arrangements, for instance), body movements, time (willingness to wait, pauses in speech), objects (clothing, jewelry, furniture, etc.), colors (hue, brightness, lighting), intonation.[109] These formats work simultaneously in exchanges. Virtual environments, however, eliminate many of those formats.

Media environments desensitize us to physical surroundings, beginning in childhood. In her work on the impact of media on children, Marie Winn acknowledges that TV programming transmits valuable information about wildlife to young viewers. In doing so, television's view of reality often conflicts with a child's perception of nature. "[I]f a walk in the woods begins to seem a bit boring when compared to the experience of lions pouncing on unsuspecting zebras in the Serengeti Plains, it begins to seem unprofitable to dwell on the educational value of those programs."[110] Conversely, physical environs teach as well as stimulate.

When we interact in community, we are aware of our habitat mentally and *sensually*. A virtual habitat lacks such authenticity, generates it artificially or, at best, metaphorically. "When someone says, 'I'm going online,' where are they going?" write authors of *Online Communication: Linking Technology, Identity & Culture*. Andrew F. Wood and Matthew J. Smith employ metaphor throughout their text to explain interactions between people in virtual space. "Why is it that the better part of society has embraced the metaphor of space rather than any other?"[111] they inquire. "After all, wouldn't something like cyber*library* be a better description of the Internet's information-rich contents?"[112] Wood and Smith posit that a sense of space helps people make sense of the world, enabling them to interact meaningfully with others, even in places that do not really exist, like a chatroom that is no "room" at all.

There is vast difference between places that exist authentically and ones that exist artificially. For example, chemists easily can create a wintergreen oil smell so that a person can imagine the outdoors—perhaps white pines on a snowy mountain slope. Technology can even generate that aroma in a computer accessory as the user listens to RealAudio of birdsong, watching digital video of deep woods, or views this via Web cam in Aspen. But a person standing under 200-foot conifers experiences the metaphysical awe of nature enhanced by rousing physical sensation: the bed of needles on the forest floor, the awning of limbs on high, the pine-scented breeze and revitalizing rush of oxygen—plus birdsong (or tranquil lack thereof). These sensations also act on us simultaneously. The sensory patterns are archetypal. James Howard Kunstler notes that they echo processes of birth and decay, stimulating us in ways that artifact replacements cannot. A hike through meadows and woods in May is exhilarating, he states, "because of the extravagance of patterns of emerging life operating in concert: the buds unfurling on the trees, the trilliums blooming, the insects buzzing in the air, the birds singing as they build their nests, the little wild mammals scurrying about, the perfumes and tantalizing stinks of the cow pastures and the sloughs. We feel more alive in places like this."[113]

We long to feel alive. But many of us have forgotten how to live in synch with biological time and physical place. Instead we seek social support from technology because marketing promises that we can find it there. As physician Esther M. Sternberg notes, "The rapid response time of e-mail and the telephone gives us a sense of true social support. But is this sense real? Or are these pale, uni-dimensional pieces of a social interaction? Peel back the rich layers of a close physical social interaction, peel away the touch, then sight, then voice, down to the electronic words—is this really a social interaction, or is it a soliloquy? What is missing in these interactions is the original meaning of the word 'interaction'—the action between people."[114]

At best, technology only synthesizes reality with varying degrees of success. That, in itself, is a miracle. Media and technology create virtual habitats, defying the laws of reality. When you are speaking on the phone, for instance, you are at two places at once: your actual space, in the living room, say, and someone else's actual space, in an office, say. Your actual space is authentic and your virtual space—the sound of your voice resonating inside the receiver—is electronic. At that moment, you may be more conscious of virtual space because you are speaking on the telephone. Subconsciously, you know you are in your home or wherever, using a mobile phone. If you are in the living room, chances are that your television and/or stereo is on adding background dissonance, the way cars and trimmers do on the streets and lawns of neighborhoods. The cars and trimmers are real, the TV talk show is virtual. And yet, there is a "there" there: the host and guests of that talk show are at two places simultaneously: in the studio (real) and in your home (virtual). If your computer is on in the next room, connected via Internet to a home shopping site showing pictures and prices of entertainment centers, there is no "there" there: your computer is virtual on your end and images are virtual on the other. You have entered cyberspace. This chapter tracks how you got there in your search for community.

To appreciate the journey, we need to measure more thoroughly how media and technology blur our sense of self, and with it our sense of time, place, and principles. That requires knowledge of media history, whose lessons recur, causing us to commit the same mistakes as others who also lived during periods of great technological change.

Journal Exercise

During the course of a week, analyze the frequency of lies on television and in real life. Watch five installments of a syndicated sitcom or current soap opera and log each lie. In your own life, note the following:

- Each lie you tell—including so-called "white lies," half-truths, and exaggerations—and predict the consequences. Be sure to note additional lies told to shore up original ones. Track the lies and document the actual consequences. Compare predicted with actual consequences.
- Each lie you believe others have told you. Note consequences pertaining to trust.
- Each lie you or others expressed in virtual habitat (from e-mail to cell phone) and each lie you or others expressed in physical habitat. Compare differences, including number of lies and scope of consequences.
- Each time you were tempted to lie but told the truth, noting where the truth was expressed (in virtual or real habitat) and again tracking consequences.

Discussion/Paper Ideas for Chapter Three

- Discuss observations from the Journal Exercise above.
- Discuss the validity of these assertions:
  1. Media and technology may inspire many things but not trust, especially when it comes to self-help.

2. Technology accelerates our biological clocks because it warps our sense of time and place.
3. The news media shape politics more than voters, a distinct phenomenon afflicting our social identity.

- Discuss central theses and themes on identity, mediated communication, and emotional balance from Suggested Readings below.

Suggested Readings from Chapter Three

Castells, Manuel. *The Power of Identity*. Oxford, England: Blackwell, 1997.

Chesebro, James W. and Bertelsen, Dale A. *Analyzing Media: Communication Technologies as Symbolic and Cognitive Systems*. New York: Guilford Press, 1996.

Sternberg, Esther M. *The Balance Within: The Science Connecting Health and Emotions*. New York: W.H. Freeman, 2001.

Wood, Andrew F. and Matthew J. Smith. *Online Communication: Linking Technology, Identity, & Culture*. Mahwah, NJ: Lawrence Erlbaum, 2001.

The Impact of Media
and Technology

Television hangs on the questionable theory that whatever happens anywhere should be sensed everywhere. If everyone is going to be able to see everything, in the long run all sights may lose whatever rarity value they once possessed, and it may well turn out that people, being able to see and hear practically everything, will be specially interested in almost nothing.

—E.B. White, *The New Yorker*, 1948

The Real and Virtually Real

History is important, the saying goes. Or else we are apt to make the same mistakes. *Media* history is important because communication has the power to change the course of events—in the world and in our lives. Personal computers have changed the nature of government, education, information, entertainment, and business with on-line access to agency reports, distance learning, databases, gaming, stock trading, and more, influencing everyday activities. In the late 1950s, television had even greater impact. The telephone had similar influence at the start of the last century. So did the telegraph a half-century before that. Each new medium was a momentous, technological wonder that transformed the most basic aspect of human relationships: *how we talk to each other.*

Humans talk. We relate. We commune. Talk builds relationships and communities, informing individual and collective awareness, through which we enhance conscience and consciousness. That is why, in our search for acceptance, we must analyze the role that media and technology plays in our lives—especially how they shape our identity as individuals who populate communities and as citizens who should contribute to them. Otherwise we are apt to commit the same social misjudgments as other generations, reliving personal and cultural histories because we are unaware of what manipulates our choices and values.

In one respect, this is old hat. Media and technology have always manipulated self-image, values, and perception. However, the current high-tech era is unique because of the power of the electronic tools, the time that we spend using them, and the influence of the corporations that manufacture them. The net result is a blurring of boundaries. The real and virtually real have blended to such degree that we cannot always correctly ascertain what is genuine and enduring from what is artificial and fleeting. That type of confusion comes with its own set of interpersonal and societal consequences, complicating our lives and relationships, not because we are necessarily dysfunctional, but because we have forgotten how to respond ethically, emotionally, and intellectually to the challenges, desires, and opportunities of life at home and at work.

Our homes and workplaces have been altered by media and technology. *Communication alters habitat.* That is the objective. When you leave a handwritten note under a refrigerator magnet, so your partner knows your whereabouts, you defy time and thus can be in two places at once: in the kitchen and in the car. You don't have to wait until your partner comes home to say you need milk. You leave word and leave. Of course you are really elsewhere, not in the kitchen. But you are there virtually, too, when your partner reads your note.

Communication defies physical laws. Consider the saying, "If a tree falls in the forest and no one hears it, does that tree actually make a sound?" The answer is decidedly *no.* The tree makes a sound *wave* of certain frequency emanating around the severed trunk. Sound requires ears (human or animal) able to pick up that frequency in the vicinity. There is another scenario, however. A tree that falls without anyone witnessing it also makes a sound if technology has been placed there to record the event. In that case, people listening to the recording can say assuredly that falling timber produces sound, even if no one was at the site to hear it. The effect is the same as that note placed under the refrigerator magnet. A person is at two places at the same time—violating physics. Many social critics influenced by Marshall McLuhan—revisited in Chapter Six—overemphasize biology and overlook physics when assessing the impact of media, believing technology extends and enhances human senses. A microphone placed beside a felled oak may seem to extend the range of the ear, enhancing hearing; it does neither.

It creates a secondary set of senses by placing an individual in multiple locations. Advocates of and apologists for media and technology embrace the biological model because it promotes extension and enhancement of senses, which, by *logical* extension, also should enhance identity and humanity. Conversely, the physics model emphasizes a violation of scientific law associated with place. McLuhan never realized that and so, despite his "global village" prophecy—touting television, not Internet—never foresaw cyberspace or the splitting of consciousness that comes with breaches of time and place. When consciousness is split, so is perception. When perception is skewed, so is identity. Symptoms develop from the overuse and consumption of technology and media, which blur and blend the real with the virtually real.

Arguably, the blending of the real and the virtually real began with written words. With the invention of written language in ancient Mesopotamia some 5000 years ago,[115] people no longer needed to be face-to-face to interact; they could express themselves in writing and their messages could be read from afar. The invention of the printing press, discussed in the next chapter, transformed fifteenth-century society as much as the Internet did twentieth-century society—precisely for this reason. Between 1450 and 1500, the number of books in Europe increased from a few mere thousands to more than 9 million,[116] transforming culture, especially religion. In addition to Bibles, Johannes Guttenberg printed papal coupons called "indulgences," forgiving sins for a fee, and freed up Vatican scribes. They wrote the coupon once, instead of thousands of times, and went to vespers. Granted, couriers still had to hand-deliver indulgences. Several centuries later, the Internet would deliver coupons and other digital messages much more efficiently. Using e-mail, senders compose a message once and post it on a listserv, for instance, clicking a mouse, and then are free to go on to other sites or pursuits, while the message is being read at multiple places simultaneously. The Internet also delivers the message without any couriers; so they are free to be elsewhere, too—so free, in fact, that as long as there are electricity and operating systems, communicators no longer need couriers. Virtual habitat has deleted them from the landscape.

Evolution in virtual habitat is similar to that in actual habitat, with a few differences. Occupations, rather than species, disappear from the cyber-landscape. Because there is no "there" there, the fittest survive not by claiming territory but by performing more tasks in less time involving fewer people. The computer software or operating system that accomplishes that goal earns a profit . . . and makes a category of people obsolete. Those folks literally disappear, replaced by others who can multitask more efficiently. In the case of extinct couriers, for instance, cyberspace replaced them with technophiles to make listserv systems function properly and automatically. The difference, of course, is that couriers made rounds in real habitat and delivered paper messages face-to-face; technophiles have no faces because they deliver electronic messages in cyberspace, whose salient feature is *invisibility*.

Because of that feature, people de-evolve in virtual environments into symbols (hypertext, pixels, and logins) and raw materials (listservs, hotlinks, and statistics). Cyberspace lacks physical dimensions, including space and time, without which, activities are simulated rather than authentic. Philosopher Andrew Feenberg states that technology incorporates people "into the mechanism" as objects with digital functions rather than true identities.[117] In virtual habitat even governments lose control of citizens and organizations. According to sociologist Manuel Castells in *The Power of Identity*, "State control over space and time is increasingly bypassed by global flows of capital, goods, services, technology, communication and information."[118] The transformation of society from the real to the virtually real has been occurring since the nineteenth century, affecting how we perceive others and their cultures, communities, priorities, activities, and whereabouts.

The Dawning of Mass Media

Modern media history begins with electricity. The invention of three devices literally transformed society and the American landscape: the telegraph, telephone, and radio. These inventions were supposed to bring prosperity to the masses. In fact, nineteenth-century "advocates of electricity claimed it would eliminate the drudgery of manual work and create a world of abundance and peace,"[119] writes Tom Standage, author of *The Victorian Internet* (i.e., the telegraph). Many prophesy the same new world because of Internet and related technologies. In any case, the telegraph, telephone, and radio set the stage for twentieth-century inventions, including television and the computer, which influenced our collective view of the world and ourselves.

With each technological wonder, our perception of community changed and with it, our way of life. The telegraph was invented in 1835 by Samuel Morse, who also devised a code of dots and dashes. Telegraph lines were placed along rail lines to test the device. On May 24, 1844, Morse tapped his famous message, "What hath God wrought?" from Baltimore to Washington, DC. The phrase is fear-based, suggesting that Morse realized that his telegraph would alter perception, compressing our sense of geography and devaluing the impact of words. The telegraph reduced words to simpler symbols. Before the telegraph, Europe was perceived as a place—a harbor, city, river, or mountain range; after the telegraph, "Europe" became a word and much easier to reach. You said "Europe" to a Western Union agent and, voilà!, you were virtually there. Fittingly, "telegraph" in Greek means "distance writing."

The telegraph increased the speed of news. Beforehand, reporters had to row out to ships steaming into New York harbor to learn the latest news from abroad. By 1858, news was arriving in America by transoceanic cable.[120] Soon telegraph lines connected the east and west coasts of the United States, enabling the Associated Press to become the world's first mass medium. The AP, to this day, is known as a "wire service." Western Union joined with the AP to create the first media monopoly. Both controlled the content of news until 1875. Finally, over objections of Western Union, the AP was able to lease its own telegraph wire.[121]

As soon as the AP established relative autonomy, using telegraphs to convey news, journalism entered a new age. Researchers have pegged the 1870s as a time when media changed from "the age of communities and place" to "the age of class and groups" (1870–1930) as corporate moguls, including Samuel Morse and Alexander Graham Bell, introduced inventions that altered the perception of physical habitat.[122] The age of class and groups differed notably from the age of communities and place. Priorities changed. Previously newspapers had been emphasizing people and the importance of community—how readers, for instance, might contribute locally to the common good. After the Civil War, however, the focus switched from the character of people to their status in society, defined by wealth or affiliation. Special interest groups, including media companies, were connected not by values, but by wires, roads, and railways. Mass communication reached millions of consumers rather than hundreds because media had lost the shackles of place, enabling tycoons to stake claims in the virtual environment and amass fortunes.

Telegraph technology empowered reporters as never before. As the AP realized, Western Union had a vested interest in coverage, attempting to shape the news so that it was in line with corporate priorities. (That conflict of interest still exists to this day.) The telegraph was a powerful communication tool, in itself; but combined with news, the medium rewrote history. Abraham Lincoln relied on the telegraph to learn the latest news from the battlefront. Lincoln was the first U.S. commander in chief to command armies from the War Department in Washington. He also relied on news coverage, much like some leaders still rely on CNN. Journalists who telegraphed details of battles influenced military strategy, for better or worse. The AP accepted that responsibility and covered both sides in the Civil War to give coverage a semblance of balance.

Meanwhile, another war was raging in America. Western Union was trying to quash all competitors, including the fledging Bell system, swiftly ascending in virtual habitat. The phone could do more tasks quicker involving fewer people interacting face-to-face. The telegraph required agents who knew Morse code. Those agents had to copy and tap messages from customers in Western Union offices and then hand-deliver messages to addressees in physical locations. That inconvenience would make the telegraph obsolete in virtual habitat. In a few decades, long-distance telephone operators working invisibly at mysterious exchanges would replace those agents. Anonymous "Ma Bell" operators would also develop "attitude"—similar to those now at computer support desks—primarily because they lacked face-to-face interaction . . . and could disconnect at will. The focus, then as now, was on the bottom line. As early as the nineteenth century, entrepreneurs realized that those who owned both the medium *and* the new technology (or established partnerships to acquire both) were destined to become powerbrokers. That rule holds true to this day. The symbiotic relationship of media and technology—especially their ability to make profit and wield influence—started with the telegraph and would define each invention to come, including the telephone and radio.

Alexander Graham Bell founded his telephone company in 1876. Within a decade, Bell created American Telephone and Telegraph and elevated it to "parent company," acquiring Western Union along with its influence and power. The telephone changed the nature of news. The media had to retool to use the new technology, just as they had to retool in the twentieth century to use computers. Like computers, telephones impacted coverage by placing reporters increasingly in virtual environments and displacing them from community. The transformation happened swiftly. A generation earlier, reporters had to "row for news," meeting ships in harbors to get the latest reports from overseas. Then reporters used telegraphs to gather facts and information but still had to travel to physical locations to interview newsmakers. With the advent of telephones, however, reporters could interview sources without traveling anywhere, relying on quotation, rather than on observation, without necessarily fact-checking assertions about issues affecting communities.

The characteristics of communication metamorphosed to suit the new medium. Telegraph messages were tapped, not spoken, as e-mail today is tapped and not spoken. But e-mail is tapped on keyboards. Telegraphs required agents who knew mysterious codes and preferred brevity, inventing "headline news" a full century before CNN. Symbols like "SOS," the international distress call, replaced phrases. The medium became the message, and users had to adapt. Language changed. The most frequently read word in the telegraph era was *stop*, which replaced periods at the ends of sentences. The telephone did not need code; it made communication easier and more convenient—the same qualities touted today, concerning computers. The greater the convenience, the greater the impulse to misuse the technology. The new device changed the nature of interpersonal communication. People did not have to visit to engage others in dialogue. Neither did they have to pen letters, a nineteenth-century art; they could save time and phone. Nothing wrong with that, of course; the sound of a loved one's voice generated joy, affirming family ties and renewing relationships. Conversely, the telephone could ease the conscience enough for a person to skip a visit or cancel a trip. Place was dispensable. Because they had options, people began aligning priorities with levels of convenience, deciding when to travel or when to use technology. That impacted their relationships. For just as we do not fully appreciate how e-mail and cell phones affect relationships, Victorian counterparts did not appreciate how new technologies would affect theirs. More important, media and technology in that epoch skewed perception about world events that would have enormous social impact. Society still respected the word, especially great books, many of which were being written at the time, including works of such masters as Walt Whitman, Emily Dickinson, and Mark Twain. Media moguls exploited respect for the printed word. Even in the aftermath of our bloodiest war, during which multitudes had perished, preserving the

Union and the Constitution, tycoons elevated corporate interests over the common interest.

A few newspaper publishers in the 1890s practiced *yellow* or sensational journalism. They obeyed the cardinal rule of virtual habitat, *speed*, the technological touchstone to this day, with computer and cable companies touting processors and delivery systems. The quicker that news is delivered, the more incredible and incorrect it becomes—another rule that still holds true. At the end of the nineteenth century, the media not only could manipulate public opinion; they could create it along with government policy and sell more newspapers in the process. Humanity suffered because of that practice. Two publishing giants in particular, Joseph Pulitzer and William Randolph Hearst, instigated political mayhem in America with overblown news about brutalities in Cuba, ultimately triggering the Spanish-American War.

That was a turning point in journalism. Moguls became more profit-minded and used technology to cut costs. Telephones decreased the need to travel, saving money. Reporters relied on phones to contact sources for information. Publishers relied on telegraphs to transmit news, coast to coast. That opened up advertising possibilities. Publishers created new media as vehicles for national brands. One publisher, Cyrus Curtis, owner of the *Tribune and Farmer*, spun off the "woman's page" of his paper—edited by his wife Louise Knapp Curtis—into *Ladies' Home Journal* in 1883. A few years later Curtis purchased the *Saturday Evening Post*, a newspaper dedicated in part to family, morality, and literature, for $1000, and transformed it into a national magazine. Magazines had a geographic advantage over newspapers because they were not bound to local economies and communities. Periodicals, circulated nationally, had longer deadlines than newspapers and so underplayed time elements, preferring "evergreen" features lacking the immediacy of "spot" news (a term emphasizing *place*). Better yet, national media could sell national brands.

The Advent of Marketing

"Branding" was invented fifteen years after the telegraph. Its purpose was to distinguish a company's product from that of competitors. William Procter and James Gamble, brothers-in-law, began making candles and soap in 1837 and marked candle boxes with P&G's legendary trademark: the moon-stars icon, which symbolized the brand. In 1886 the company spent $11,000 in a campaign to promote the purity of Ivory Soap. Branding expert Martin Lindstrom notes that within a decade, "P&G became advertising innovators, regularly placing product advertisements in national newspapers and magazines."[123]

Advertising became as indispensable as news. Companies sold brands in nationally distributed magazines. That also homogenized culture. In short order, Coca-Cola became the national drink. Ivory Soap became the cleanser of choice and its maker, Procter & Gamble, the first company to place a color ad in *Cosmopolitan* in 1896. Westclox kept Americans on time. Westclox was the first corporation to advertise its popular alarm clock "Big Ben" in a national campaign, noting in a 1910 advertisement in the *Saturday Evening Post* that this "punctual sleepmeter" would awaken American families with "a deep musical voice . . . on your sleepiest mornings."[124] Overnight, media grew, especially magazines, infiltrating American homes because advertising funded new start-up publications distributed to wider geographic regions, based on those national brands. Soon items on shelves, in medicine cabinets, cupboards, and rooms began to look alike; eventually, occupants of these homes began to think alike about issues *and* products.

Success came at a cost. Consumers were eager for national brands, and companies like Procter & Gamble wanted to serve that need. In the past, a manufacturer generally made one product and competed with other companies that made a similar product. Competition happened in real habitat—on shelves of local stores. What if one company made two similar products, like soap bars? Would one product cannibalize the other? Procter & Gamble faced that problem with Ivory Soap and Camay, and the company figured out how to sell both without one product winning out over the other: *marketing*. Ivory was billed as a cleanser; Camay, as a beauty bar with moisturizers. This way, both products could compete within the same category but not within the same segment. That approach led P&G to develop a system still being used today: *brand management*. Marketers manage competing products made by the same company, devising strategies for each brand.

Marketing also relied on media and technology. Brand management systems sold products more efficiently, using technology not only to advertise but also to generalize wants and needs. Just as publishers had used technology to shape public opinion and government policy, marketers used technology to shape desire and standard of living. Magazines like *Saturday Evening Post* and *Life* regularly showcased lifestyles at a level above that of their readerships, whetting appetites for consumption during the age of "class and groups." The 1920s has been called the decade of advertising. "The admen went wild," writes Juliet B. Schor in *The Overworked American*, associating consumerism with higher workloads, noting "everything from walnuts to household coal was being individually branded and nationally advertised."[125] That stimulated the U.S. economy, generating jobs for the masses and fortunes for mass media, setting the stage for broadcasting.

In 1898, the Italian-born Guglielmo Marconi had fashioned a crude radio prototype. Two decades later, Westinghouse radio station KDKA was broadcasting the results of the 1920 Harding-Cox presidential election. Two years after that, American Telephone & Telegraph Company—another technology behemoth at the time—sponsored the first paid radio advertising commercial, broadcast on AT&T's New York City outlet, WEAF. Almost everyone found the idea of paid advertising over public airwaves repugnant—so much so, writes journalist Ben Bagdikian, that then Secretary of Commerce Herbert Hoover warned, "It is inconceivable that we should allow so great a possibility for service, for news, for entertainment, for education and for vital commercial purposes to be drowned in advertising chatter."[126]

A quarter-century after its invention, the medium of radio had spawned quandaries impacting us even today:

- The influence of broadcasting on the electorate and commerce.
- The power of corporate ecosystems on people and society.
- The use of technology for commercial gain rather than for social enlightenment.

Radio accelerated America's social clock more than Westclox ever could. The new catchword was "progress." By now the corporate world recognized how technology could make or break fortunes. Western Union proved that in 1877, committing one of the biggest business gaffes of all time. It dubbed the telephone "an electrical toy" and rejected an offer to buy Bell's patents for $100,000.[127] That mistake created a precedent. AT&T eventually gained control of Western Union and marketed both technologies, encouraging customers to use telephones to order telegraphs. The rule of acquisition—buy out, duplicate, or integrate new technology—dominates corporate thinking today.

In the first half of the twentieth century, the radio became as popular and as powerful as the telephone. Radio targeted the *individual* listener rather than the entire community. The focus was on the consumer in a house, not on the house in a geographic place. Radio programs like *Captain Midnight* targeted youth and offered boys and girls such premiums as "Flight Patrol" membership cards, "Ringo-Jumpo" bean games, and "Mysto-Magic Weather Forecasting" badges.[128] By 1940, Ovaltine sponsored *Captain Midnight.* Campbell Soup Company was more interested in the New York Drama Company's *The Mercury Theatre on the Air,* founded by entertainers Orson Welles and John Houseman. Welles had proved that mass media could create mass hysteria with his broadcast of "The War of the Worlds" on October 30, 1938. The infamous hoax about a Martian invasion reportedly struck terror "at the hearts of hundreds of thousands of persons in the length and breadth of the United States."[129] Two years later, when Campbell Soup acquired the radio show, *Mercury Theater on the Air* became *The Campbell Playhouse.*

Mass marketing was established. The media of choice were magazines and radio because they could target segments of the audience, identifying potential customers. That practice undermined the media's perception of the importance of community. Until then, newspaper advertising sold to an eclectic mix of folks living in a geographic area—thereby implying community. Companies sold products and services to families rather than to specific members of families. Radio- and magazine-based marketing took aim at those members by luring them with programming or content suited to their lifestyles and then targeting them with specific name-brand products and premiums. Marketing, once a business practice, was now a media tool—just in time for television.

Vision and Values

Television made its public debut at the 1939 World's Fair—an apt forum, as TV would span the globe within a few decades. The essayist E. B. White had prophesied the future of television, maintaining that it would become "the test of the modern world, and in this new opportunity to see beyond the range of our own vision, we shall discover either a new and unbearable disturbance of the general peace or a saving radiance in the sky. We shall stand or fall by television—of that I am sure."[130] White foresaw, perhaps more clearly than any other social critic, how this powerful new medium would homogenize our vision and values.

Television did not gain popularity until after World War II. In 1949 only 2 percent of households had television; within six years, 64 percent of U.S. homes had at least one TV set.[131] By 1959, 90 percent did, a phenomenon that political scientist Robert D. Putnam believes to be "the fastest diffusion of technological innovation every recorded," including Internet access.[132] (Pippa Norris, author of *Digital Divide*, reports that in 1994 about 3 million people, mostly living in America, had access to the Internet, a figure that increased to 26 million the next year, with worldwide estimates roughly doubling each year after that through 2000.[133]) Television not only spread faster than the Internet; it also transformed home life more thoroughly. As Bagdikian observes, "Educational, cultural, and political patterns changed as the new electronic box moved into homes. Habits of reading, of doing homework and housework, and of eating family meals were rearranged to place the television set into the daily schedule."[134]

People who did not own televisions in the pre-Sputnik era of the early 1950s lived mostly in remote areas unable to receive a signal. By the end of that decade, however, the number of televisions was fast approaching 85 million, or nearly one set for every two citizens.[135] Americans were also on the move in the 1950s, with families relocating across the country to secure jobs and moving into new suburban neighborhoods whose houses featured garages. People without cars could not fully use their environment, creating two classes of people— those with and without motor vehicles—much like Pippa Norris claims about computers, responsible for the digital divide. However, access to automobiles in the 1950s differed significantly from access to computers in the 1990s. The computer industry competes with the auto industry as people decide which large purchase to make in any given year. The auto and television industries complemented each other because television advertising showcased the mobility of cars, featuring them across the expanse of the new U.S. highway system.

Families moved into homogeneous homes in ersatz developments with TV antennas, watching television an average four hours per day. Before television, children would learn about their communities by playing in, growing up in, and contributing to them. They engaged in after-school *activities* (rather than passivities). That was soon to change as television-viewing habits increased each decade after the 1950s, with programming wielding more influence on viewers than the neighborhoods in which they lived.

In his book, *The Fifties*, Pulitzer prize–winning journalist David Halberstam notes that what people saw in real life and on television began to merge, affecting awareness, mainly about community. "[M]any Americans were now living far from families, in brand-new suburbs where they barely knew their neighbors. Sometimes they felt closer to the people they watched on television than they did to their neighbors and distant families."[136] Congress, wary of the impact of the new medium, held hearings in 1952 to determine whether TV was corrupting morals by overemphasizing crime and violence. More hearings occurred two years later because of concern about growing crime rates.[137] The hearings generated some debate, but did not significantly change public attitude. At the time few definitive studies could be cited to make a case for or against television; however, by the 1970s, evidence about TV's influence on children was becoming as indisputable as tobacco's influence on health.

An important study was done in 1973 by Tannis MacBeth Williams of the University of British Columbia. Williams, a psychologist, had studied habits of three Canadian towns: one dubbed "Notel," which had no TV reception but would soon acquire a transmitter; another, "Unitel," which had only one government channel (Canadian Broadcasting Company); and the last, "Multitel," which had the CBC and U.S. network channels. Williams and other researchers analyzed viewer behavior in all three towns before Notel had television and then again, approximately two years later.

The results affirmed the worst suspicions, especially about TV's effect on children. While there was no significant difference in physical and verbal aggression among Unitel and Multitel children, Notel children exhibited nearly twice as much aggression toward each other after television as before. The experiment is explained in detail in Williams' book, *The Impact of Television: A Natural Experiment in Three Communities*. Williams' study not only showed that television triggered physical and verbal aggression among children; it also affected adult relationships and activities—even sleep. Jane Ledingham, director of the Child Study Centre at the University of Ottawa, has summarized Williams' study, and television's impact on community, in her paper, "The Effects of Media Violence on Children":

> [Williams' study] found that people spent less time talking, socializing outside the home, doing household tasks, engaging in leisure

activities such as reading, knitting and writing, and being involved in community activities and sports after television became available. They even slept less. . . . It is clear that television's impact on children arises not only from the kinds of behaviour it promotes, but also from the other activities it replaces.[138]

Television viewing impacts community engagement. Some critics argue that TV viewing promotes aggression and some, including Herbert J. Gans, dispute that idea. Gans asserts that his "reading of the existing research suggests that the media encourage violent attitudes and acts only for some people at some times."[139] That may not reassure many in an era of high school shootings; but Gans misses key points about TV-inspired violence. The news media hype and overplay such violence; communities are typically safer than those depictions. Television viewing not only reduces civic engagement with fewer hours being spent in physical habitat; it alters the perception of that habitat in a continuing cycle of displacement. Robert D. Putnam documents that in his research about the collapse and revival of American communities, noting that "the average American's investment in organizational life (apart from religious groups . . .) fell from 3.7 hours per month in 1965 to 2.9 in 1975 to 2.3 in 1985."[140] Those statistics are the inverse of television statistics in U.S. homes.

As studies still document, television alters reality and with it, consciousness. Marketing exacerbates that effect. In his aptly named book, *The Culture of Marketing, the Marketing of Culture*, social critic and magazine journalist John Seabrook documents the omnipresent, transparent role of marketing. Until recently, marketing analyzed products before promoting them. That ensured accuracy but was not cost-effective. Now campaigns for products are developed while the products themselves are being developed. In fact, campaigns frequently have become indistinguishable from products. "It was said of the movie *Godzilla* that the marketing campaign was better than the movie but in the prerelease hype surrounding *The Phantom Menace*, the marketing and the movie have become the same thing," writes Seabrook. "I go to the supermarket to buy milk, and I see Star Wars has taken over aisle 5, the dairy section. There are figurine mugs of Han Solo and Princess Leia, nine-inch collectibles featuring Emperor Palpatine, an R2-D2 dispenser filled with Phantom Menace Pepsis, and down from that, another big display case filled with Star Wars–themed Frito-Lay potato chips. Pepsi has sunk over $2 billion into promoting the new trilogy. Each of Pepsi's three fast-food franchises—KFC, Taco Bell, and Pizza Hut—has licensed a different planet and festooned their containers with its characters."[141]

Marketing strategies homogenize America as much as subdivisions and chain stores. Our identities no longer are associated with community but with psychographics—statistics categorizing us according to the products that we purchase and the services that we perceive to need. Sociologist Manuel Castells observes that the obliteration of shared identities is equal to the dissolution of society as a meaningful social system. "At first sight," he writes, "we are witnessing the emergence of a world exclusively made of markets, networks, individuals, and strategic organizations, apparently governed by patterns of 'rational expectations' (the new, influential economic theory), except when these rational individuals suddenly shoot their neighbor, rape a little girl, or spread nerve gas in the subway. No need for identities in this new world."[142]

Marketing similarly afflicts the news industry and with it, community journalism, undermining our collective sense of place. Hodding Carter III, chief executive officer of the Knight Foundation and an award-winning journalist and commentator, says, "Making money is no longer what [corporations] do so you can afford to do journalism. Making money is what you *do*."[143] Carter believes that media conglomerates—ecosystems that view news as content, cable as delivery, broadcasting as entertainment, new media as revenue source, and so on—focus on yearly profits nearing 30 percent, forgetting that that they once were "part of the entire civic enterprise in this country. The public is not an outsider," Carter observes. "The public is the point of the enterprise."[144]

Marketing used to focus on building relationships with people. Now it focuses on building relationships with other corporations. Computerization has altered priorities. In its "Brand Report," the Ashton Brand Group notes that technology has transformed traditional marketing relationships. The report states that the practice of "co-marketing" used to mean that a conglomerate like Philip Morris with two competing divisions, Kraft and Oscar Mayer, would target consumers jointly and combine products to create a new product like "Lunchables." According to the Brand Report, "Now, virtually all technology offerings are comprised of products manufactured by multiple companies. Think of broadband Internet access. IBM makes the PC (with Intel, Mitsumi,

Microsoft et al.), Ericsson makes the cable modem, Time Warner provides the pipe (and subscriber base) and Roadrunner brings the service to the home."[145] This type of "brand ecosystem" requires more investment in marketing and affiliated network systems, most of which facilitate communication across corporations rather than interactions between those companies and consumers.

As a result, corporate values have changed. Because of technology, companies can downsize and downplay the importance of interpersonal customer service, emphasizing strategic relationships with other companies. Typically those companies are media-related or use media to relate. Because we use the same tools to communicate, consumers believe that they are valuable, only to learn that they are not. Customer service requires use of e-mail to lodge complaints, with lagging response time. The irony of that does not escape us. We have the power to interact with officials of corporate ecosystems that influence our lives, but the technology that empowers us also ignores, delays, or deletes us in virtual habitat. Nevertheless we keep on e-mailing. There is a degree of desperation in the attempt to contact companies electronically and speak to human beings, as there is in repeatedly pushing the buttons of an elevator, attempting to hasten its arrival. The difference is that the elevator, eventually, responds. When companies do not, because they have downsized staffs and automated service, we question ourselves as individuals in an environment purported to be interactive, responsive, and empowering. At stake is our identity in the high-tech media world.

Journal Exercise

Many social critics and historians note that the automobile in the 1950s homogenized the planning of neighborhoods and the architecture of houses, with main thoroughfares featuring billboards, national chain stores, gas stations, and fast-food restaurants, and with garages altering living space in residential housing. Can the same be said of media and technology with respect to living space? Test that in your own or a relative's house by:

- Taking an inventory of media appliances (televisions and video recorders, etc.) and technology (computers and telephones, etc.) in each room of the household.

- Naming the specific room according to its primary architectural function: bedroom (for sleeping), parlor (for conversations), living room (for family time), kitchen (for meal preparation), dining room (for eating meals), guest room (for hosting visitors), recreation room (for exercise), and bathroom (for hygiene).
- Determining the primary habitat—virtual or interpersonal—that defines that living space according to activities there during the course of a week. Ask yourself such questions as:
  1. Is the room mostly being used for its architectural or electronic function?
  2. How many face-to-face interactions occur in each room vs. electronic interactions?
  3. Are media appliances and technology equipment left on during interpersonal exchanges?
  4. After taking an inventory and analyzing how each room is being used, determine whether interactions in the household are primarily interpersonal or mediated.

Discussion/Paper Ideas for Chapter Four

- Discuss observations from the Journal Exercise above.
- Discuss the validity of these assertions:
  1. Media history is important because communication has the power to change the course of events—in the world and in our lives.
  2. With each technological wonder, our perception of humanity changes, along with our way of life.
  3. Shared identities in current society are associated more with marketing profiles than with cultural profiles.
- Discuss central theses and themes on media, technology, and social change from Suggested Readings below.

Suggested Readings from Chapter Four

Halberstam, David. *The Fifties*. New York: Villard Books, 1993.

Norris, Pippa. *Digital Divide*. Cambridge, England: Cambridge University Press, 2001.

Standage, Tom. *The Victorian Internet*. New York: Berkeley, 1999.

The Blurring of Identity and Place

And even my sense of identity was wrapped in a namelessness often hard to penetrate. . . . [T]here could be no things but nameless things, no names but thingless names.

—Samuel Beckett, *Molloy*, 1953.

The Disembodied Self

The blurring of identity occurs when technology places an individual in two or more places at once. That defies time and physical law. When identity and time are blurred, so is our sense of place. We live in a three-dimensional universe, existing as physical entities in linear time at specific locations. Defy that law, and the self actually divides. Consciousness focuses in varying degrees on our physical and virtual environments. For instance, a person may be more aware that he or she is in the kitchen on the phone dealing with a tiresome telemarketer during the dinner hour. The same person would dwell more in the virtual environment if he or she were in a car on a cell phone arguing with a partner. The self can handle such moments sparingly, with split consciousness driving the vehicle so that the person, shutting off the cell phone, does not even recall the geographical miles traveled during the argument. Sometimes, though, drivers are not that lucky—especially when real habitat asserts itself, from pothole to ice patch, causing an accident. In any event, as stated earlier, our habitats must be primarily *actual* for the self to be *actualized* or whole psychologically.

When that happens, we are *grounded*. That's an interesting word. It suggests that people who know *where* they are also know *who* they are. It is also an electrical term. Electricians attach one wire of a device to a nonconductive substance, like wood, thereby preventing short circuits. People short-circuit when they lose a sense of place. For ages, that place had been home, school, or community. Media inform us daily about these endangered environments, sponsored by advertisements telling us what technology to buy for home, school, and community. For much of the twentieth century, writes historian Theodore Roszak, magazines were devoid of advertisements for data processing equipment, "let alone books and articles celebrating their inventors and manufacturers. Compare this with the situation today, when the slickest, most futuristic ads in print and on television are those touting computers. . . ."[146] Homes, schools, and communities are *wired*—another intriguing word, suggesting loss of perception—and so are we.

Many people lose perception because of conflicting depictions and stereotypes about identity. The older the person, the more metamorphoses he or she will have endured, influenced by the expansion of media and technology. These include:

- *The cheapening of personhood because of military threat.* During the Cold War, when technological innovations were being developed, including Internet prototypes, people felt inconsequential because entire countries could be vaporized by button-click in a megaton flash. During the Vietnam War, the U.S. government used *birthdays* to rank-order and draft men into the armed forces—many of whom would return home in body bags, the prevalent media image of the early to mid 1970s. For many television viewers, Russia, China, and Vietnam were virtual places that could kill us or our loved ones at any moment. (Today leaders still speak of axes of evil.) To be sure, the cheapening of personhood because of military threat is not confined to these historical periods, nor shall we circumvent future warnings about threats; elements exist in any era because of weapons of mass destruction. The question here concerns how media cover those weapons and how the coverage influences identity.
- *The generalization of personhood because of computer-assisted marketing.* People who survived the trauma of war had to cope with the feel-better optimism of the 1980s' *Me* Generation, known for its greed and materialism. Marketing had a hand in that, too, targeting individuals for specific products by using census and lifestyle data. (A better name for the "Me Generation" might have been the "Me *Generalization.*") "Home," once a refuge from the world, had become a virtual target stereotyped by income level and purchasing power. Television, infomercials, telephone pyramid schemes, telemarketing, direct

marketing, and more permeated American homes. With the advent of more invasive methods, powered by computers in the 1990s, marketing strategies continue to homogenize individuality. The question here concerns the cumulative impact of marketing messages from a variety of sources and how those generalizations influence personal and collective identity.

• *The overglorification of personhood because of media and technology.* Personal computing became popular in the 1990s, shortly after the end of the Cold War, marking the advent of the Information Age. Technology made a person seem important again because entire communities could be linked by mouse-click in a megabyte flash. And eventually so would the world. Media invite viewers to telephone their questions or e-mail their opinions while shows are in progress, as if only dozens—instead of tens of thousands of viewers—were watching or listening. Our phone calls are routed by automated operators, giving us keypad instructions that seldom lead to a human voice. Likewise our e-mails are scanned by artificial intelligence that mocks our own unintentionally, misreading syntax or synonym in electronic replies from "customer service"—replete with more advertising, naturally—thanking us for visiting their domain. The question here concerns the promise of personal attention via media and technology and the impact on identity when our demands go unfulfilled.

Mainstream media have blurred identity and community so much in recent years that "identity" is synonymous with "consumer" and community, with "market share." Round-the-clock coverage sensationalizes events or repackages them as entertainment for celebrity talk shows. According to a Knight Foundation report, other troubling trends include "a great focus on scandal and celebrity, a 'gotcha' philosophy of investigative reporting run amok; loose strands in mainstream publications about accuracy; gossip, rumor; plagiarism; privacy, fact-checking, using multiple sources, breaking confidences."[147] Helen Thomas, the United Press International reporter who covered the White House for nearly thirty years, agrees with that assessment, associating similar trends with media ecosystems. She writes, "Now we see newspapers owned by large faceless conglomerates, and major television networks by industrial giants or big entertainment corporations. The twenty-four-hour news cycle that used to be the sole province of the wire services is now standard operating procedure, with the explosion of all news cable channels, the Internet and other innovations. There used to be a line between what is known as the 'mainstream press' and the tabloids, but that line has become blurrier."[148]

The blurring of news is a technological phenomenon dating back to the 1960 presidential race between John Kennedy and Richard Nixon. Media historians typically focus on Kennedy's charm versus Nixon's beard in the first of four televised debates. From a technological standpoint, however, the third debate was the most influential because candidates were positioned in studios on each coast, blurring place in an event that discussed, among other pressing topics, the obliteration of place in the nuclear era. Moderator Bill Shadel of ABC News introduced the candidates and the new technology:

> In New York the Democratic presidential nominee, Senator John F. Kennedy; separated by three thousand miles in a Los Angeles studio, the Republican presidential nominee, Vice President Richard M. Nixon; now joined for tonight's discussion by a network of electronic facilities which permits each candidate to see and hear the other.[149]

Television, as we have come to know it, had arrived. And it did so in record time. Only three years earlier the industry had logged its first nationwide broadcast. Now it was helping to determine the outcome of a presidential election. After the Kennedy-Nixon debates, television became the agenda-setting medium for American politics.[150] The United States was quickly becoming a virtual community defined by the number of television sets in homes—more than 23 million by 1957—rather than by the number of Americans in those homes. (The same is occurring at present with reports on the number of computers in homes.) In the third Kennedy-Nixon debate, the new medium was showcasing virtual habitat, hyping technology, the essence of which threatened to delete *real* habitat and humanity during the Cold War. The stakes were never higher. Both candidates accused the other of being "trigger-happy." At one point Kennedy asserted: "I think the fate not only of our own civilization, but I think the fate of the world and the future of the human race is involved in preventing a nuclear war."[151] Such a holocaust would nearly happen two years later during the Cuban Missile Crisis, covered extensively by television. Already by 1960 television was changing how society perceived reality and our place in it; the medium was changing collective conscience, too: *how we saw our enemies, how we saw ourselves.*

That vision is still at the crux of our search for community in the high-tech media world. Indeed, the very definition of "new media" not only excludes physical place but also pivots on marketing terminology associated with clusters of like-minded people, undermining idealistic prophecies of the mid-1990s about an informed, global society. In *Media Debates: Great Issues for the Digital Age*, authors Everette E. Dennis and John C. Merrill distinguish old from new media according to real rather than virtual habitat. "Old media were largely geographic, aimed at people in particular physical places, whereas new media were demographic seeking clusters of like-minded individuals with similar interests and passions, much like specialized magazines, but with broader reach and genuine interactivity."[152]

Despite that scope and interactivity, the world seems smaller because of personal computers. Is it really, or is our vision merely blurred? Certainly we can access home pages or message people almost anywhere on the globe. But have we genuinely become "world citizens," as marketers of the latest technology would have us believe? Do we interact with international visitors more civilly now and respect their cultural values more willingly, because of the World Wide Web? Or do we visit sites that target our lifestyles, ambitions, or needs? Do we speak more languages because of e-mail or chat more in English than ever before? Do our children use technology the way computer makers advertise in commercials, with well-dressed boys and girls doing homework in a shared living space as parents glance over their shoulders admiringly? Or is this a misleading advertising depiction, much like commercials that showcase jeeps on mountaintops instead of in traffic jams?[153] In reality, then, do children today hide out more than ever in their rooms, arguing with parents about their privacy—as they violate their own and their family's privacy—filling out interactive surveys in exchange for free premiums?

For many, the latter depiction has proved to be more prevalent in typical U.S. homes. Even Pippa Norris in *Digital Divide* acknowledges that "free Internet services, e-mail and Web hosting services are already widely available, albeit with advertising strings attached."[154] Marketers would pull those strings, having us believe more ideal portrayals. When reality at home differs from that ideal, families may infer that something is wrong with them or their loved ones. That fear is artificial, by and large. However, marketing targets that fear at optimum levels to sell products and services, continuing cycles of inappropriate disclosure and blurring of identity and place.

The impact of marketing hits home because "home" is the target. Of all words, perhaps, marketing most alters the meaning of "home." James Howard Kunstler makes that observation in *The Geography of Nowhere*, noting, as Americans in the twentieth century thought less about building towns—"in the sense of creating coherent communities—they thought more and more about acquiring a product called a 'home.'"[155] Kunstler recalls a marketing trick used by real estate agents who encourage prospective buyers to think of their purchase as *home* and sellers to think of the same dwelling as *house*, "just a thing made of wood where the family happened to sleep and eat, nothing to be attached to. It was most emphatically not *home*. Home was where one was born and raised, a place in time called the past, gone forever. You can't go home again."[156]

Home used to be "where the heart is," a phrase that suggests *security*. Home used to be a castle or refuge, a place or a room of one's own away from the hustle and bustle of the workaday world. Many have lost that sense of security due to the blurring of place. If you own a computer, you have two addresses: a real one in which the computer is located and a virtual one in which the computer operates. If you have more than one computer, you have a real address where both machines are located and two virtual portals into and out of your home. If you buy a domain name to operate a business or promote an association from your home, chances are you work at a real company or association and come home to virtual ones. Your personal "home" page is yet another portal into and out of your home. Your portable phone with e-mail and Internet functions also contains a virtual address that follows you into and out of your home. Like most conscientious readers, you may still believe that your home is the source of warmth and security—just a bit more connected, is all. A genuine feeling of connectedness is self-affirming. Do you feel that? In another era, not terribly long ago, you could provide safe haven for yourself and your children, providing that you locked the doors or joined a local neighborhood watch or, if appropriate, installed security equipment to notify authorities of a break-in. At present, in thousands of homes, parents are locking doors *inside* rooms of their dwellings where computers are found to keep children off them so that everyone can go to sleep or participate in family or other necessary activities. In thousands more homes, however, parents are allowing children unrestricted access to virtual portals for a variety of reasons—because they believe that the Internet is educational and their children are engaged in wholesome activities, because they want time to use their own computers away from the children, or because they want to e-mail relatives in virtual habitats while their family operates in isolation under their own roofs.

Family members may share the same home and DNA, but their lifestyle habits are influenced by other factors.

Mapping the Consumer Genome
In his book *Popular Culture & High Culture*, Herbert J. Gans argues that mass media really do not exist, in terms of behavioral influence:

> Several studies have shown that people choose media content to fit individual and *group requirements* [emphasis added], rather than adapting their life to what the media prescribe or glorify. They are not isolated individuals hungering for and therefore slavishly accepting what the media offer them, but families, couples, and peer groups who use the media when and if the content is relevant to group goals and needs. Thus the audience cannot be considered a mass.[157]

Gans is correct, but he misses the point about marketing. The audience is not a mass; it is a *cluster*. To sell merchandise, marketers routinely stereotype people by cluster analysis and database. As noted in Chapter Three, illustrating the range of self-help, from A to Z—or "Abuse" to "Zen"—marketers also categorize individuals from A to Z—or "Already Affluent" to "Zero Mobility." This method, conceived in the 1970s, began with a real place: San Francisco. Researchers had analyzed four decades of U.S. Census data in the Bay Area and found that voter preferences remained the same even though families had moved in and out of that community during the period. "In other words," writes Jock Bicket in *Marketing Tools*, "not only did birds of feather flock together, but successive generations of those birds flocked in similar fashion."[158] Direct marketing has since perfected cluster analyses so that marketers not only generalize where specific birds flock, according to census data, but also the perceived needs, desires, and hopes of each individual bird.

The goal of marketing is to persuade. Literary and social critic Kenneth Burke, discussing the power of persuasion, quotes the famous maxim: *It is not hard to praise Athenians among Athenians.* Aristotle took heed of that logic, cataloging virtuous traits, from courage and self-control to prudence and wisdom. Among Athenians, a simpleton can be depicted as lovable, earning praise. Among enemies of Athenians, a prudent person can be depicted as cowardly. That is why, cautions Aristotle, we should not only consider the source of persuasion, but also the *audience* at whom rhetoric is directed. Notes Burke, "You persuade a man only insofar as you can talk his language by speech, gesture, tonality, order, image, attitude, idea, *identifying* your ways with his."[159] Marketing is based on the same tenets, amplified in virtual habitat.

Computer technology promises to become more invasive with marketing programs that break down households into DNA-like "cells" and "super cells." This method employs the Darwinian paradigm of virtual habitat, focusing on household income and eliminating people on that criterion from the cyber-landscape. People are targeted in each home according to the number of adults, their children and their ages; the family's buying power, based on income, type of dwelling, and category of home ownership; and spending patterns, based on surveys, credit card use, and new car/truck purchases. The system was developed in the 1990s when the "consumer genome"—behavior in shopping malls and stores—was mapped.[160] Marketers continue to map the consumer in cybermalls and stores, using interactive technology.

This kind of marketing involves sensitive issues of privacy in an Internet age, especially with children willing to divulge information about their parents in return for free gifts, as studies alarmingly show. For instance, a University of Pennsylvania study showed that only 22 percent of children age 10–17 said they would give out such information in exchange for a "great free product"; however, another 23 percent said "yes" as the premium rose in price from $25 to $50 to $100.[161] Gone are innocent days of Captain Midnight merit badge premiums, whose text, by the way, read: "As a Junior Pilot of the Captain Midnight Flight Patrol, I pledge myself to be Honest in all things, Fair to all others, Brave in the face of danger, Courteous to my superiors and elders and Alert at all time to the fine principles of our Flight Patrol."[162] These days media and marketing do not foster such values. "Popular culture now routinely mocks and undermines basic values: the work ethic, faith, family, honesty, integrity. It bombards us with carnality and blurs the distinction between right and wrong,"[163] write Gerry Lange and Todd Domke, noting influences that shape behavior at home and at work. Family issues associated with privacy—what used to be kept secret "among ourselves" or "in the house"—now are violated routinely, especially by teens. Parents reared in less technical eras remain more protective of their privacy. According to the University of Pennsylvania study, "American parents and youngsters are often of very different minds when it comes to giving personal information to Web sites. Kids' release of information to the Web could well become a new arena for family discord."[164]

Families traditionally view privacy as sacred in their communities. Media law still prevents journalists from disclosing facts about people that are embarrassing but true, such as a dread disease, for instance. Privacy plays an integral role in reputation and social mobility. It allows families to overcome obstacles or achieve in spite of them, without censure or gossip from neighbors and competitors. In traditional hometowns, "neighborhood gossip" not only violated privacy but also undermined acceptance, causing social stigmas, especially ones associated with sex, race, lifestyle, and religion. Those stigmas still abound. The difference is, they used to be perpetuated in and confined to physical place. Now gossip is posted worldwide on Web pages or stored in personal computers downloading group e-mails. Worse, marketing further violates personal privacy with intent to sell data that can be accessed by anyone anywhere electronically. Marketers often acquire such data by offering free gifts in exchange for information; providing access to software or upgrades via the completion of digital surveys; or by placing "cookies" (computer tags) in the hard drives of users, to track movement on the Web and collect more private data. Much of this is done deceptively with seemingly innocent downloads of euphemistic "shareware." For instance, almost half of parents do not realize that Web sites gather information without users knowing it.[165] And while Internet browsers can warn users of stealthy placement of cookies and so-called "data miners"—applications that search computers for specific information—that function hinders quick navigation, the chief selling point of faster computers and broadband connections.

Television, which remains the most powerful media tool, in terms of influence, operates similarly in some homes, especially ones with personal video recorders allowing users to rewind or fast forward cable programming. Communication ecosystems—networks of media companies, telecommunications and software firms—have designed technology to collect data about viewers based on show selection, age, income, household, and other profile facts. Data are collected to send "personal" messages into user homes. According to the report, "TV That Watches You: The Prying Eyes of Interactive Television," from the Center for Digital Democracy, "To advertisers, the development of a technology that combines the Web's interactivity with television's element of dedicated spectatorship is a dream come true for they will now have access to a new breed of couch potato, one that both enjoys the warm glow of the tube and craves the personal touch of the Internet."[166]

More invasive methods that rely on converging technologies have been developed. Minute transmitters employing "radio frequency identification" may replace bar codes, notifying consumers when they run low on Country Fresh milk or out of Playtex hose. Functions can be added to the chip to work in tandem with the Internet so that marketers can analyze data from distant sites, ascertaining a family's eating and hygienic habits.[167] RFID technology has distinct benefits when used properly. Initially transmitters were used to safeguard security, allowing employees with coded cards to unlock office doors. Later the military relied on chips in wristbands of soldiers to track their whereabouts or to disclose medical histories. Doctors using handheld computers could decode histories for quick treatment of wounded. Information could be added to chips to help triage on battlefields or in field hospitals. In the home, however, RFID technology can threaten the good name of a family, violating privacy.

The marketing culture views data both as product and vehicle to sell product. Companies amassing consumer profiles can vend sensitive information to other parties, including the health care industry. Because of converging technologies, Internet and TV or transmitter and decoder, personal data can be gathered from a variety of high-tech gadgets and sources. For instance, a person who watches medical shows about a disease or purchases coded products about the disease or orders health-related merchandise on-line or during infomercials may be at risk. Richard Smith, chief technology officer of the Privacy Foundation, writes that a person's genetic predisposition for Huntington's disease might end up in her medical records, preventing her from getting health insurance or even finding employment. "Such medical records are intensely personal," he asserts, "but when big economic interests and systems are involved, they can become just another commodity."[168]

Because of the Internet, the concept of privacy has changed. Privacy used to pertain to people and principles. Virtual homesteader Howard Rheingold acknowledges this, calling for ethical and legal principles to preserve individual autonomy in cyberspace. He admits that sophisticated technology usually circumvents the law, adding that profit and power—combined with tracking difficulties in virtual environments—may be so significant that "no laws will ever adequately protect citizens."[169] Perhaps this will cease to be a concern. "You have zero privacy anyway," proclaimed Scott McNealy, chief executive officer of Sun Microsystems in January 1999. "Get over it."[170] Many already have because media and marketing have altered the meaning "privacy." For typical consumers, privacy pertains to credit cards and encryption so that we can order items without worrying about our identities being stolen by cyber thieves, as reporters warn us on the news. Our identities are threatened in other ways in virtual habitat.

Invasion of privacy makes a big impact on our psyches and way of life. The effect on the family is threefold:

• *Family members interact less.* Media divide the family via programming, requiring multiple television sets and/or computers so that each member has access to shows or sites of his/her own choosing and, as a consequence, lives apart from others for several hours per day in the same home.

• *A divided family buys more products.* Marketing targets each member by breaking down the family into units and pitching products directly to individuals of similar lifestyle and/or age bracket, providing a false sense of belonging or an exaggerated sense of importance.

• *A divided family divulges information more readily.* Media develop programming and marketing devises strategies that segment the family and isolate members in front of monitors and screens. Consequently, parents cannot always warn children about offers too good to be true. Conversely, parents who visit adult-only sites risk having cookies placed in computers that transmit information to children touting pornography, for instance, or any number of digital sins.

Inevitably, discord results. Discord is not the goal, of course. Data collection is, allowing teenagers access to chat, free gifts, music downloads, and myriad other virtual temptations. In turn, data gathering—from surveys to instant messengers—exposes minors to inappropriate material (cult propaganda, peer sex practices, racially offensive lyrics) or introduces a behavior (body piercing, tattooing, binge drinking) that can cause divisions within families. True, questionable social behaviors also emanate out of interpersonal contacts—from meeting on street corners to mingling with criminals. However, that is not the issue. Never before in our society have such behaviors been affirmed by ubiquitous media and technology, implying norms that may or may not exist in the actual community. As such protection of privacy ceases to be a familial priority; access to programming and the pursuit of lifestyle, from spouse to teen to child, typically takes precedent.

Naturally we feel confused or dysfunctional. It's easy for experts to make that case because symptoms are so widespread that we see them in each other and ourselves. Symptoms, of course, emanate out of fear—a human survival trait associated with fight/flight response in real habitat. Symptoms also may be associated with the blurring of identity and place, caused by media and technology. Fear empowers media, particularly in commercials, which warn us daily that unless we buy elixir products, from deodorant to self-help, our quest for acceptance will fail. For many, that quest becomes a paramount concern. Typically, though, it is conducted in an electronic rather than a physical environment, virtually inviting failure.

Moral and Social Upheaval

Society, we have noted, periodically experiences significant change. In that respect, the current era does not differ dramatically from dozens of others throughout history. When society undergoes upheaval as happened, say, during the Bolshevik Revolution, so does communication. We say "comrade" when we mean "friend," incorporating political diction into everyday vocabulary. Technology also changes communication. The latter has greater impact because it alters our perception, priorities, and principles. Social change is confined to an area—from community to continent; technological change is not confined to a specific location because its goal is to transcend locale. During the Vietnam conflict, America exaggerated the so-called "domino effect," fearing Southeast Asian countries would become communistic if South Vietnam fell. South Vietnam fell, but dominos did not. More recently, a different domino argument was made to justify the 2001 invasion of Afghanistan and the 2003 invasion of Iraq—regimes that had to fall, the U.S. government claimed—or else support of terrorism would proliferate worldwide. Terrorism, to be sure, changed parts of the world in addition to our vocabulary—Al Qaeda to Ground Zero. However, the real domino effect—the one that should command our attention—typically occurs not with socio-political but with *techno-logical* change. That occurs because machines skew people's perceptions of the world, altering fundamental aspects of the life experience. Not only do vocabularies change, entire cultures do. "When a new major communication technology is introduced into a culture that shifts the bias from time to space"—increasing the speed of human interaction from one place to another—"this new technology could have profound cultural consequences,"[171] observes Susan B. Barnes, describing effects of mediated communication over the Internet.

Automobiles changed the landscape along with architecture and community planning. But automobile technology also fostered mobility and interpersonal contact, connecting communities and people. Communication technology displaces people, forcing change in our interpersonal relationships. The last comparable such change in Western culture occurred in fifteenth-century Europe with the invention of movable type by Johannes Guttenberg, a German metallurgist. Guttenberg began his career by peddling trinkets to religious pilgrims and later made metal molds to print thousands of "indulgences," slips of paper sold as coupons to sinners to shorten their stays in Purgatory. Guttenberg, of course, is best known for his press and Bible; media scholars, however, note that the indulgences—the junk mail of the fifteenth and sixteenth centuries—afflicted the collective conscience in Europe and led, ultimately, to a revolution in thought, word, and deed.

In the sixteenth century, the Roman Catholic Church shaped the collective conscience, dictating moral values and, on occasion, ignoring Scripture to promote special interests. Scholars like Martin Luther, father of the Protestant Reformation and a Catholic monk, had ready access to printed Bibles. Soon he became aware of the discrepancies between the Bible and Church teachings. His own writings, including the famous Ninety-five Theses nailed to the door of Castle Church at Wittenberg in 1517, challenged papal authority "out of love for the truth and from desire to elucidate it." Luther, as activists before him, understood that nothing sparks the collective conscience as effectively as the truth. Unlike activists before him, Luther also realized that his own excommunication—*execution*, even—could not throttle community debate, for though Luther himself could be silenced, his theses against indulgences could not, because the power of truth combined with the power of the press. Both would usurp the infallible power of popes. One could still kill the messenger, but *not* a message as powerful as this one by Luther:

> Why does not the Pope deliver all souls at the same time out of Purgatory for the sake of most holy love and on account of the bitterest distress of those souls—this being the most imperative of all motives—while he saves an infinite number of souls for the sake of that most miserable thing money, to be spent on building a church—this being the very slightest of motives? [Thesis 82]

Theses like that spawned the Protestant faith and eventually transformed society on a global scale, spreading to Puritan America and shaping many of our values. As the case of Martin Luther attests, the domino effect of technological change is substantial. Such upheaval is occurring today with the Internet. The difference, however, lies not in the tool or the toolmaker but how the tool is used, and *by whom*. Are we using media and technology to enrich our lives and reaffirm our values, or are media and technology using us to program our lives and influence our values?

Let us be clear on the following: There is nothing inherently wrong or immoral about technology and media. This book is part of mass media and was researched, edited, rewritten, updated, and produced efficiently because of technology. To damn innovations as awe-inspiring as immediate global communication would be a tragedy of immense social proportions, for media and technology can help us evolve into an enlightened, compassionate multicultural community, liberating the oppressed and sharing information and ideas for the universal good. Without these electronic tools, we could not tap into the immense knowledge base now at our disposal, nor teach new generations futuristic methods to address historic problems, from health care to human rights, for what we know as a species—every fact of science, art, culture, and more—doubles amoeba-like every eighteen months or so. In fact, those who malign media and avoid technology because they offend or cause discomfort are themselves the first victims of the electronic era. They are closer in conscience and consciousness to news junkies and technophiles, for all these types, as we shall learn, cannot deal effectively with challenge because their dominant character trait is to bypass issues that trigger emotional distress. These "cultural totalitarians"—including those we label Luddites or curmudgeons—

disenfranchise themselves, not the way news junkies and technophiles often do, through lack of literacy, but through detachment from the paramount issue of our era: how to use media and technology wisely so that they help rather than hamper our intellectual and spiritual growth.

In *Questioning Technology*, Andrew Feenberg comes to the same realization, noting that ideals and economic interests can merge in a proactive process of technical change. "In that process," writes Feenberg, "potentialities that appear at first in ethical or ideological form are eventually realized in an effective consciousness of self-interest" that makes such a change possible.[172] After all, the Information Age is still in its infancy. It took a generation, about sixty-five years, before Martin Luther emerged to aright the new medium of moveable type and set it on a more balanced path. Luther proved that truth is greater than authority 218 years before German émigré John Peter Zenger's acquittal on charges of seditious libel for criticizing the royal governor in the *New York Weekly Journal*. As such, Bill Gates is to Guttenberg as Luther is to some yet unnamed mogul. That person is likely to be a media expert or computer specialist because she or he will use one or both mediums "out of love for the truth and from desire to elucidate it." Nobody can predict what will be invented or transformed to meet this challenge; but there will be distinct hallmarks: a shift from economic toward transcendent truth, from corporate toward collective empowerment, and from social disenfranchisement toward civic engagement. Until such a person uses media and technology to affirm that truth is greater than market or market share we will suffer a diminished sense of community.

To attain such growth, we must use media and technology to *expand* community rather than be used by them to *replace* community. When used appropriately, media and technology reaffirm our values, advance our knowledge, and improve the quality of our lives. Television keeps us informed during breaking news, as does the Internet; when used in tandem, the Web expands on news, providing statistics and databases. Media and technology also empower a select portion of the populace—those who have the requisite education, discernment, and skills to utilize instant access to information. Until recently, even the social elite relied on such authority figures as researchers or physicians to explain data or treatments; now more of us can do so ourselves, locating records or facilities to suit our personal needs. The prestigious

Knight Higher Education Collaborative concludes that interactive technology "empowers the end-user" at every turn, connecting "an individual to any source of information, anywhere, anytime. In making possible this set of linkages, technology is effecting profound changes in the sense of self, in work, in social structures, in the economy—and in higher education."[173] Information, once an academic or social privilege, has become an everyday commodity, shifting the balance of power away from the institution and toward the educated, discerning, and diligent individual. However, in the hands of children or those without adequate education or self-control, media and technology deepen the learning divide. Policy analyst and author Dinesh D'Souza believes a "digital divide" exists, but has little to do with access to computers or the Internet. "The real digital divide is that some people and some groups know how to use these tools to get information and put it to use, and others are not as adept in doing so. In the United States, the information and knowledge are available; the problem is one of teaching people the value of knowledge, how to obtain it, and what to do with it."[174] Without such education, computer access can be as dangerous as controlled substances when misused and overconsumed, resulting in psychological imbalance.

An analogy may help argue the point. Medication, used properly, bestows balance. Physicians prescribe drugs to ease pain and restore vitality or perception so that we can go about our daily routines at home, at work, and in the community, maintaining robust relationships with family, friends, colleagues, and neighbors. If we abuse medication, however, we become addicted and experience withdrawal pains and loss of vitality and perception. According to substance abuse experts noticeable physical symptoms include a pale face, imprecise eye movements, and neglect of personal appearance, with less noticeable symptoms exhibiting themselves in reduced ambition, a decline in the quality of schoolwork, shortened attention span, impaired communication skills, and less care for the feelings of others.[175] These symptoms resemble those of media addiction. As early as 1977, *Wall Street Journal* columnist Marie Winn established such a connection in her influential book *The Plug-In Drug*, in which she compares excessive TV-watching to heroin use. "The television habit distorts the sense of time. It renders other experiences vague and curiously unreal while taking on a greater reality for itself. It weakens relationships by reducing and sometimes eliminating normal opportunities for talking, for communicating."[176] Now television-viewing has combined with computer use, adding hours to the time that we spend looking at screens rather than each other. That affects us emotionally, ethically, and spiritually. At best we are forgetting basic problem-solving skills requiring tact, patience, civility, mutual trust, and respect. Lacking these values, social skills deteriorate. Without such skills, we complicate our lives and relationships. Too many of us have become addicted to media and technology, wasting precious years in lonely but wired rooms or in oblivious virtual environments. That has a domino effect on our values and awareness without which there can be no empowerment, even with the world at our fingertips.

Endangered Habitats

Media and technology not only have displaced us, disembodying the self; they have endangered our traditional residential habitats, including schools, hospitals, and homes. Nowhere is such endangerment more apparent than in wired universities whose leaders understand the necessity of media and technology as learning tools but who themselves are educated, discerning, and diligent—precisely because they are socially active within several communities—from student bodies and professoriates, with which they interact; from local to national service organizations, on whose boards they sit; from alumni to corporate networks, from which they solicit support; from state to federal agencies, within whose budgets they must live. However, the very students whom they recruit—those weaned on media as babysitter and technology as guardian—lack the education, discernment, and, most importantly, *attention span* to use these tools conscientiously.

In *The Cult of Information* Theodore Roszak notes that computers are only the most recent educational product billed as the ultimate teaching machine. "More to the point," he writes, "an increasing number of educators have begun to recognize that classroom technology is emphatically *not* neutral but carries with it significant (if subliminal) cultural, ethical, and epistemological presuppositions."[177] Students intuit this, too, especially in wireless classrooms, where they click away in surreptitious "back-channel" chat as likely to be off-topic as on. While it is true that conscientious students often enhance discussions by noting appropriate links or data associated with the topic, others heckle lecturers or hurl digital spitballs at each other without the consequence of paper-era note-passing. According to a *New York Times* article titled "In the Lecture Hall, A Geek Chorus," some "ignore speakers entirely by surfing the Web or checking their e-mail—a practice that has led some lecturers to plead for connectionless auditoriums or bans on laptop use."[178] In sum, misuse of wireless and computer technology has become a moral and behavioral issue in academe.

Engineering major Parker Synder was among the first of his generation to write about the misuse of computers at Wake Forest, an exceptional institution that stresses the importance of ethics as well as technology. Even at such a campus, writes Synder, students lacking moderation and self-discipline can transform an information-gathering assignment "into an endless escapade through pages of consumer intended marketing gimmicks."[179] Synder believes that technology nurtures "addictive behaviors by providing a pipeline to the source of the addiction" and "the framework to introduce negative behaviors" to the campus community.[180]

Synder focuses on pornography:

> College men are presented with the opportunity to habitually abuse sexually explicit material because of the ease with which it is accessed over the Internet and the anonymity and privacy associated with residence life. Habitual abuse introduces a number of negative consequences with ramifications to the campus community. For example, healthy relationships are devalued by habitual exposure; the woman may be looked upon strictly for physical gratification at the expense of personal commitment. A man is more likely to engage in behaviors that are self-fulfilling at the expense of his partner while developing a more shallow conception of personal fulfillment.[181]

In the early 1990s, Synder reminds us, students had to go to great lengths in real rather than virtual community to procure pornography, renting or purchasing videos and magazines and then hiding them from roommates and partners. Using a computer, a person can avoid the awkward glances of passersby at local sex shops. In some sense, this is ironic in that pornography is determined by *community standards*. Internet has blurred that, too, for what used to be pornographic in Topeka, for instance, now can be accessed virtually anywhere. In a word, misuse of Internet to access pornography—including child pornography in residence halls—fosters addiction in an environment that ought to stimulate the intellect rather than the libido. Students become addicted to pornography because they underestimate the consequences of accessing such material. Consequences affect personal development—the sole objective of a college education—with larger ramifications in more uncontrolled settings at home or at the workplace, whose penalties often include divorce and dismissal. In sum, universities that provide and/or encourage computer access also must assume responsibility to promote ethics and character development, especially on residential campuses where community, traditionally, has been emphasized.

Without ethics, we rely on instinct instead of values. The more we rely on instinct, the easier marketers target us, because we lack discretion and violate our own privacy. If something tempts us on-line, we visit the site. If we want a "free" premium, we fill out the surveys. We do this instantaneously because the technology operates best that way, with a mouse-click. The sole authority for many people these days has become instinct, says psychologist Mihaly Csikszentmihalyi. "If something feels good, if it is natural and spontaneous, then it must be right. But when we follow the suggestions of generic and social instructions without question we relinquish the control of consciousness and become helpless playthings of impersonal forces. The person who cannot resist drugs or alcohol, or whose mind is constantly focused on sex, is not free to direct his or her psychic energy."[182]

College students, above all, must learn to direct their creative and psychic energy. This, like most learning, is best done face-to-face without mediated communication. However, colleges continue to promote distance education via information technology, in which they have heavily invested. They also tout collaborative and service learning on residential campuses. The two don't mix. Even educators who promote distance learning, such as Robert P. Ouellette, director of technology-management programs at the University of Maryland, acknowledge this on some level. Ouellette, who has conducted studies about experiences in on-line education courses, remarks that students learning on-line tend to be more distant and abrupt when they communicate. "It's easier to tell somebody where to go online. It's very difficult to do that face to face."[183] Ouellette also believes trust is established more slowly in the virtual habitat because of different time zones on-line and lack of physical presence. He notes the importance of teamwork in collaborative learning, disclosing, "The students in the face-to-face environment worked well in groups. The students online found it very difficult."[184] On-line students also may find it difficult to foster meaningful interactions with their professors who appear animated only at designated transmission times and are otherwise as artificial and downloadable as any other file on the learner's hard drive. This, too, devalues the value of education. Thomas J. Watson, professor of religion and distinguished professor of philosophy, emeritus, at Syracuse University, puts matters into perspective with this anecdote:

> In my college days we students were in and out of our professors' homes all the time. The logical limit of today's personalized education is courses that proceed entirely by Internet. One of my graduate students devised such a course. Unable to land a face-to-face teaching position, he seized the initiative and created a course on world religions, which the University of California Extension continues to offer for credit. In the five years it has been online, he has yet to lay eyes on a single one of his students.[185]

The same phenomenon is happening in other professions, including medicine. Physicians used to make house calls. Then they requested that patients come to them. If they ever return to making house calls, they will do so virtually through telemedicine. "The day is fast approaching when a doctor equipped with nothing more than a handheld computer can do medical checkups or even perform surgery on patients thousands of kilometers away,"[186] writes Wallace Immen in "Healing without the human touch," touting telemedicine in the *Globe and Mail*. Immen notes as well that the technology is evolving more rapidly than people who want to take advantage of it. That makes sense. When our health or well-being is at stake, we require face-to-face dialogue and human contact. Telemedicine eliminates both. Telemedicine uses electronic communication to transmit X-rays, ultrasound, and other data and facilitates doctor–patient consultations. Telemedicine does save lives in remote areas where availability of physicians is limited. That is the proper use of technology, able to overcome issues of physical space, especially vital during medical emergencies. However, as we might have anticipated, the appeal of telemedicine is cost-effectiveness. "The cost-containment dimension of telemedicine is an added impulse for its adoption,"[187] asserts one government specialist. Cost containment can be easily documented. Effectiveness, however, cannot. Moreover, proper use of technology involves *a real product* as much as virtual information—something that telemedicine cannot provide but that physicians, working with medical engineers and technicians, can. Bionic appliances are expensive. But they help humans touch, see, walk, bend, and hear. "In the not-too-distant future, doctors will be able to replace or assist almost every part of the body,"[188] *Newsweek* reports. The insurance and health care industries are less likely to promote such achievements because they do not involve cost-containment via communication technology.

In every facet of life, virtual habitat is intruding on real habitat. That includes crime. Within the last decade of the twentieth century, the United States has added to its geographical population of some 275 million inhabitants a virtual community with a population equal to that of Mexico and Germany—or some 181,500,000 Americans with access to the Internet. Crime, of course, happens in physical and virtual community. According to the FBI, a total of 11,417 special agents were assigned to cover actual habitat—the towns, cities, and states in which crime occurs physically in three dimensions. Fewer than two hundred agents in field offices nationwide, however, were assigned to investigate cyber crime.[189] Worse, the FBI anticipates 50 percent of its caseload to require computer forensic examinations. Because there is no "there" in cyberspace, criminals are able to elude authorities with alarming nimbleness.

In a report to Congress on cyber crime, the FBI notes that one network intrusion case involving espionage required analysis of 17.5 terabytes of data. "To place this into perspective," the report continues, "the entire collection of the Library of Congress, if digitized, would comprise only 10 Terabytes."[190] In 1999 alone, cyber crime cost businesses some $123.7 million, in large part because of security breaches. Granted, these statistics may spiral out of control or come under control in the future. The lesson here involves crime in an environment that exists electronically rather than physically. Moreover, all categories of virtual crime are on the rise—from information warfare by enemies of the United States, including terrorists eluding homeland security, to organized crime by credit card scammers and identity thieves.[191] "There are more threatening scenarios" involving the access to information about individuals, writes Tim Berners-Lee, creator of the World Wide Web. "Burglars could find it very handy to know who has been buying what recently."[192]

Law enforcement, not to mention the judicial system, is currently not equipped to handle virtual community with the same standard of protection as real community. "There are jurisdictional issues yet to be resolved,"[193] states Theodore Jones, former director of Campus Security at Ohio University, an institution which, like dozens of others, purchased computers for residence halls. Like Wake Forest, OU also has a strong ethics program. But sometimes that is not enough. For instance, a virus launched from an OU residence hall closed down an entire computer system in the United Kingdom. "Who has jurisdiction?" Jones asks. "State, federal, local, Interpol?" Moreover, he adds, the new technology has created a new set of victims. "We recently executed a search warrant on a computer in a residence hall which was being used to launch 'bombs' (viruses). We seized the computer which was an inconvenience to the students, and it turned out their computer had been hacked into and they were guiltless." Criminal rules have not been established because physical evidence is especially difficult to gather in an artificial community. "There have not been enough court cases, especially at the appellate level, to know what the rules are. For instance, how do you prosecute violations that originate in another country?"

The blurring of place—what comes in and out of your home, virtually or otherwise—affects our peace of mind. For we are not only social creatures in search of acceptance; we are *territorial* creatures every bit obsessed with place as wolves. We have our dens, just as they do. We have familial hierarchies, just as they do. We protect our kin, just as they do. That explains why many of us experience a persistent sense of uneasiness in a house with real and virtual gates of entry. At bedtime some of us not only lock front doors but also program the security system, shut off the cell phones, program the caller identifications and call blocks, shut down or leave on the computer systems, lock or leave unlocked the rooms containing computer systems, and then go to bed to stare at the entertainment center until we drift to the only genuine virtual reality associated with the conscience and consciousness: *dream*. Who or what can awake us?

Journal Exercise

Computer-assisted marketing collects data on individuals to build "customer profiles." Marketers match people of similar profile and target them in applications, promoting products or services. To assemble profiles, specific data must be collected, including:

- *Demographics*, or personal facts as found in a census survey: sex, age, race, marital status, annual income, vehicles, education, citizenship, disabilities, housing—physical and financial characteristics.
- *Psychographics*, or lifestyle facts as found in credit and credit card reports identifying debt, brand-name purchases, and other financial/consumer information; magazine subscriptions; television viewing habits; and product warranties.
- *Attitudes*, or reasons for lifestyles choices or consumer-spending habits, including why a person chose one brand over another; how the person views the product; why the person subscribes to certain magazines or consumes TV programming; why the person goes on diets, exercises, or uses beauty products, and so on.

It is one thing to say a consumer is a twenty-six-year-old college-educated man renting a two-bedroom dwelling in Washington, DC. It is another to say he is a twenty-six-year-old business school graduate of Hampton University with a $22,000 debt from student loans renting a $2,000-per-month townhouse in Georgetown. It is another to say that he is active in his alumni association because he values his Hampton education; aspires to own his own accounting firm because wealth bestows status; and donates time in a nearby homeless shelter because volunteering enhances leadership skills.

A consumer profile detailing personal facts, lifestyle choices, and attitudes—just illustrated—is usually more extensive. Does such a profile actually define or stereotype that person? Does it violate privacy when data like these are collected on-line and sold to companies or other interested parties?

To answer such questions, assemble a consumer profile about your personal, lifestyle, and attitudinal traits. Provide answers concerning:

1. Your sex, age, race, marital status, income, vehicles, education, citizenship, disabilities, and living quarters—including how many and what type of rooms, whether you rent or own the dwelling or live with others, how much you pay in monthly rent or mortgage, and so on.
2. Your existing loans or debt; your bank accounts or stock and other investments; six months of credit card purchases, noting brand names; magazine subscriptions; and merchandise bearing product warranties.

3. Why you made each lifestyle choice enumerated in No. 2, chose one brand over another; subscribed to each magazine; and anything else that explains your attitudes.

After you assemble your marketing profile, ask yourself:

- Does the profile actually define or stereotype me?
- What other attributes about my character are omitted that define me as an individual?
- How would I feel, with respect to privacy, about others having access to my profile and/or about companies that collect and sell such data?

Discussion/Paper Ideas for Chapter Five

- Discuss observations from the Journal Exercise above.
- Discuss the validity of these assertions:
  1. Many people have lost perception because of conflicting depictions and stereotypes about identity, including:
     ✓ The cheapening of personhood because of military threats.
     ✓ The generalization of personhood because of computer-assisted marketing.
     ✓ The overglorification of personhood because of media and technology.
  2. Virtual habitat intrudes on real habitat, especially with respect to health care, education, and crime.
  3. Computer-assisted marketing involves sensitive issues of privacy in an Internet age, especially concerning children.
- Discuss central theses and themes on marketing, privacy, and social consequences of computerization from the Suggested Readings below.

Suggested Readings from Chapter Five

Dennis, Everette E. and Merrill, John C. *Media Debates: Great Issues for the Digital Age*. Belmont, CA: Wadsworth, 2002.

Lindstrom, Martin. *Clicks, Bricks & Brands*. London: Kogan Page, 2001.

Rochlin, Gene I. *Trapped in the Net: The Unanticipated Consequences of Computerization*. Princeton, NJ: University of Princeton Press, 1997.

Roszak, Theodore, *The Cult of Information*. Berkeley, CA: University of California Press, 1994.

The Medium Is the Moral

[T]he medium is the message. This is merely to say that the personal and social consequences of any medium—that is, of any extension of ourselves—result from the new scale that is introduced into our affairs by each extension of ourselves, or by any new technology.

—MARSHALL MCLUHAN, *Understanding Media*

McLuhan, Revisited

"The medium is the message," wrote media critic and theorist Marshall McLuhan, coining a phrase that seems more prophetic now, in the Internet Age, than poetic. McLuhan, though, may be more poet than prophet. His oft-cited phrase acknowledges the impact of media on messages; however, McLuhan fails to predict the future of mediated communication. Like a line from a poem, his aphorism merely explained pop culture so cogently that his words came to define communication in the television era. McLuhan also coined the phrase "global village," believing that electronic media "retribalized" people from various cultures and countries so that they became citizens of the planet, rather than of a place, and hence tended to know more about world events, say, than happenings in their hometowns. "The new electronic interdependence recreates the world in the image of a global village,"[194] McLuhan wrote, noting the impact of media in the Telstar period of the 1960s.

Historian Theodore Roszak believes that many of McLuhan's prophesies are based on "zany media metaphysics" predicting generations of cozy technophiles engaged in worldwide civic participation.[195] The idea of telecommunication as human liberator harkens back to this particular McLuhan proclamation. According to Roszak, "McLuhan primarily had television in mind; he insisted that people sitting passively in front of cathode ray tubes, watching a steady display of images from around the world, were somehow becoming more participative citizens."[196] The expression "global village" has become as popular as "the medium is the message." Again the phrase encapsulates truth poetically, bestowing new perspective on an extant aspect of media, rather than predicting new technologies to come.

With the publication of *Understanding Media: The Extensions of Man* (1964), in which the famous phrase "the medium is the message" appears, McLuhan became better known as a media critic than as a professor of English literature, which he was. In addition to *The Medium Is the Massage: An Inventory of Effects* (1967) and *Culture Is Our Business* (1970), McLuhan also edited *The Selected Poetry of Tennyson* (1954) and *Voices of Literature* (1964). It was only natural for him to tap the universal truths of literature via clever metaphors—a poetic tool—than to measure media's impact on culture, the way a journalism researcher might. Conversely it was not natural for him to test his theories or gather quantitative data to support them. Appropriately, McLuhan's singular talent befitted the times—the literary sound bite at the beginning of the television era—as powerful as any Shakespearean line. McLuhanisms include such gems as:

- "'Time' has ceased, 'space' has vanished. We now live in a global village. . . ."
- "When you are on the phone or on the air, you have no body."
- "All advertising advertises advertising."
- "The future of the book is the blurb."
- "News, far more than art, is artifact."

In many respects, McLuhan's aphorisms are literary artifacts reminiscent of Renaissance masters like Francis Bacon, the great English scholar and poet recognized for these truisms:

- Knowledge itself is power.
- The remedy is worse than the disease.
- Virtue is like a rich stone—best plain set.

McLuhan, of course, digested the works of Sir Francis early in his academic career. Indeed, McLuhan's biographer Phillip Marchand acknowledges Bacon's influence on McLuhan in "the art of the aphorism." According to Marchand, "Bacon maintained that the aphorism—the pithy, arresting statement—was useful precisely because it did not explain itself. In its incompleteness and suggestiveness, it invited 'men to enquire further' into a subject. The McLuhan who later became famous for his aphorisms—notably, 'The medium is the message'—was intrigued by this use of language."[197]

McLuhan's interest in Francis Bacon is significant from another aspect, concerning knowledge and technology. Bacon believed that truth and utility were synonymous, directly associated with mechanical invention, meant to ease humankind's fallen state, restoring a sense of transcendence.[198] Policy analyst and author Dinesh D'Souza dubs Bacon "the patron saint of our technological civilization," noting that Bacon believed that "true knowledge is not that which enables us to rise above our wants, it is that which allows us to gratify our wants."[199] Technology embraces such a materialistic philosophy, at least from a marketing standpoint. Poets, however, are known to be positively monkish in their pursuit of knowledge rather than possession. McLuhan, like Bacon, resists that stereotype. The poet in him may have created the aphorism; however, McLuhan the materialist uses it as sound bite in the media.

"I may be wrong," McLuhan once remarked, "but I'm never in doubt." In retrospect, concerning his media predictions, McLuhan was wrong about as often as he was right—standard fare for a typical poet—whose truths are hit and miss. But when they hit, they hit *home*, possessing the power of epiphanies. As such, they endure and become clichés until time resurrects them. McLuhan enjoys such a legacy, recently resurrected. Because of the World Wide Web, his stature has grown from media guru to prophet. But the poetic term "global village" refers primarily to broadcast technology, which he deemed superior to books as an educational tool. Television, he believed, stimulated rather than dulled our senses:

> In television there occurs an extension of the sense of active, exploratory touch which involves all the senses simultaneously, rather than that of sight alone. You have to be "with" it. . . . Television demands participation and involvement in depth of the whole being. It will not work as a background. It engages you. Perhaps this is why so many people feel that their identity has been threatened. This charge of the light brigade has heightened our general awareness of the shape and meaning of lives and events to a level of extreme sensitivity.[200]

Guido Stempel, distinguished journalism researcher and contemporary of McLuhan, calls himself "data oriented," and so he is predisposed to question McLuhan's theories. As Stempel puts it in an interview, "I'm guilty of not having completely analyzed the theories of my published research. McLuhan, on the other hand, doesn't bother with data and is guilty of oversimplification,"[201] particularly his idea of "hot" and "cool" media. McLuhan believed that a hot medium is high definition, like a photograph. Conversely a cartoon is a "cool" medium of low definition, requiring viewers to interact imaginatively to receive the message. (One wonders what McLuhan would say about high-definition television, or HDTV, which generates picture quality similar to that of film and sound quality similar to that of a compact disc.) In any case, Stempel doubts the validity of McLuhan's theories. "Television is not a 'cool' medium of lines and dots that force the viewer to interact with the screen," Stempel says. "Television is passive. Except for the remote control. In that sense," he quips, "television is interactive."

The more one contemplates McLuhan's hot-cold motif, the more unlikely it seems, more reminiscent of oxymoronic poetry than of media. Several theorists have criticized or modified McLuhan's metaphor, including his most famous legator Neil Postman, distinguished author and communications professor, who believes the medium *biases* the message. All media, however sophisticated, are mere tools, according to Postman, and embedded in every tool is an ideological bias, prodding the user to envision reality "as one thing rather than another," causing him or her to value one thing over another and amplifying one or another particular skill or mindset over another. [202] This, adds Postman, is what Marshall McLuhan meant when he said the medium is the message. Postman acknowledges that the truth behind the aphorism was not really new but "in short an ancient and persistent piece of wisdom, perhaps most simply expressed in the old adage that, to a man with a hammer, everything looks like a nail. Without being too literal, we may extend the truism: To a man with a pencil, everything looks like a list. To a man with a camera, everything looks like an image. To a man with a computer, everything looks like data."[203]

Similarly to a man with a metaphor, everything is extended. Part of the problem with McLuhan's metaphor is his core belief that technology extends the human senses. To some extent, this is arguable. But the metaphor is inexact. A hearing aid, for instance, extends the capacity to hear within a physical radius because its purpose is to amplify sound into the ear canal, directly stimulating that sense. A telephone, on the other hand, extends the capacity to hear over tens of thousands of miles. However, it is the distance traveled, rather than the capacity to hear, which is impressive. This eludes McLuhan. He uses a biology rather than physics paradigm, as articulated in this book (i.e,. "real vs. virtual habitat"), and thus never truly foresees cyberspace—a genuine metaphysical environment with domains and digital divides—that engages as it splits awareness, so we can "visit" new realms, as one does a Web site, or diverts attention, so we can drive and use cell phones. Technology puts a person in two or more places simultaneously and, therefore, impacts consciousness and conscience, also as previously discussed. McLuhan discusses the impact of electronic media on consciousness and conscience with oracular fervency. He believed that "technological extension of consciousness" metamorphosed humans into mighty beings of expression, enabling us "to reverberate the Divine thunder, by verbal translation."[204] McLuhan prophesied the development of external conscience—in itself, an implausible oxymoron—that would complement and shape individual conscience, instantaneously advancing culture. "No further acceleration is possible this side of the light barrier."[205] In essence, McLuhan theorized that electronic media would evolve human beings biologically into "information systems," extending the reach of physical senses around the globe.

McLuhan's mistake was to focus on humans *as* information systems rather than on humans in information *space*. Thus he never foresaw the splitting of consciousness accompanying new technologies. Here is where McLuhan's biological model breaks down. McLuhan emphasizes sense instead of space, arguing that the telephone extends the human ear; film, the eye; and television, touch. The notion that television extends the sense of touch has always been problematic, metaphorically and literally. McLuhan's metaphor is based on his unscientific belief that television does not dull but actually supercharges the senses. TV does so, according to McLuhan, because moving images are made up of low-density lines and dots—unlike high-density photography or film—that the TV viewer must learn to decipher in "creative dialogue" with the screen. "By requiring us to constantly fill in the spaces of the mosaic mesh, the iconoscope is tattooing its message directly on our skins," McLuhan asserts in a famous 1969 *Playboy* interview.[206]

Despite mixed metaphors and a penchant for puns (as in "the medium is the *massage*")—another incurable Shakespearean trait—

McLuhan does deserve respect and attention. He is especially insightful asserting that we must understand how technology changes culture. McLuhan is perhaps singularly responsible for teaching the audience to put less emphasis on content (what a newsmaker says) and more emphasis on the medium (what a newsmaker says on *television*). That kind of education is needed today, especially in the schools which, historically, help shape character and build community. Otherwise, the medium becomes the moral. Content usually is biased because messages enter homes via virtual portals with specific electronic rules, depending on the medium. For example, a sage philosopher promoting civic virtue on C-SPAN does so on the same set that transmits Jerry Springer, using similar camera angles, cuts, pans, and fades in the director's booth. This fact, though, typically eludes educators who overplay content and underplay the format and production of content, viewing the latter as technical rather than as scholarly. James W. Chesebro and Dale Bertelsen in their book on mediated communication believe that academics tend to treat the content and structure of a presentation as the totality of its message. "In this regard," they write, "communication critics have traditionally failed to give the channel, format, and medium of communication the same attention they have devoted to the ideational presentation of a message."[207]

Education impacts communities. Without adequate scholarly information on how communication systems alter messages, officials of school systems investing heavily in media and technology often are unaware of their impact on face-to-face interaction and civic engagement. In his research about the collapse and revival of U.S. communities, Robert D. Putnam notes that computer-mediated communication transmits much less nonverbal information than face-to-face communication. This affects our interactions, Putnam states, because people "are remarkably effective at sensing nonverbal messages from one another, particularly about emotions, cooperation, and trustworthiness."[208] Ethical values, collaboration, and mutual trust are essential building blocks of both character education and civic engagement. Media and technology may be ends to such goals but not without educators explaining the impact of mediated communication, balancing instruction on converging media and software applications with equal emphasis on civic virtue and interpersonal participation.

Instead, many educators put faith in media and technology as information providers without which emerging generations will tumble into the digital divide, disenfranchised in the global village. As they did at the advent of the television era, purchasing sets for classrooms and trumpeting technology, educators are doing it again, renovating and rewiring buildings to house computers, without stopping to question:

- *How learners perceive the computer.* Do they see it as many educators do—as a tool of information—or as a video arcade, jukebox, and/or all night cyber café? Does any disparity in perception affect learning pedagogies and, if so, what adjustments might be made?
- *How process is transformed via the computer.* Does the information-gathering process encourage personal exploration and intellectual discovery the way that the process did once in libraries? Or does the computer transform the experience into a mechanical exercise on par with data processing?
- *How content is biased by the computer.* Do computer databases and hotlinks to reservoirs of text mean that learners will access information because it is available? Or will they be prone to (a) visit more appealing sites associated with their lifestyle statistics, (b) contact proxy sites that deliver information for a fee, (c) simply copy, paste, and reformat material, passing it off as their own?

One would think that journalism, of all academic disciplines—noted for its emphasis on content, especially concerning news—would ponder ramifications of such questions. In the late 1990s and early 2000s, thousands of media outlets went virtual with the focus on posting news on their Web sites rather than covering cyberspace with dogged rigor. To this day "technology journalists," by and large, are more like movie reviewers than investigative reporters, previewing new Internet sites or rating new electronic gadgets. In response, dozens of prestigious journalism schools have inaugurated "new media" initiatives. Those initiatives typically circumvent questions about content and coverage, or how they are altered, via computer technology. Instead they advertise, as one representative journalism school recently did, for new media specialists "with the talent and commitment to develop a new generation of journalists who are confident in using and stretching the communication potential of new technologies."[209] Even journalism educators are seduced by the processing power of personal computers, emphasizing their ability to design pages or reach new audiences. Many journalism schools with on-line sequences are teaching "a new generation of journalists" how to sit in front of computers and use software—a talent that most already possessed in high school. Worse, journalism professors buy into marketing hype about the necessity of new media, which automates jobs in communication ecosystems, keeping reporters in front of monitors in newsrooms rather than in front of sources in communities. In time, given the right hardware and digital networks, even these practitioners will be displaced, victims of the virtual environment whose apologists continue to bemoan digital divides.

The New Generation Gap

Digital divides exist, not only between people of particular social classes or ethnic backgrounds, based on those with and without computer access; the divide is generational and interpersonal and as pronounced as any other gap in the twentieth century, including Vietnam–era ones. Marshall McLuhan, of course, based many of his media theories on the philosophical gulf that separated youth from their parents in the 1960s–1970s. Television, McLuhan believed, played a major role in the erosion of family values. Electronic media, he said, "far surpasses any possible influence mom and dad can now bring to bear."[210] McLuhan believed the gap then was so wide that genocide likely would ensue. As his biographer Phillip Marchand notes,

> To be sure, profound social change begun in the sixties continued in the seventies, primarily in the sexual sphere; but the apocalypse hovering around the corner, the long-haired, Day-Glo, ultimate revolution spearheaded by youth, was evidently postponed forever. . . . Despite the back-to-business air on campus—which spectacularly falsified his predictions of increasing student violence—he still believed, as he told one audience in 1976, that our society stood on the verge of "another binge of slaughter."[211]

What broke out was a media pandemic of such proportion that no one, including McLuhan, could have foreseen. The gap widened with each generation of techno-kids. Children of the "Nintendo generation" (those born since 1990) view technology primarily as portable modes of entertainment. In fact, many do not distinguish between entertainment and communication—they are one and the same. Why not? They have been reared with speaking toys, interactive keyboards, cable TV, arcade consoles, Internet play, game handsets, cellular phones, virtual reality goggles, and chat rooms. The younger set sees technology the way Roman peons saw free corn at the Coliseum—amusement as birthright—else they bore. Conversely, their parents and *grandparents*—those Day-Glo revolutionaries cum day traders—view technology as they do books: repositories of fact. Those born between 1950 and 1980 generally do not distinguish between information and communication. Their mistake, alas, has been to associate both with accumulation of wealth rather than of knowledge.

Therein lies the gap eroding educational standards. Baby boomers have become our moral decision-makers whose principal sin was to abandon the noncommercial values of their youth in favor of net worth and profit margin. Indeed, it is laughable to hear how McLuhan described youth in 1969: "These kids are fed up with jobs and goals, and are determined to forget their own roles and involvement in society. They want nothing to do with our fragmented and specialist consumer society."[212] Many of those kids would become media moguls of the likes of Bill Gates, Ted Turner, and Ted Leonsis. They made their fortunes by creating technology that realized the dominant motif of their youth: *information and communication are synonymous.* If you have or desire one, then you must invent means to acquire the other and as many outlets, platforms, and protocols required to fund and maintain it. As a result, marketing evolved as a hybrid of information and communication whose goal was not to inform but to *finance.*

Entertainment was the quickest means to do that. As described in the last chapter, marketing strategies separate children from their parents in front of personal screens. Children chat and play, guardians encrypt and pay, and seldom do family members speak as meaningfully to each other as they did before access. That is the true divide, involving a breakdown in interpersonal communication. There is also a generational divide between baby boomers who view technology as virtual library and their children who view technology as virtual arcade. In his latest book, titled *Smart Mobs: The Next Social Revolution*, virtual homesteader Howard Rheingold acknowledges cultural and generational gaps that accompany technology use. He covers "killer apps," software applications that transform an underused technology into an industry. Rheingold discusses the impact on education of Napster, an on-line music trading site. He notes that millions of college students overloaded the carrying capacity of major university Internet connections when they began sharing MP3 music files. This, in turn, "alerted the vested interests in the existing intellectual property industry that a frontal assault had been launched on their livelihood, and demonstrated that teenagers can ignite world-changing . . . ad-hocracies."[213]

Another youth-driven frontal assault has occurred in public and campus libraries, traditionally since ancient times an architectural symbol of enlightenment. A library housed knowledge, from pillar to catalogue. Oak chairs invited patrons to stay awhile. Librarians, by turn, demanded silence—a chilling notion for the Nintendo generation—or served as literary tour guides, introducing us to great works and ideas. For many impoverished children, especially in cities, public libraries bestowed a sense of security in a wholesome atmosphere. The physical environs—the slight mold-scent of old paper, the lumpy feel of it between fingers, the arc-light and shadow of lamps, the hushed whisper of voices similar to parental ones at bedtime, the polished and sturdy wood—stimulated the conscience and titillated the consciousness. In such an environment, nobody felt disenfranchised. If you misapplied the Dewey Decimal System and looked for a book in the "wrong" aisle, you might pull down a tome that sparked lifelong learning in a completely different subject. If you asked for help, a librarian often served as mentor and usually knew more than your teachers and could chart your growth, from elementary school to college, based on the aisles you frequented and the books you checked out. McLuhan's biological model—technology as extension of the senses—cannot live up to the experience. Using a computer search engine to access library files, patrons not only are deprived of the physical sensations but also the intellectual ones. Librarians now spend as much time explaining software as they did the great works. Such is the legacy of "killer apps" as educational tools.

Gene I. Rochlin discusses that phenomenon in *Trapped in the Net: The Unanticipated Consequences of Computerization*, focusing on the destruction of library card catalogues. Rochlin notes that the card catalogue not only was more flexible and versatile than digital data searches, but also instilled in users a respect for well-developed, efficient research skills. "Computerized data searches, on the other hand, are inherently structured. The first search might be refused (too many entries), or result in a dump of thousands of listings; any attempt to narrow it can be an exercise in frustration that would try the patience of Job."[214] While students can access information at any hour, putting off reading

Les Miserables to download Eminem, they now must be taught how to think like computers rather than like scholars.

Increasingly, college students no longer speak the language of scholarship. A frantic student at Ohio University's journalism library went from librarian to professor asking for "Carol." The student insisted she had been told to "find a Carol" in the library so she could take her makeup exam, which she had in her hand. A librarian and professor listened carefully and attentively, confused, until the librarian figured out that the student had been told to "find a carrel"—or cubical—so she could take her test on trust. The librarian, Jason Whited, figured out what the student was trying to convey because, he says, "This generation of kids is computer literate but not socially literate, especially in how to ask questions. They can find things on the Internet but not in card catalogues. They are used to searching by keyword rather than by concept."[215] Librarians like Whited have become techno-translators as much as information mentors, understanding better than the professors who assign research how to speak with youth trained to think like Pentium rather than like Plato. In a digital library, the databank, not the book, becomes the message.

The databank has an economic purpose that often supercedes the informational one. Even Tim Berners-Lee, inventor of the World Wide Web, expresses concern about that. The smarter search engines become, the more marketing drives the search, he says, using a shoe store analogy. A consumer wants to buy shoes, Berners-Lee says, and uses a search engine to locate addresses of stores. The search engine does not return listings of every available store—only those that have deals with it or with its parent company. Berners-Lee writes, "It's like having a car with a Go Shopping for Shoes button on the dashboard; when pushed, it will drive only to the shoe store that has a deal with the carmaker. This doesn't help me get the best pair of shoes for the lowest price, it doesn't help the free market, and it doesn't help democracy."[216]

Internet providers rather than scholars and scientists, like Berners-Lee, are shaping the media message, along with educational and moral standards. In 1997, for instance, Ted Leonsis, then president of America on Line, chastised content developers for giving the audience what developers believed it needed rather than what the users wanted. The AOL executive proclaimed: "It's better to be successful than to be right,"[217] another modern-day marketing mantra. Being successful rather than right undermines ethics in particular and education in general. Teachers and librarians should give learners what they need rather than want, and new technology should facilitate that. What learners need is knowledge. What they want is entertainment.

America, more than any other society since ancient Rome, embraces entertainment, perhaps to circumvent the human condition. James Howard Kunstler, in particular, makes that observation in his work on community life in the twenty-first century, maintaining that no other society has been so preoccupied with instantaneous make-believe and on-demand fantasy. Americans, he believes, demand fantasy to distract themselves from the hardships and tragedies of life, and because reality is unrelenting, "we must keep the TVs turned on at all waking hours and at very high volume."[218] Kunstler concludes that the emphasis on fantasy in virtual community only deepens our hunger for authenticity in physical community.

That phenomenon escaped Marshall McLuhan, who, at the height of his popularity, pontificated poetically about the new technology: "We have now become aware of the possibility of arranging the entire human environment as a work of art, as a teaching machine designed to maximize perception and to make everyday learning a process of discovery."[219] This was not in the cards. McLuhan was fooled, perhaps, because the Baby Boomer generation did not distinguish between information and communication, especially during the Vietnam War. Nobody then could foresee generations of Internet enthusiasts flooding AOL in 1997 with traffic greater than CNN and MTV combined. On one day users sent almost a million instant messages over AOL. They weren't discussing current events. Leonsis quipped that 99 percent of those messages asked, "Hi, male or female?"[220]

Reports about such usage have been available for many years now, although educators seldom acknowledge that. Instead, they continue to stress content without considering how learners use electronic media and how, in turn, those media use learners in a symbiotic marketing relationship. Content becomes biased in the process. According to Chesebro and Bertelsen in *Analyzing Media*, specific biases include:

- The medium actively helping to determine meaning.
- The medium generating different knowledge than the content of a message.
- Each medium producing a distinct view of reality.
- Media systems reflecting and creating their own culture.[221]

Tim Berners-Lee emphasizes the importance of separating content from the medium. He wants to turn on his television without the channel jumping to a host site selling merchandise or a particular channel providing better picture quality only because it contains commercials targeted to his needs. Berners-Lee states, "I expect my television to be an impartial box. I also expect the same neutrality of software. I want a Web browser that will show me any site, not one that keeps trying to get me to go back to its host site."[222] But that is what browsers and search engines do when content melds with media driven by marketing rather than by knowledge.

This aspect of Internet escapes layman and educator alike. For instance, a committee of the American Association of University Professors developed guidelines addressing utilization of new technologies in higher education. They posed such questions as, "How can educators ensure that the content of courses offered via this new medium is as rigorous as the content offered face-to-face in a classroom?"[223] The issue does not concern rigor but content transformed by media. A better question might have been, "How can educators ensure that the content of courses offered via this new medium will be authentic, applicable, and effective?" McLuhan clearly understood this situation. "By placing all the stress on content and practically none on the medium," he asserts, "we lose all chance of perceiving and influencing the impact of new technologies on man, and thus we are always dumfounded by—and unprepared for—the revolutionary environmental transformation induced by new media."[224]

In the 1960s, new media and technology complicated America's "revolutionary environmental transformation." A beloved president had been assassinated and his assassin murdered live on national news. Reality programming was born accidentally. The Johnson administration was escalating U.S. involvement in the Vietnam War, during which some 58,000 Americans died (along with more than a million Vietnamese military and civilians). To report the war on the other side of the world, the media relied on facsimile and telex transmissions. Those technologies altered the message but delivered it quickly, as the telegraph had done in the Civil War. News, however, was often discouraging. The administration claimed one truth, the media reported another. More assassinations followed, claiming the lives of civil rights activists Malcolm X and Martin Luther King, Jr., and of Democratic presidential candidate Robert Kennedy. Television documented race riots, student protests, sociopolitical mayhem, and more. Truth, for many baby boomers, became relative—an ethical conundrum to this day. What they saw on TV defied the natural order of things: rebellion and military defeat.

The Unnatural Order of Things

Access to information is vital during war and rebellion. In World War II, the British developed the first all-electronic digital computer, Colossus, to cipher Nazi codes. Textbook authors Joseph Straubhaar and Robert LaRose note in *Communications Media in the Information Society* that "the need to calculate detailed mathematical tables to help aim cannons and missiles led to the creation of the first full-blown, general-purpose computer, the electronic numerical integrator and calculator (ENIAC), at the University of Pennsylvania in 1946."[225] Likewise the need for quick, reliable communication during the Vietnam War led to faster telex and facsimile technology, which eventually led to electronic mail and modems.[226] Support for computer development, from World War II to this day, continues to be a military priority. Gene I. Rochlin states that the U.S. government "remains heavily invested in supporting fundamental, forefront research, particularly in high status areas such as artificial intelligence."[227] David F. Noble examines this in depth in his influential work, *The Religion of Technology*, noting that the pioneers of artificial intelligence "have been sustained by the U.S. military—together with their disciples in Artificial Life, cyberspace, and virtual reality."[228] The military continues to utilize technology to wage war, surveil and control enemies of the state. Meanwhile government officials have encouraged application of these technologies to stimulate the U.S. economy, defending military expenditures by noting social benefits. As Noble correctly asserts, "And they also have placed their technological means at the disposal of manufacturing, financial and service corporations, which have deployed them the world over, to discipline, deskill, and displace untold millions of people, while concentrating global power and wealth into fewer and fewer hands."[229]

Marshall McLuhan, the leading media critic during the Vietnam War, did not fully factor into his theories the impact of military technology on communication networks. As is generally known the ARPANET—precursor to the Internet—was implemented in 1969 to link researchers at laboratories, universities, and military sites. At the time, McLuhan was prophesying the demise of the car, the Dow, and mass marketing:

> The automobile, too, will soon be as obsolete as the cities it is currently strangling, replaced by new antigravitational technology. The marketing systems and the stock market as we know them today will soon be dead as the dodo, and automation will end the traditional concept of the job, replacing it with a role and giving the breath of leisure. The electric media will create a world of dropouts from the old fragmented society, with its neatly compartmentalized analytic functions, and cause people to drop in to the new integrated global-village community.[230]

Suffice to say that McLuhan's vision was poetic, at best. The natural order of things, considering the speed of progress and the promise of technology, was that people would enjoy more leisure time in the global village. That was turned on its head. McLuhan did, however, foresee how the new technology would undermine the maxim, "a place for everything and everything in its place." As he put it, using an Oz metaphor, *You can't go home again.*[231] Ironically, however, during the Vietnam War, television reemphasized the importance of place because it had to generate video (although, via the wonders of technology, producers routinely operate in one place, reporters in another, and anchors in another). Place had become associated with television when the networks began broadcasting half-hour news segments in 1963, the year that President John F. Kennedy was assassinated. Most middle-aged Americans recall where they were when they heard news of JFK— somewhere in the community; likewise, most readers remember where they were when they heard news of the 9/11 terrorist attack on America—somewhere near a television. Yet, concerning television, both examples illustrate how the medium emphasizes geography *even as it condenses it.*

That effect dates back to 1963. A year earlier the communications satellite Telstar I was launched, enabling reporters to transmit news to a network hub. Communication had become instantaneous and global. Increasingly Americans relied on TV news to shape opinions and provide information.[232] Those news programs brought home brutalities of the Vietnam War, from napalmed children in Trang Bang to public executions in Saigon, sparking student demonstrations across the United States. Thousands protested the violence; tens of thousands protested the draft that would make them accomplices in that violence. During that time, television produced an eerie montage of explosions, burning buildings, and troops fading in and out on TV screens. That defied the natural order of things, too, including the credibility and security of America, which was about to lose its first war.

Much has been made of the difficulty that U.S. troops faced, determining who was friend or foe in a divided Southeast Asian nation. But the same could be said of coverage of anti- and pro-war movements as viewed on television in the United States. Because it made for good video, TV analyzed the violence and destruction rather than the arguments and viewpoints of each side. Watching the news, viewers had difficulty distinguishing between buildings bombed in Hanoi and ROTC buildings firebombed on campuses, including Kent State University, where National Guardsmen fired on students, killing four and wounding nine others. Reality television had become surreal. Certainly the architecture of war-torn Hanoi and academic Kent, Ohio, differed dramatically; but not through the television zoom lens, which altered the message, de-emphasizing place. Electronic media had both biased and become the message. Truth was lost in the mix.

Each medium has its viewpoint (or slant on the news) and, hence, on the message by virtue of its technology. Television, for instance, not only views the world through camera lenses but also through production crews, gatekeepers (editors), time slots, advertising, anchors, general managers and other factors affecting content and delivery. In our time, satellite hookups have heightened the impact of those effects so that the world not only enters our living rooms; the world has *become* our living rooms and every other room that contains a television set. We invite the world into our homes and lives but also neglect those who dwell in our homes and those who share our hometowns. Nothing illustrates the point more than handheld computers and cellular telephones, baby boomer embodiments that assume society requires smaller, faster, and ever more mobile information and communication. Thus, we are drowning in information and so continually focus on what messages to block out of consciousness and what to let in. That behavior, however necessary, displaces us from community *and* people.

Until recently in some small towns, especially in the South and Midwest,[233] it had been customary to say hello to strangers who shared our physical environs. The practice honors the importance of place, with Southerners known for their hospitality and Midwesterners for their congeniality. Granted, such hospitality and congeniality are factors of agriculture and weather—from blizzard to twister—as much as manners. Nonetheless, the emphasis was on *place*. Friendly greetings are especially important at local stores whose clerks are typically hometown high school and college students, earning their first paychecks or paying tuition. Heidi Nyland, one such college student, worked during college breaks at a drive-through photography shop in Columbus, Ohio. An avid horsewoman, she bought a cell phone in case she needed to contact someone during an emergency on the trail. She soon found, however, that she was carrying her cell phone with her at all times, tending to it as an electronic pet, shutting it off during classes and turning it on during walks across the campus green. But the real impact of the cell phone occurred at work. Interviewed in 2002, during a period of cell phone proliferation, she stated,

> Yesterday at work I waited on three (one, two, three) customers who were at the drive-through window, driving SUVs, wearing sunglasses, talking on cell phones, and combining various hand gestures to communicate what they wanted from me. The kicker was that every single one apologized to the person they were talking to on the phone. Only one attempted to apologize to me (attempted—meaning she mouthed the words while the person she was talking to continued their conversation). I decided to resign from drive-through service until I could contain my disbelief. This belief? People do seem to be forgetting the communication (and the people) under their noses and are replacing reality with a ringing in their ears.[234]

As Nyland implied, the medium was becoming the moral. Noting that her patrons paid more attention to the "ringing in their ears" than the people "under their noses," she felt socially displaced and affronted by the split consciousness. To some her 2002 anecdote might seem quaint. Since then, social mores are being defined as much by virtual as by physical reality. Consumers view cell phones as social necessity. New behavioral norms have arisen with that change in attitude, responsible for the diffusion. A typical store clerk generally does not feel insulted when patrons using cell phones continue their discussions during purchases, barely noticing the person at the register. The cell-phone user would likely feel socially affronted should the clerk (or anyone else, for that matter) request his or her attention in physical place, and the phenomenon is not limited to behavior in stores. A person speaking aloud in a restroom stall used to startle others in the facility; now the assumption is he or she is using a cell phone there. Cell phones resound digitally and regularly during worship, wakes, births, graduations, hearings, trials, and board meetings—interrupting life-changing spiritual moments or secular proceedings—with most people present accepting the intrusion with mild annoyance, if any. These subtle social transformations provide evidence that the medium not only is the message, but the moral; and "virtual morality"—as the phrase suggests—is borne out of mechanism rather than humanism.

Equally as important is the marketing of cell phones as necessity. In the 1990s, the news media hyped cell phone safety, publicizing stories of car drivers surviving natural and man-made ordeals because of the phone in their pockets. Of course, as more and more drivers purchased cell phones for safety reasons, increasing numbers of drivers became distracted using them. A recent study suggests that using cell phones while driving is as dangerous as driving while intoxicated. The research also adds weight to banning cell phone use by car drivers. "A mere half second of time lost to task switching can mean the difference between life and death for a driver using a cell phone,"[235] the report said.

Of course, there is nothing wrong with using a cell phone as a safety device, as long as we remember that reason. And who can forget the chilling cell phone calls that happened during the 9/11 tragedy, with passengers on doomed airliners leaving messages of courage or of occupants in doomed buildings leaving messages of love? More than any other technology, the cell phone epitomizes the key concern of this book. Juxtaposed to the 9/11 use of the cell phone, our typical use to order pizza while driving on the freeway seems, well, frivolous. Granted, such use may quell appetites quicker—and imperil us and others in the process. We bought mobile phones for safety reasons and then use them for trivial reasons, putting lives at risk. That is why this device in particular illustrates how we are manipulated by the optimal level of fear—the marketing message that prompts us to purchase an item. Once we do, marketing touts convenience over utility. Convenience, however, often trespasses on common sense.

Common sense is associated with consciousness—the essence that communication technology is said to enhance, connecting us to friends, relatives, and associates anywhere in the wireless world. Common sense is a distinct American virtue associated with character and conscience. The United States, in fact, is founded on common sense, dating back to the 1776 pamphlet by that title. "[T]here is something very absurd," wrote Thomas Paine, "in supposing a continent to be perpetually governed by an island. In no instance hath nature made the satellite larger than its primary planet. . . ."[236] Alas, in our time, technology has reversed the natural order of things, elevating satellites over the primary planet, eroding common sense and, with it, our perception. How can we recover that and repatriate to our communities?

Journal Exercise

To determine how the medium changes the message, conduct two sets of interviews, one using e-mail and another, in person. Identify six sources—two elementary school teachers (fourth through sixth grades with selected teachers at the same grade level), two public librarians, and two computer scientists—and divide them into two groups: virtual and interpersonal. Use e-mail to interview one teacher, librarian, and computer scientist. Schedule appointments and interview in person the other teacher, librarian, and computer scientist.

- Ask the same set of questions:
  1. For the elementary school teachers: *In general, how do learners perceive the computer—as a tool of information or entertainment? How much time per day do you believe your students use computers as information tools versus entertainment tools?*
  2. For the librarians: *How has the library process been transformed via the computer? How do computerized searches differ from traditional card catalogue searches, especially with respect to research skills?*
  3. For the computer scientists. *How does electronic mail change the content of messages? Do educators in other disciplines—the humanities, say—typically overemphasize content of messages without fully taking into account the medium's impact on messages?*
- After your interviews, collect your e-mail responses in one document and transcribe your face-to-face responses in another document. Ask yourself:
  1. Which set of responses conveyed more information—virtual or interpersonal?
  2. What kind of information (anecdotal, factual, sensory) was conveyed in each set of responses?

3. What, if anything, was different about the information in the two sets?
4. Which set of responses was more memorable—virtual or interpersonal? Why?
5. Which set of responses presented a more complete overall representation of the interview—virtual or interpersonal? How?
6. Which type of interview was easier, more convenient to do? Why?
7. How, if at all, did the exercise validate or refute assertions about mediated communication as covered in this chapter?

Discussion/Paper Ideas for Chapter Six

- Discuss observations from the Journal Exercise above.
- Discuss the validity of these assertions:
  1. Without adequate scholarly information on how communication systems alter messages, officials of school systems investing heavily in media and technology are unaware of the consequences, especially as they affect face-to-face interaction and civic engagement.
  2. Those born since 1990 view technology primarily as portable modes of entertainment and generally do not distinguish between entertainment and communication—they are one and the same.
  3. Internet providers rather than scholars and scientists like Tim Berners-Lee, creator of the World Wide Web, are shaping media messages and, in doing so, overinfluening educational and moral standards.
- Discuss central theses and themes on the effects of mediated communication and educational technology from Suggested Readings below.

Suggested Readings from Chapter Six

Marchand, Phillip. *Marshall McLuhan: The Medium and the Messenger.* New York: Ticknor & Fields, 1989.

McLuhan, Marshall. *Understanding Media: The Extensions of Man.* Cambridge, MA: The MIT Press, 2002.

Postman, Neil. *Technopoly: The Surrender of Culture to Technology.* New York: Vintage, 1993.

Icons and Caricatures

It is possible that, some day soon, an advertising man who must create a television commercial for a new California Chardonnay will have the following inspiration: Jesus is standing alone in a desert oasis. A gentle breeze flutters the leaves of the stately palms behind him. Soft Mideastern music caresses the air. Jesus holds in his hand a bottle of wine at which he gazes adoringly. Turning toward the camera, he says, "When I transformed water into wine at Cana, this is what I had in mind. Try it today. You'll become a believer."

—NEIL POSTMAN, *Technopoly: The Surrender of Culture to Technology,* 1993

Icons and Idols

The meanings of words change rapidly during technological change, transforming communication, not only in how messages are sent but also in how they are deciphered. Historian Theodore Roszak notes that alterations in meanings of words have occurred throughout the history of science. Scientists take a commonly understood word from the public vocabulary and then corrupt it with an esoteric definition, Roszak states, causing confusion among scientists "who may forget what the original word meant."[237] Roszak refers here to the meaning of "information," which used to be *fact*-based—a fact that few information scientists recall anymore, seeing information as quantifiable data. *The Random House Unabridged Dictionary* defines *icon* as "a picture, image, or other representation" or "some sacred personage, as Christ or a saint or angel," and *idol* as "a mere image or semblance of something, visible but without substance, as a phantom." The word "icon," of course, is more popularly known now as a computer desktop image which, when clicked, opens up an application. Few folks regard that as sacred. The issue is, do we idolize media icons—mere images, visible but without substance—or put them in perspective, as common sense dictates?

We glorify celebrities. They also are made of image, visible but without substance, for we cannot get to know the typical personality, athlete or actor, three dimensionally, in time, space, and person. Instead, we get phantoms. Case in point: Early in his career the great basketball star Michael Jordan endorsed athletic footwear to generate publicity about the rightness of athletic achievement, hoping to influence young people to work hard at what they love, contributing to community. In response, many adopted Jordan's work ethic as their own. He was their role model. Others idolized him as a media icon. Like most such icons—Madonna, Elvis, among others—Jordan came to be known by one name: Mike. Several youths ignored his role model aspirations, robbing others wearing the Jordan brand sneakers. They didn't want to "Be like Mike," a nifty advertising slogan: They wanted to *be* Mike. They wanted those shoes.

Several sports magazines reported this in the late 1980s. *Sports Illustrated* even reprinted an article, "Your Sneakers or Your Life," in May 1990, about Michael Jordan feeling distraught about his role-modeling efforts. He had delivered the right message at the right time to the right target audience; however, Jordan could not control how that message was being received. First of all, the medium—television commercials—promoted footwear, not guidance. Jordan may have wanted the message to be about personal values; instead, it was about branding. The icon had become the message. Moreover, if readers subscribed to *Sports Illustrated* around this time, they received as a free premium or gift, a "sneaker phone," more evidence that media feed our idol worship without their or our even knowing it.

When we fail to monitor media, pop culture has the last word. Perhaps that is why "reality" shows, from *Cops* to *Survivor*, became popular at the end of the twentieth century. Reality shows play upon conscience and consciousness in a unique way, according to the rhetorical concept of "consubstantiality," or vicarious involvement. That concept helps explain the public's appetite for reality programming, a two-dimensional but nevertheless powerful depiction of the world. When we watch a police chase, anticipating the imminent crash, we can put ourselves in the speeder's car and simultaneously participate in and survive the accident. Such shows bore many viewers, but usually not ones who have been in chases, namely officers or speeders. For them, consubstantiality kicks in, and viewer involvement intensifies. Kenneth Burke, rhetorician and social critic, points to the Abraham-Isaac story in the Old Testament as an example of consubstantiality. Commanded by God to slay his son Isaac, Abraham simultaneously would be destroyed and saved. That phenomenon, according to Burke, occurs when we look down from great heights and wonder, "What if I jumped?" causing nausea in some people. But that feeling is intensified acutely if a parent, say, accompanied by a beloved child, asked, "What if I pushed the child over?" In that case, the person would be reliving the archetypal Abraham-Isaac story and "could have, simultaneously, both the jumping and the not-jumping."[238] Such thoughts are universal and intensely private. Because of those attributes, reality programming is marketable to a receptive audience eager to live vicariously in the virtual safety of their homes.

Homes have several virtual ports of entry. Safety is not assured. Privacy is at risk—not only in what we transmit but also in what we surveil inside our domiciles. Surveillance technology has combined with computer software, adding new meaning to the word "monitor." George Orwell, considered a social prophet with his dystopian *1984*, depicted a Big Brother dictator using technology to spy at all hours on ordinary citizens. Orwell foresaw how media would violate privacy; but he underestimated people's oxen appetite for acceptance and the lengths that they would go to attain it via such technology as twenty-four-hour web cameras. Several Internet sites feature college students in residence halls going on-line via inexpensive web cams, producing and on occasion *staging* their own "reality" shows. Visitors eavesdrop and "chat" with uninhibited students nicknamed "attagirl" or "luckyguy," allowing the general public to experience voyeurism through Microsoft Windows rather than bedroom windows—another example of virtual consubstantiality.

Orwell did not prophesy the entertainment quotient of invasive technology. However, that is not to say that the bleak vision of his *1984* still cannot occur. Howard Rheingold, more cautious in his latest work about virtual communities, *Smart Mobs*, observes:

> The surveillance state that Orwell feared was puny in its power in comparison to the panoptic web we have woven around us. Detailed information about the minute-by-minute behaviors of entire populations will become cost-effective and increasingly accurate. Both powerfully beneficial and powerfully dangerous potentials of this tracking capability will be literally embedded in the environment.[239]

Alas, the word *environment* is one of those terms whose original meaning, appropriated by scientists, has become blurred. It used to mean "living space"; now, just as often, it means "information space." Rheingold, in the excerpt above, refers to both spaces—physical and virtual environment—with surveillance technology planted in one habitat and transmitted to another, an ominously new blurring of physical place. Privacy, he cautions, can be obliterated in an Orwellian minute.

We all require a modicum of privacy. Adults need it to work out personal problems, protect assets, and advance aspirations. Privacy is especially important for children, beginning with time-outs for younger ones to contemplate the impact of their misdeeds, a better punishment than spanking, because it exercises the conscience of the child rather than the hand of the adult. As such, privacy teaches patience to child *and* adult. Teenagers need privacy, too, to break free of parental influence so that they can exercise their rights as individuals. That is why many teenagers often react angrily when parents trespass on the boundary of bedrooms. Privacy is also pegged to community, concerning what others may or may not know about us *even if true*. That is a boundary, and we draw it for a reason, because it allows us to make mistakes and rebound from them, without undue condemnation from others, so that we can contribute to community.

Respect for privacy begins in childhood. In past eras child rearing—always difficult—was, by some standards, simpler. As long as parents were reasonably sure that their children had been exposed to strong values and good coping skills, including reflection and patience, they could trust their children's judgment. That fostered *mutual* trust, which flourished in the confines of one's home. What happened there was private, family business. If parent or child made a mistake in judgment, which is only human, both or all parties would acknowledge and discuss that and learn a valuable lesson—not only about the mistake in question but also about the importance of dialogue. Access to technology, however, has made child rearing more complex because the home has several portals now and many influences and dialogues beyond the familial. Teenagers use computers in their bedrooms, bastions of privacy, and routinely divulge personal information about their households in return for premiums, as previously discussed. Because the teen years can be rebellious, some parents purchase "spy gear" to monitor behavior of offspring. Hidden cameras not only transmit within the confines of the house but also directly to the Web so that parents can eavesdrop at any hour from any place. Perhaps some teenagers require invasions of this magnitude when addiction or behavior becomes a health or a criminal concern. Intervention is best done by parents interacting face-to-face with their children rather than from a distance with machines. Invasive technology not only violates privacy, it subverts trust in mediated households.

Technology appeals to the ego. The ego is its own idol—visible, without substance—a phantom image of our true identity, which we come to know through conscience and consciousness. Our true identity, a wellspring of acceptance, is a natural gift born out of innocence and extant within us, although the ego typically will not acknowledge this. Social activist Parker J. Palmer writes in *The Active Life*, a book about work, creativity, and caring:

> Our tendency to identify ourselves with our acquired skills rather than our natural gifts is one of the less desirable habits of the ego. It is the ego that decides what skills it prizes, the ego that exerts the effort to develop those skills, the ego that manipulates and markets those skills once it acquires them. . . . Indeed, the very fact that we have gifts that the ego did nothing to earn is threatening to the ego, which desperately needs to believe that nothing comes into being without its own authorization or agency.[240]

The ego, conscious of itself, yearns for self-promotion. As such it loves the Internet because that medium showcases pomposity, simulating the Andy Warhol standard of "fifteen minutes of fame." That phrase refers to extraordinary moments in a person's life—a bystander witnessing crime or surviving a natural disaster. The media would capture the event for posterity. Now, because of technology, *we have become the media*. Technology enthusiasts of late, including Howard Rheingold, acknowledge the good *and* bad about that cultural transformation. Rheingold notes that people in virtual communities do not need to be professional writers or reporters to publish their views. Internet elevates you to that status, and you do not have to be "civil, capable of communicating coherently, or know what you are talking about in order to express yourself to others."[241] Professional writers and reporters realize that electronic expression comes with consequences beyond ones that Rheingold cites. Uncivil, incoherent, idle communication distributed worldwide via a powerful medium like the

Internet also violates privacy—*of both the creator of a work and others named therein.* Nevertheless we capture snippets of ordinary life and post them on-line for all to see, inflating the Warhol standard from fifteen minutes of real fame over the course of a lifetime to fame-on-demand over the course of any hour on-line.

The ego thrives in a culture of self-promotion. Marketing blurs culture along with identity (which it generalizes). As John Seabrook, magazine journalist, confides,

> The culture of marketing, the marketing of culture: What really was the difference? It used to be, or so it seemed to me, one could say reliably that this was culture and that was marketing. Culture came first. Culture was the way you made the apple crumb cake because your grandmother made it that way. Then came marketing, which was Martha Stewart's recipe for your grandmother's apple crumb cake. Marketing attempted to exploit culture for commercial ends. Culture was a spontaneous enthusiasm, a genius of an individual or a people; marketing tried to manipulate that genius—to sell culture back to itself.[242]

Marketers want us to believe that we can have it all. By design, advertising targets the ego at the expense of the conscience. Huston Smith, professor of religion, believes that advertising, in particular, works against moral needs. "It presses for immediate gratification," he observes, "and thinks that will benefit oneself instead of the general public."[243] Religion and secular ethics emphasize the community of faith or community of man. Because human beings are social creatures, our moral values typically emphasize mindfulness of others from a "made-in-God's-image" perspective or from a "made-in-genome" perspective. We are programmed spiritually and biologically to rely on each other so that we rise in the afterlife or in the food chain. Religion asks us to share resources with others because the God light in "me" also shines in the "other." Likewise our genome requires us to share resources because teamwork of the few ensures the survival of the many. Truly religious people work everyday to kill the ego, risking their lives doing missionary work in dangerous environs for the betterment of humankind. Humanists do likewise, accepting the same risks and honoring the same social tenet. As reward, believer and nonbeliever experience the rhapsody of the soul or the endorphins of the collective consciousness. In both cases the enlightened individual elevates the importance of community and devalues the importance of possessions.

The ego covets possessions. It amplifies self-worth above that of others and measures "net worth" according to wealth and material goods. Advertising encourages that. Consumers are profiled according to demographics, psychographics, and attitudes, as we have learned in previous chapters. By accumulating such data, marketers can detect the lifestyle that we lead in real life and the one that the ego covets for us in our dreams. Knowing that, advertisements are created and targeted at us and at others with similar profiles, lifestyles, and dreams.

Icons and Advertising

Advertisements send two basic messages: *You need this product* (manifest message) and *What happens when you use this product* (latent message). Those messages typically differ dramatically from the social message—what the product really does and what happens when we use it. Latent messages are powerful because they appeal directly to the ego. We not only covet the flashy sedan that a flashier supermodel drives on a country road; we also want the model or to look like the model. We want it all. The manifest message suggests that we need this "make" and "model"—words that relate to car *and* woman; and the latent message suggests that if we drove that car, we would seduce that woman or look like her. The ego believes that we would. Advertising relies on that impulse across product lines. Fundamentally, then, advertising pivots on fantasy and exaggeration and, as such, is almost impossible to regulate, writes Joshua Meyrowitz in *No Sense of Place.* "If a diet soft drink commercial *said*, 'Drink this, and you'll be beautiful and have beautiful friends to play volleyball with on the beach,' they could be prosecuted for fraud."[244] Maybe we should use fluoride toothpaste for hygienic reasons; but we buy a brand because the ad portrays a couple who kiss because of fresh breath. Consciousness reminds us of the social message: flashy cars do not necessarily seduce supermodels nor fresh breath procure their kisses. There may be other interpersonal factors involved. The ego downplays those factors and holds the conscience at bay to get what it wants.

Children, in particular, are prone to such advertising because their conscience and consciousness are not yet fully developed. They cannot see through or resist the pitch. According to the American Academy of Pediatrics, children between the ages of two and eighteen spend on average six hours and thirty-two minutes per day consuming television and other media, including the Internet.[245] That adds up to almost forty-six hours per week or almost one hundred days per year. Because there are variables associated with lifestyle, work, and social class, statistics cannot reliably predict how much media and technology Americans on average will consume in the future over a lifetime; however, if the rate at which they begin is any indication, the total exceeds eighteen years between ages two and seventy. In some respects, though, the early consumption of media and technology is more important because this has a huge impact on a child's moral development. Not surprisingly, the current generation of schoolchildren is experiencing emotional dysfunction at record rates—with estimates as high as a quarter of all school-age children suffering from some sort of behavioral problem. The American Academy of Pediatrics notes that the suicide rate for children between 1950 and 1990 rose 300 percent, with youth at increasing risk because of media exposure and clusters occurring after programming depicting teen suicides.[246] The Academy also calculates that children by age eighteen are exposed to more than 200,000 televised acts of violence.[247] True, the violence is virtual and so the harm is debatable, depending on how well- or ill-adjusted individual children are, media notwithstanding. But the accumulated effect is not. Although the AAP does not directly link higher rates of emotional dysfunction to increased media consumption, the correlation is still there.

By some measurements, anxiety in college students has reached record levels. According to psychology professor Jean M. Twenge, writing in *The Chronicle of Higher Education,* "[A]nxiety that would have put a student in the top 16 percent in the 1950's made a student merely average in the ratings for anxiety in the 1990's. Students' anxiety began to rise in the early 1950's, and the increase has continued at a steady pace ever since."[248] Although her research and that of others do not directly correlate anxiety levels with increasing use of media and technology, one seems directly proportionate to the other. Twenge states that among other symptoms, students suffering from anxiety tend to "hole up in their dorm rooms for days at a time."[249] Those dorms, of course, contain computers—sometimes required or even supplied by universities—along with televisions with cable hookups. Because college students consume Internet and media, they are targets of marketers seeking optimal levels of fear. Add to that the media emphasis on campus safety and the myriad news reports about crimes and assaults. Institutions have responded with more police, emergency telephones, and hidden security monitors—all meant to help students feel safe. As Twenge notes, however,

> Of course, an overabundance of campus police and call boxes on an already safe campus could create the appearance of danger. Perception of one's environment is often just as important for anxiety as reality is.
>
> Like feeling safe, having meaningful relationships is a good buffer against anxiety.[250]

Students suffering anxiety often search for acceptance in the wrong place—cyberspace—a virtual montage of latent messages. They log onto sites to buy textbooks, only to be dazzled with pop-ups offering credit cards for spring break and Mardi Gras. They visit a homework site to do research, only to be tempted by term papers on sale. They browse music sites for free downloads, only to fill out registration cards allowing access and promising "chat, friends, party, travel, dating." Latent messages abound. Many students seek fulfillment, longing to love and be loved and have meaningful relationships with peers, difficult to do when holed up in dorms accessing chat rooms and downloading so-called "freebies." Those services and gifts may seem free but are laden with advertisements or targeted specifically at users by "cookies," files that track usage or compile consumer information, placed in computers, often without users even aware of it. Thanks to such files, technology has added a new layer of latent message, hidden in hard drives.

Add to this the commercial aspects of television. The Center for Media Education reports that by the time American children graduate from high school they have already viewed an estimated 360,000 broadcast commercials. According to the Center, "Children are bombarded with marketing from the moment they wake up until bedtime. And there's growing evidence that it's harmful to them."[251] Such exposure influences ethics. One of the first to address that was poet and scholar Hayden Carruth in a 1981 essay in the literary magazine, *Georgia Review*:

> Constantly we are told that this or that commercial product or service, or even this or that candidate for office, is "better," when we know it cannot be true. . . . Children today are taught, in lessons compounded every five minutes, that untruth may be uttered with

impunity, even with approval. Lying has become a way of life, very nearly now *the* way of life, in our society. The average adult American of average intelligence and average education believes almost nothing communicated to him in language, and the disbelief has become so ingrained that he or she does not even notice it.[252]

Lying, of course, undermines ethics and with it, a sense of trust and acceptance. However, a more worrisome factor is the number of hours that children spend indoors instead of in community. Neighborhoods that once bustled with voices of children on Saturday mornings now are eerily silent until the electric lawn mowers and trimmers kick in. A sedentary lifestyle due to media overexposure contributes to obesity and retards moral development. Worse, children do not learn during critical developmental stages the importance of interpersonal dialogue.

This is evident by displacement associated with the high-tech gaming phenomenon. Video games used to be large and located in mall arcades. The problem there, of course, was the inability of marketers to target children playing with others in community, even if their attention spans were shortened by Pac Man, Donkey Kong, and Zaxxon. Soon those games were replaced by computer and console software, moving video arcades out of the community and into kids' homes. But they still gathered according to play dates and schedules to interact in front of a television. Then, with the introduction of consoles that allow Internet play, children no longer gather in entertainment rooms of houses but stay home in their rooms to interact with each other and strangers on-line. The migration of children from playground to playroom to computer room illustrates in micro what is happening to us in macro. We leave the public arena first. Then we gather in our homes. Then we are home alone in our rooms. There is a reason. The more isolated we become, using technology to access programming, especially video games, the easier marketers can target us with typical promotions and services like these:

- Advertisements and coupons inside game boxes and software.
- On-line sites selling new releases and other services, including technical support.
- Warranties that generate spam via e-mail and pop-up messages via cookies and data miners.
- Subscriptions to magazines promoting more gaming software and upgrade applications.

- Games requiring access fees to play on-line, forcing consumers not only to pay for the cartridge or software but for the "opportunity" to use it, thus generating more profit by selling the same product monthly instead of once, with fees apportioned to the various arms the multimedia corporation.

Marketing notwithstanding, few parents stopped to ascertain the impact of this everyday displacement. In the mall at video arcades children had to wait their turns to play the most popular games. They had to interact, too, with attendants, patrons, peers, other parents, and strangers. Kids played games according to parental and arcade schedules rather than their own. That, too, required interaction and patience. When arcades went out of business, video games moved from mall to home. That necessitated fewer interpersonal skills. However, even using consoles in front of living room TVs, children still had to interact with each other face-to-face. What game to play? What level of difficulty? Who gets what controller? They also had to interact with parents about when play began and ended, which required tact and negotiation. When gaming went on-line so that kids could access it on demand, they no longer had to gather with friends or interact with them and parents. They just had to hop out of bed or off of the school bus and rush to their computers and consoles to play each other on-line. Often they multitask while doing this, speaking to friends on headsets while playing with them on-line and chatting with others in on-screen windows, a poor substitute for real contact. Literally and figuratively, they are paying the price to play video games on demand, losing perspective along with social skills, chief among them, *patience*.

Media scholar Michael Real discusses the phenomenon by comparing board games to video games and the impact on children's psyches:

> Board games such as *Monopoly* and *Clue* tended to teach young people to develop strategy, think and plan ahead, be patient, play fairly, take turns, and follow written directions. Video games are based instead on classical conditioning theory: the sights, sounds, and colors are reinforcers. They are fast-paced and entertaining. They teach some of the same abilities as older board games, yet they reduce, without necessarily eliminating, the interpersonal interaction.[253]

LEGO learned this lesson the hard way in the late 1980s when handheld video games were introduced from Japan into the U.S. market, eroding LEGO's sales. Branding author Martin Lindstrom notes that by 1996, when the gaming migration began to move from arcades in malls to personal computers and consoles at home, LEGO's fifty-year record of increasing sales reached a turning point. LEGO finally reversed that trend in late 2000 when officials realized that children lacked patience and, perhaps, the creativity to build structures out of plastic blocks that matched pictures on the box. "In the past you needed lots and lots of the smaller blocks to make the model depicted on the box," Lindstrom notes. "Now you only need a few blocks to make the model."[254]

Children weaned on Internet gaming and easy LEGOs eventually enter college, and many of them exhibit questionable interpersonal skills. The Pew Internet & American Life Project reports that computer, video, and on-line games are a substantial part of students' social life with almost half of all gamers in agreement that gaming keeps them from studying "some" or "a lot."[255] The project surveyed 1,162 students on twenty-seven campuses and discovered, among other things, that 32 percent of students "admitted playing games that were not part of the instructional activities during classes."[256] Wireless classrooms provide more gaming opportunities during lectures with laptop-toting students pretending to take notes. Such overindulgence undermines community interaction on residential campuses known for lovely landscape, historic architecture, and renowned professoriates. Remaining indoors in front of monitors, students miss opportunities to develop conscience and consciousness in real rather than virtual habitat, locating mentors there.

Mentors and Caricatures

In the past parents, teachers, mentors, and others in the community set the moral agenda along with standards of behavior, based on interaction. Sometimes the moral standard was high, fostering inclusiveness; sometimes it was low, fostering exclusivity along social, class, or racial lines. *Expectations were overt*. Neighbors knew where they stood—on terra firma. They may not have been able to resolve every dispute or meet every challenge; but at least they acknowledged the interpersonal dynamics required to do so. A case in point concerns Martin Luther King who mastered these dynamics. King relied on them to assemble followers in his "March against Fear through the South" and in other marches in the North, trying to end racial discrimination in housing, schools, and employment. Had the technology been available in King's day, those protests could have been organized via the Internet, as protestors against the World Trade Organization did in the "Battle of Seattle" in November 1999, deploying disruptive "swarming" tactics that included "mobile phones, Web sites, laptops, and handheld computers."[257] But King transformed U.S. society, raising consciousness and deepening awareness, because of his oral prowess and interpersonal skills, evidenced in his "I have a dream" speech that emphasizes the value of community and role models, from the "red hills of Georgia" to the "content of character." To be sure, arguments can be made for Internet's combating racism and exclusion; just as many can be made for its promoting those evils. Martin Luther King relentlessly focused on *community*, from peace marches to dreams, because he and other civil rights activists realized that equality, much like acceptance, was found in real rather than mediated environments. King also understood that human relationships were complex and took time, as did everything in community. That lesson is not yet lost on us. To this day those who interact primarily in real environments usually develop interpersonal skills, discerning in others an array of motives and emotions, from greed to grace. Many also acquire "content of character," not because they study philosophy or subscribe to self-help, but because they perceive situations and challenges more fully, sensing subtle cues that suit time, place, and occasion.

People spending too much time in virtual habitat—network, Internet, cell phone—may have blurrier standards, as discussed in previous chapters. Estranged from parents and mentors, their moral agendas are programmed in part by media and technology. Their standards are erratic—at times inclusive, at times, not. *Expectations are covert.* Users may not know where they stand because there is no "there" there. True, they may know how to disrupt as a "swarm" in information space but not how to enlighten as an assembly in living space. They may be smart mobs, but they are mobs nonetheless, routinely overlooking the social dynamics needed to resolve problems without creating greater ones. Mobs tend to be better at severing relationships than at restoring them.

No where is this more apparent than in celebratory riots on college campuses which, alas, mostly revolve around partying than around the social issues of so-called "smart mobs." In comparison, then, those participating in celebratory riots might be labeled "dumb mobs." At Ohio University, for instance, riots typically occurred at Daylight Savings Time when bars on the campus strip closed one hour

earlier, spilling out partiers into the public streets, where they protested the loss of an hour's alcohol on a weekend—a far cry from the
social causes of smart mobs. Dumb ones also are equipped with cell
phones, a technology used to summon fellow students out of residence halls to the riot scene so that they, too, can watch the reality
show of police clashes, overturned cars, and burning dumpsters.
Former Ohio University President Robert Glidden, who combated
celebratory riots for several years while in office, notes that cell-phone
technology increases numbers at any party quickly and also plays a
role in increasing numbers at riots.[258] That technological phenomenon
was apparent in a 2004 celebratory riot at Iowa State University.
Police arriving at the scene were momentarily stunned by what ap-
peared to be a phantom image of an earlier, more natural age. As the
Ames (Iowa) *Tribune* described it: "At one point, police say what
looked like a sea of fireflies actually was rioters calling their friends
on cell phones to draw more people into the mob."[259] In the aftermath of the riot, some students pepper-sprayed by police claimed to
be innocent bystanders merely watching the drama unfold. Unfortunately, because they were in physical rather than virtual space, they
suffered physical consequences, not the least of which was a lesson
about reality showdowns vs. reality shows. Students may not have
fully perceived the danger of their situation, nor had time to, showing up at the disturbance in mere minutes, because of the immediate
access of cell phone technology that thrust them into real time and
place. Some students felt that they should not be held accountable
for being swept up in the celebratory riot, claiming that they were
victims of circumstance, unjustly targeted.

Maybe so. In the aftermath of the riot, they responded to news reports depicting them as revelers or vandals, reducing them to caricatures. In reality, members of techno mobs are as three dimensional as
anyone who ever marched with Martin Luther King. Moreover, media
often stereotype disturbances by overplaying violent spectacles rather
than probing social consciences. This is especially true with smart mobs,
typically portrayed as "ethical but oblivious." Conversely, officials are
portrayed as "unethical but aware." That perception is flat because the
medium is. Few people are truly *ethical but oblivious* or *unethical but
aware*. Most of us possess value systems placing us somewhere between
the polarities of conscience and consciousness. However, the media—
especially talk shows, tabloids, and news—create caricatures because

they are two dimensional, with clear antagonists and protagonists, as in a melodrama.

The world witnessed such a melodrama at the turn of the century, transfixed by the impeachment of Bill Clinton, America's first celebrity president. Clinton had lied under oath about sexual encounters with then White House intern Monica Lewinsky. Television portrayed Clinton as the classic unethical but sensitive man. His nemesis, Independent Counsel Kenneth Starr, was viewed as an ethical but oblivious man causing a moral crisis in his relentless, $50-million-plus prosecution of the president. Both lived up to their media billings. Clinton, surrounded by members of his cabinet, looked cameras straight in the lenses and proclaimed, "I did not have sexual relations with that woman, Monica Lewinsky." Starr, outraged by the lie, investigated intricate details of the sex acts in encyclopedic, semipornographic detail available on-line.

Media saturated us with updates, bulletins, documentaries, and twenty-four-hour news. Although the scandal broke on the Web, thanks to the aptly named "Drudge Report," most Americans relied on television for information. Producers, of course, were skilled at televising sexual content; they had just never done so to this extent with a president. So politics combined with sex for powerful but shallow coverage that stunned parents. The outcry was swift and immediate, even in an age of media hype and idol worship. Social critics scolded producers for candidly noting sex acts between intern and president during prime-time segments, concerned that children would overhear them. In a newspaper report titled "Sex, Lies: What to Tell the Kids," Bill Womack, professor of child psychiatry at the University of Washington, noted that television news could be as sexually explicit as network soap operas. Womack advised parents not to let school-age kids watch Clinton scandal coverage "without sitting in the same room with them."[260] In her op-ed titled "The Little Clintons," published in the *Wall Street Journal*, author Peggy Noonan observed that thanks to media coverage, "fifth-graders now know that oral sex is not . . . talking about sex." More important, Noonan also observed that media had replaced family and community as the primary shaper of children's values. "There is really no escaping the American culture anymore," she wrote. "Once, you could live on a farm and raise your children with your own truths and information. Once not so long ago, in our lifetime, you could live in a big-city suburb and do pretty much the same."[261]

Noonan, of course, was a former speech writer for Republican President Ronald Reagan. Fact is, Independent Counsel Kenneth Starr made a big impact on children, too—perhaps even greater than Bill Clinton. The impeachment taught a generation of schoolchildren that powerful adults could lie with relative impunity, as the president did; unfortunately, because of Starr, it also taught children that there was no mercy or grace. Clinton, media idol, became an icon of compassionate immorality; Starr, an icon of moral cruelty.

Literature typically circumvents those caricatures. Unlike popular media, the moral of many great books emphasizes the importance of grace. During the impeachment, print media like the *Washington Post* and *Time* compared Kenneth Starr and Bill Clinton to Inspector Javert and Mayor Jean Valjean of Victor Hugo's 1862 classic, *Les Miserables*. In that masterwork Javert, Starr's counterpart, is convinced that the mayor is a fugitive parolee and former thief and so hounds Valjean with ceaseless ethical conviction. Valjean has survived childhood deprivation, as Bill Clinton did (although circumstances naturally differed), and has spent almost twenty years in prison for taking a loaf of bread. Valjean becomes a true thief upon his release, stealing silver from a kindly bishop. When Valjean is arrested and brought before the bishop, however, the cleric tells authorities that he also meant to give the fugitive the candlesticks as well as the silver. Subsequently, the prisoner is freed—both from bondage and from his conscience—because of the bishop's transcendent act of grace. As a result Valjean becomes increasingly aware of the impact of a person's actions on others and is empowered by conscience, and eventually viewed by the community as an ethical, sensitive role model. Valjean is elected mayor. Inspector Javert, unable to deal with his demons, does not evolve in *Les Miserables* because he mistakenly believes that he does not need others—just his convictions—ethical and legal. But that, alas, is not the moral. *Les Miserables*, along with many other great books, informs readers about the importance of grace to inspire spiritual growth and social acceptance. As is also widely known, author Victor Hugo drew character traits for Javert, Valjean, and the bishop from aspects of his own conscience and consciousness. Each individual is that complex and three-dimensional. Kenneth Starr and Bill Clinton were that complex, too, although the media—along with a partisan Congress *created by media*—overlooked that moral message. Instead of role models, we got idolaters.

This is also a media effect. "[E]ven when the idols remain relatively untarnished," write the authors of *Good Work: When Excellence and Ethics Meet*, a book by three world-renowned psychologists, "it is becoming increasingly difficult to know just how to draw inspiration from models in vastly changing circumstances."[262] Who are our role models in media other than idols and caricatures? Who are our role models in technology other than icons and mobs? Such questions are not rhetorical but ethical, and we are obliged to answer them for the well-being of future generations.

Social critics, including Howard Rheingold, are contemplating these conundrums. Rheingold, in particular, wonders how our communities would have evolved had others in the early twentieth century paid more attention to the power and convenience of automobiles, which transformed the American landscape. "Before we start wearing our computers and digitizing our cities," Rheingold asks, "can the generations of the early twenty-first century imagine what questions our grandchildren will wish we had asked today?"[263] Perhaps those grandchildren will ask how we might safeguard interpersonal skills in a technological milieu, promoting the importance of character and community. As we shall see, it is possible to live a full life in an otherwise flat hightech media world.

Journal Exercise

To determine the magnitude of difference between virtual and authentic environments, with respect to advertising,

- Analyze advertisements in ten issues of a popular general magazine, such as *People*, a repository of icons and idols. Choose ads that feature people interacting with each other rather than depictions of merchandise. Decode messages in each advertisement according to *manifest* (what the product does/why we need it), *latent* (what happens when we use the product), and *social* (what the product does in real life *and* what happens). For example, in a toothpaste advertisement depicting a couple kissing, messages would be as follows:
  1. Manifest: *You need this product to freshen breath.*
  2. Latent: *You use the product to get the gal (or guy).*

3. Social: *You use toothpaste to clean teeth. Teeth remain clean until the next meal.*

- After decoding messages, write a short account in your journal describing the media world according to manifest and latent messages. Example: *In the media world, people buy toothpaste to freshen breath and end up kissing stunning women (or men).*
- After writing about the "media world," write another short account describing reality according to social messages pertaining to the content of each ad. Example: *In the real world, people buy toothpaste to prevent decay and clean teeth until the next meal.*
- Compare accounts from No. 3 and No. 4 above, noting the extent of hype and hyperbole between mediated and social depictions and postulating the cumulative impact on conscience and consciousness.
- Analyze how advertisements appeal to the ego rather than to consciousness by noting instances of idolatry, fantasy, stereotypes, and caricatures. Ask yourself:
  1. What is the cumulative impact of ads on conscience and consciousness?
  2. How, if at all, does advertising copywriting affect our trust of language?
  3. How, if at all, do ad depictions reinforce unhealthy notions about the real world?

Discussion/Paper Ideas for Chapter Seven

- Discuss observations from the Journal Exercise above.
- Discuss the validity of these assertions:
  1. Privacy is increasingly at risk because new media combines surveillance technology with computer applications.
  2. Access to technology has made child rearing more complex than in other eras because the home has several portals now and many influences and dialogues beyond the familial.
  3. A sedentary lifestyle due to media overexposure contributes to obesity and retards moral development. Worse, children do not learn during critical developmental stages the importance of interpersonal dialogue.

- Discuss central theses and themes on persuasion, technology, and media culture from the Suggested Readings below.

Suggested Readings from Chapter Seven

Burke, Kenneth. *A Rhetoric of Motives*. Berkeley, CA: University of California Press, 1969.
Rheingold, Howard. *Smart Mobs: The Next Social Revolution*. Cambridge, MA: Perseus, 2002.
Seabrook, John. *Nobrow: The Culture of Marketing, the Marketing of Culture*. New York: Vintage, 2001.

Living Three-Dimensionally

The modern world needs people with a complex identity who are intellectually autonomous and prepared to cope with uncertainty; who are able to tolerate ambiguity and not be driven by fear into a rigid, single-solution approach to problems, who are rational, foresightful and who look for facts; who can draw inferences and can control their behavior in the light of foreseen consequences, who are altruistic and enjoy doing for others, and who understand social forces and trends.

—ROBERT HAVIGHURST, QUOTED IN *The Learning Child*, BY DOROTHY H. COHEN, 1972

Virtues and Environments

Ethics evolve innately when the conscience is clear and consciousness, unobstructed. Both must inform each other harmoniously to make sense of the world. Ethics also emanate out of community when people interact meaningfully with each other, nurturing relationships that transcend self-interest and contributing to the public good. With proper role models, we welcome the diversity of human discourse and treat others as we wish to be treated across the broad social spectrum, living three-dimensionally. We develop perception and discretion, seeing reality as it is, not as we wish it might be. Others who rely on media and technology to fill the void in their lives eventually succumb to myopic vision, perceiving reality through screens and lenses, displaced in their homes and hometowns.

An objective depiction of reality is difficult to convey through the filters of media. Authors of a book exploring the media's impact on perception—*It Ain't Necessarily So: How Media Make and Unmake the Scientific Picture of Reality*—ask, "Why are we so often anxious about the state of our world? Do we encounter dramatic research findings whose significance troubles us but also perplexes us? Do we suspect that we are in some measure captive to a largely hidden process that shapes

161

our 'conventional wisdom'?"[264] Reality experienced firsthand is complex, the authors add; but news creates simple, conclusive portraits of events, producing anxiety or perplexity. Moreover, people tend to believe what media tell them when content falls outside of their immediate personal experience, increasingly the case, given global coverage.

That tendency disenfranchises the audience locally and globally. Media condense geography in part to simplify complex issues. That shapes the conventional wisdom about the role of physical place in our lives, with the emphasis on crime, tragedy, calamity, social discord, and other troubling news. People overinfluenced by media begin to distrust their communities and so cannot easily experience the benefits of interaction, chief among them, the ethics of mentors who set the standards for success—in business, relationships, and life in general. Without mentors, people look to virtual substitutes—idols and icons—in their search for acceptance, covered in the last chapter. Role models leave the calligraphy of rightness on our conscience; idols, the graffiti of estrangement, as portrayed on the nightly news. Idolaters covet power, people, and possessions—the source of crime, tragedy, and calamity in society. Role models lead lives based on moral principles, practicing kindness, fairness, civility, and discretion—concepts difficult to portray in quick, conclusive outtakes and sound bites. Ethics are too abstract to capture in high-definition video and streaming audio because moral behavior entails mindful attention to the minutiae of life over linear time and is only rarely revealed through heroics at a particular point in time. The media wait patiently to document moments of high drama and then hype them as "reality" programming, conveyed as the social norm. The norm may be much different for those who encounter role models in community. In sum, coverage of reality in typical hometowns omits the cumulative effect of mindfulness and, as such, is morally thin and two-dimensional.

Role models live three-dimensionally at peace with their neighbors. They measure the quality of the world:

- *linearly*, in the time spent interacting meaningfully with others in community, from clerks at the checkout counter to VIPs at the country club.
- *horizontally*, in valued relationships that transcend race, sex, and class, acknowledging the insights of others across a broad social spectrum.

- *deeply*, in contributions made to community through those interactions and relationships.

Conversely idolaters live two-dimensionally in disharmony with others and measure the quality of their world:

- *flatly*, characterizing others as worthy or unworthy, based on their race, class, religion, culture, politics, or belief.
- *episodically*, gauging the quality of life based on outcomes of incidents or reacting to others based on past incidents taken out of context.

Flat characters in episodic events are mainstays of media. According to the authors of *It Ain't Necessarily So*, one of the most common depictions concerns that of the villain, the victim, and the hero. "If a story can be arranged in this format," the authors write, "it will get media attention, often without a great deal of scrutiny as to who, exactly, the respective players are and by what criteria they were assigned their roles. Nevertheless, journalists are ready to assign both black and white hats in order to render a morally satisfying narrative."[265] Virtual role models, victims, and villains portrayed in such news are as two-dimensional as Hollywood celebrities because we cannot know them or their circumstances interpersonally in physical place.

Authentic role models are an endangered species not because Hollywood erodes family values but because media erode perception of community, depicting a flat and episodic world. To transform that view, we need news that reaffirms the importance of place and the interpersonal transactions that occur there. Authors of another insightful journalism book, *Good News: Social Ethics & The Press*, advocate civic transformation that "aims to liberate the citizenry, inspire acts of conscience, pierce the political fog, and enable the consciousness raising that is essential for constructing a social order through dialogue, mutually, in concert with our universal humanity."[266] As noted here and elsewhere in *Interpersonal Divide*, community is the wellspring of universal humanity—a lesson worth revisiting from a philosophical perspective.

The Moral Importance of Place

Growing up, we meet many role models and idolaters. Few of us are shaped solely by one or the other, but many of us share a mix of their values willingly or obliviously. Again, it is important to note that everyone's value system is complex and varies, requiring lifelong care and continual analysis. That is why each person has to *live ethics*, rather than preach ethics or judge others because of ethics. There are no easy answers because the development of everyone's conscience and consciousness differs, depending on what has been transcribed there by others and how we have interpreted that moral data. The right path to peace and empowerment for one person may be the wrong one for another.

This is not relativistic dogma about the absence of absolute right and wrong. Although some philosophers believe in a few absolute truths— *it is wrong to steal or lie and right to be charitable and generous*[267]— most would agree that truth is relative to particular individuals living at a point in time at a specific place (yet another definition of "community"). No philosopher can prescribe a set of values upon which everyone, regardless of culture or circumstance, might base their lives to derive happiness and achieve acceptance. Therefore value systems vary dramatically from person to person. That does not mean that "anything goes," which moral relativists maintain, especially in college settings, even though the professors that espouse such beliefs have consented to rules governing tenure, behavior, course content, and more. They have agreed to be citizens of specific learning communities whose values differ according to institution. Likewise employees working in various business environments also must accept codes of conduct or values of mission statements. Similarly we must adhere to laws on how to comport ourselves in our hometowns, states, country, and world. *Virtues are pegged to environments.* Granted, they are not absolute or uniform. But we agree to them to earn livings or to live peaceably among others so that we can pursue the priorities of life. That is why we must evaluate the virtues of our myriad habitats at home and at work and endeavor to enhance them so that they become more inclusive. That standard especially applies in a multicultural era featuring a plethora of viewpoints. Nonetheless, the search for acceptance, in community with others, remains embedded in our psyches. We focus on it for guidance the way mariners do the North Star.

The reason is simple: Both the evolved and the encumbered conscience register and respond to words and deeds in every interaction, momentous or insignificant, assessing outcome and impact but only guessing at motive, because we cannot know completely what lies within the hearts of adversaries, partners, relatives, friends, peers, supervisors, and neighbors. Unless we are fully conscious and honest with ourselves, we may not even know our own hearts. So we decipher our own and others' motives, accurately or inaccurately, based on the drumbeats of conscience and the insights of consciousness. Those drumbeats require us to acquaint ourselves with value systems of others as well as our own. Those insights require us to acquaint ourselves with viewpoints, lifestyles, and cultures of others as well as our own. In other words, *others* are as important as ourselves. We either grasp or reject that core tenet of community. Doing so, we either simplify or complicate our lives.

Media have acquired unprecedented power over our lives, cultures, and minds, according to authors of *Good Work: When Excellence and Ethics Meet,* who believe that we rely on media for perception of the outside world, from weather to international politics. "It is not quite true that the media have replaced real life," they write; "but they have become a predominant determiner of what people attend to, how they interpret it, and how they experience it."[268] In other eras media had less to do with the making of role models or idolaters. Typically family members, clergy, peers, teachers, and neighbors—and the elderly, especially grandparents—transferred values or lived out fears without fanfare in community. The elderly now are culturally displaced. As Ram Dass puts it, "In a culture where information is prized over wisdom . . . old people become obsolete, like yesterday's computers. But the real treasure is being ignored: wisdom is one of the few things in human life that does not diminish with age."[269] Wisdom is a product of three-dimensional living, steeped in interactions across a wide spectrum of community, to which one contributes for future generations. Those generations will overpopulate the virtual environment as well as the physical one, where they, as we all, must dwell and which, traditionally, has been the source of knowledge and shaper of civic virtues. Place was where one found acceptance and to which one pledged allegiance, honoring neighborhood, hometown, state, and country.

Now we are too mobile electronically and geographically to find lasting acceptance or to nurture the families and friendships that traditionally provide it. As physician Esther M. Sternberg observes,

> With all this mobility, we lose our extended families. And then we lose those friends we had found to replace the families left behind. Yet humans are affiliative animals—biologically not meant to spend

their lives too far from the pack. We crave affiliation, we seek it—in fantasy, in art, and in all the devices we have invented to overcome the social isolation that our mobile lifestyle generates. So now, stoked by the Internet, telephone, and e-mail communications, we have adapted to a lifestyle and have begun to take for granted commuting spouses and "LDRs"—long distance romances. . . .[270]

Of all the devices that mobilize society and flatten relationships, from data to dates, the mobile telephone leads the pack. Mobile phones not only blur place but obliterate it because the source of a disembodied voice can be anywhere, literally. Make no mistake: there are times and occasions where such a trait is a blessing, as so many witnessed during the 9/11 terrorist attacks, with calls for help from rubble and with expressions of love and final goodbyes. Again, in the wake of such use, the frivolity of ordering pizza while navigating traffic only documents the overselling of mobility. Statistics are staggering and portend more displacement in the future. In 1990 some 6 million people were using mobile phones, mostly for business purposes, worldwide. That figure skyrocketed to almost 270 million in 1999, according to Martin Lindstrom, who notes that manufacturer Nokia predicts that "there will be 1 billion mobile phone users in the world by the end of 2002, and by 2003, the annual sales of mobile phones capable of Internet access will exceed the sales of personal computers."[271]

Such mobility could not have happened at a worse time, concerning displacement. Convenient, mobile communication diverts our attention from real to virtual habitat, decreasing awareness about community. The technology also appeals to impulse—contact on demand—violating the prerequisites of effective interpersonal discourse: time, occasion, and place. Worse, the mobile phone explosion has happened and will continue to occur during a phase of (a) unreliable media coverage about community, (b) rampant housing development in suburban and rural areas, and (c) corporate focus on ecosystem rather than on community service. The combination of these factors will likely lessen civic engagement and undermine the influence of neighbors on community standards, especially when "community" is apt to be virtual in the typical U.S. domicile. Once almost kin, a neighbor had to be conscientious about community standards or risk scorn and alienation.

We should not be nostalgic about neighborhoods. As social activist Parker J. Palmer asserts, "True community, like all gifts, involves true risks."[272] Through the 1970s communities were often clannish or prejudiced. However, even these vices influenced our collective awareness. We got to see our bigots up close instead of on monitors and screens and understood the depth of their unfounded fears and the lengths that they would go to validate them. In response, conscientious citizens could concentrate clearly on civic issues of the day, enhancing their social responsibility, as evidenced during the Civil Rights Movement. For better or worse, directly or indirectly, such neighborhoods informed the conscience, inspiring many, particularly baby boomers, to commit to equality or social justice. Others derived a sense of acceptance and security. Typically back then one did not organize a neighborhood watch to fight crime; such a watch came with the territory. Now we wire our homes with alarms rather than rely on neighbors. Often neighbors are mere acquaintances; sometimes, even strangers. Technological advancement may have put the world at our fingertips, but these days we push more buttons than doorbells.

Indeed, when we hear doorbells now, we are as apt to encounter as many solicitors, city workers, and delivery personnel—from pizza to FedEx—as family, friends, and neighbors. We usually feel anxious or "put out" when the doorbell rings and we are not anticipating any visitors. In the 1990s we experienced the same discomfort with telephones and spared ourselves such emotions by purchasing caller-ID and call-block products. To this day, advertisements promoting caller-ID services feature consumers relieved to sidestep troublesome individuals. We literally do not *accept* them but identify and block them out of our lives. We still answer our front doors, by and large, even though security companies now equip cameras with doorbell-ID and visitor-monitoring devices.

For many people, the net effect on the conscience is disconcerting:

- *An epidemic desire to avoid unpleasant emotions.* This is associated with episodic living, facilitated by technology, emphasizing the circumvention of problems rather than interpersonal skills required to resolve them.
- *An elitist affinity to identify and prejudge people who, we believe, generate such emotions.* This is associated with "flat" living, programmed by media, reducing people to caricatures in order to justify our actions, reactions, and opinions.

- *A disturbing inability to communicate authentically face-to-face with others.* This is associated with overuse of technology and overconsumption of media, eroding relationships and contributions at home and work and in community.

The net effect of the above on consciousness also is threefold:

- *Shorter fuses* when confrontation is unavoidable, complicating our interactions and, hence, our lives at home and at work, especially when we lack the interpersonal skills to resolve problems without creating greater ones.
- *Shorter attention spans* because of (a) television overexposure, with hundreds of channels from which to select, requiring use of remotes; (b) on-demand access via mobile phone, requiring split awareness to navigate physical and virtual place; (c) increased Web use, with tens of thousands of sites to surf, requiring use of a mouse; (d) impatience and/or perceived lack of time because of (a), (b), and (c) fueling our rush to prejudge others or overreact.
- *Shorter and/or less substantive relationships* with spouses, children, and colleagues, because of a growing inability (a) to interact meaningfully with others, (b) to resolve mutual but complex interpersonal problems, and (c) to focus attention on others, rather than ourselves, apprehending the dynamics of relationships and problems.

People suffering these symptoms often distrust their lovers, families, colleagues, neighbors, and their own emotions, embarrassing or disappointing themselves when encountering confrontation—a fact of life in community. Otherwise they simply pretend that their emotions and/or irritating people and complex problems do not exist. Media and technology facilitate that desire because they entertain and distract us, not only shortening attention spans but also collective memories.

Fading are days in middle-class neighborhoods when children played in the street year-round—hide-and-seek, kick-the-can, stickball, jump rope—especially in summer, when lightning bugs would spark the sky and parental voices would summon offspring reluctantly inside. In urban areas with ethnic neighborhoods or rural areas with distinct cultures, boys played with girls from kindergarten through high school and left the group on obtaining driver's licenses. Now children play inside more often than not. When children do meet in physical habitat, parents usually have arranged "play dates" or recreational sports. Children play with kids of similar age, sex, and school district, according to the marketing clusters that define us. Children said to be bullies or hyperactive—with millions diagnosed now with attention deficit disorder (ADD)—usually are not invited on play dates because of the same parental tendency to circumvent unpleasant emotions and potential confrontations. Typically, parents identify high-maintenance children as early as preschool, gossip about them at PTO or ballgames, and collectively block them out of lives, along with their children's ability to deal with emotional and physical challenge. As David Brooks notes in his watershed article on elitist values in the *Atlantic Monthly*, titled, "The Next Ruling Class,"

> I suspect that before long, law schools will begin sponsoring courses in the new field of play-date law. A generation ago of course, children did not have play dates; they just went out and played. But now upscale parents fill their kids' datebooks with structured play sessions. And they want to make sure not only that the children will be occupied at somebody's house but also that the activities undertaken will be developmentally appropriate, enriching, and safe. Parental negotiations over what is permissible during these sessions can take on a numbing complexity. Americans being Americans, surely it won't be long before such negotiations end up in a court of law.[273]

The community is the ultimate teacher of developmentally appropriate activities. Children with proper mentors learn how to negotiate disputes interpersonally in inclusive environments and usually end up socially enriched, able to meet future challenges, especially ones created by media and technology. However, the emphasis on the digital divide rather than the interpersonal divide has resulted in recommendations to put computers with on-line access in "community centers" for instant public access across social classes.[274] While it is true that some segments of society do not use Internet because of income, race/origin, education, and household type, among other factors, the notion of segregating youth at computer work stations in recreation centers is particularly disturbing and antithetical to the spirit of inclusive community. Youth require communities that not only have access to technology but also to role models interacting ethically in diverse environments. Otherwise, because of technology use, children may segregate according to lifestyle and marketing data in virtual environments that elevate consumption over community. It is true that children now enjoy more access to information than any previous generation; but they may lack the conscience to use it for the common good and the consciousness to discern that there even is a common good . . . apart from the consumption of goods.

Role models appeal to and otherwise inform the conscience and consciousness. Idolaters covet power, people, and possessions whereas idols are "objects" of worship. Media create idols now; in other eras, communities did—the high school majorette or quarterback, the college homecoming king and queen, the town matron or gallant. Those are caricatures in cinema and situation comedies now. Many people experienced such caricatures not by viewing them on monitors or on movie and television screens but by interacting with them in hometowns. Doing so they registered the degree of their wholeness or hypocrisy. Granted, some of us worshipped their popularity or lifestyles; but many of us also saw through such pomp. They had lives like ours with ups, downs, joys, and sorrows—many of which, with passage of time, we witnessed. In many ways, they evolved into living aphorisms on the human condition. We saw them grow older, fatter or frailer, and bitter as often as wiser, fitter, and kind. They passed on with or without contributing to the community; but when they did *not*, they were remembered for what they failed to do rather than what they accomplished.

The Internet has changed our collective memory concerning real-life caricatures. Pippa Norris, author of *Digital Divide*, discusses the impact of Internet on society, noting that optimists believe it will reduce inequalities between people and societies and pessimists believe that it will widen those divides. She also notes that skeptics believe the hopes and fears of optimists and pessimists are exaggerated because technology typically adapts to the social and political status quo. Norris asks, "What evidence would help to settle these claims? How can we move from the Frank Capra and the Ingmar Bergman visions toward a more systematic understanding on the impact of the Information Society?"[275]

Perhaps Frank Capra's famous, optimistic film about the meaning of community, *It's a Wonderful Life* may be apropos. Capra's 1946 masterpiece depicts an earnest but destitute George Bailey who helps others—including those of ethnic heritage—finance homes through his failing savings and loan. George longs to see the world but his conscience prevents him from leaving his hometown of Bedford Falls.

George competes with, is deceived by, and eventually triumphs over banker Henry F. Potter, the richest and meanest man in Bedford Falls— a caricature, to be sure, known for his interpersonal failures rather than for his influential affluence. That plot is driven home when an angel visits George and shows him how his contributions to community have, in fact, saved the community, along with many lives. Nostalgically to this day we watch *It's a Wonderful Life!* because it sates our need for acceptance during the holidays. How might that movie be depicted today when George, the would-be world traveler, can visit any place on the globe at the click of a mouse, using the technology and Internet access that Mr. Potter, undoubtedly, would vend? Moreover if George as on-line loan officer risked losing his fortune and reputation, who in the S&L listserv would come to his aid in his darkest moment? What user would remember with gratitude and affection his contributions in virtual community? If deleted from cyberspace, angelically or otherwise, would George's life have made the slightest on-line difference? Granted, metaphors and allusions here are extended to make a point. But they speak volumes about the value of real community and the absence thereof in the virtual world where most people dwell for much of their lengthening lifespans, yearning for what they intuit but cannot locate.

Perhaps this inner longing explains why we continue to seek peace and empowerment through which we might meet challenges and contribute to something greater than ourselves. Those challenges and contributions require deft communication skills honed in real community and experienced on three levels:

- *linearly*, in the time that we spend interacting with others.
- *horizontally*, in the relationships that we keep, transcending race, sex, and class.
- *deeply*, in the contributions that we make through those interactions and associations.

Living three-dimensionally, we find acceptance, if not in relationships with others, then in our own relationship with the self.

Dimensions of Community

Role models not only teach us to live three-dimensionally but also to deal effectively with the human condition. Desire for acceptance is part of that condition whose salient features are fundamental: *We will die, and we need others.* Prophets and philosophers through the ages have addressed this, with Jesus of Nazareth perhaps most eloquent when he states in Luke: *You shall love the Lord your God with all your heart, with all your soul, with all your strength, and with all your mind, and your neighbor as yourself* (10:27). The teaching of Jesus, especially about community, did not brand him as revolutionary in the ordinary sense, according to ethicist Donald W. Shriver, Jr., in *An Ethic for Enemies*, "but it does make him revolutionary in an extraordinary sense: before he stood before Pilate, he had taught his disciples that the humane form of *power* was *servanthood*,"[276] or service to those in community without regard to status, gender, ethnicity, and culture. Reference to Jesus here is historical, not religious, because of the mention of neighbors across social lines, implying inclusive community. Albert Einstein makes the same case, stating that a person's "value to the community depends primarily on how far his feelings, thoughts, and actions are directed toward promoting the good of his fellows."[277]

There is no other path to the oracle. Without emotional and social mentors, informing our conscience and consciousness, the search for acceptance is as episodic as any "reality"-based TV show. We enjoy it for a few hours when the "object" of desire invites us into his or her home to spend the night. We might possess it a while longer—a month while on a cruise, a year while at college, a decade while married—and then, with or without warning, acceptance withers like leaves on deciduous trees, in response to autumn, or early frost on fruit blossoms, killing hope for a harvest. We may lose jobs or be reassigned or inherit difficult bosses with new priorities and different favorites. Mentors teach us how to cope with change and accommodate the human condition which, like the seasons, is cyclical. Namely, mentors teach us to *live in* rather than *react to* the moment, dealing with difficulty; to comprehend our various inner selves, from worst to best; and to leave a contribution to the community, as evidence of our life and time on earth.

When we live linearly, interacting conscientiously with others, we appreciate each moment and encounter. Time, after all, is linear with beginning, middle, and end. Einstein, who redefined the concept of time, understood its communal implications. "How strange is the lot of us mortals!" he wrote in his essay, "The World as I See It," noting

Each of us is here for a brief sojourn; for what purpose he knows not, though he sometimes thinks he senses it. But without deeper reflection one knows from daily life that one exists for other people—first of all for those upon whose smiles and wellbeing our own happiness is wholly dependent, and then for the many, unknown to us, to whose destinies we are bound by the ties of sympathy.[278]

Because of the brevity of life, every person should be respected as an individual and "no man idolized,"[279] Einstein stated. (He called his own icon status, created by media, an irony of fate.) Einstein, keenly aware of the human condition, believed that technology had the power to liberate people from tedious work, resulting in more time to engage in and otherwise experience community. That remains the goal to this day.

To attain it, we need to spend more leisure time in the real rather than virtual world, restoring *interpersonal* as well as emotional intelligence. People who live in the moment do not routinely rush through grocery lines or traffic lanes, ignoring or insulting others en route to more pleasing encounters or vital destinations. They come to enjoy the talkative clerk at the checkout counter rather than take offense. They delight in walking an extra block to work rather than compete aggressively for parking spaces in the lot. They deal face-to-face with adversaries, when appropriate, seeking resolutions or common bonds. Simply, they learn to live linearly again and go "with the flow" rather than "against the tide"—or ebb and flow of life—anticipating each encounter, pleasant or unpleasant, as a test of conscience or an affirmation of consciousness.

When we live horizontally, welcoming others across a wide multicultural spectrum, we apprehend that each person is also similar to the next, biologically and emotionally. Cultural values may vary and be the source of interracial or even religious conflict. Universal values do not vary in their emphasis on community. Such ethical abstracts as trust, justice, generosity, gentleness, courage, and even poise (magnificence—Gk, *megaloprepeia*) imply our social obligation to neighbors and form the foundation upon which communities are built over time. These principles emanate out of conscience and are expressed through "the best self," an essence found in people across social classes and cultures. The great nineteenth-century essayist Matthew Arnold believed that mentors who embodied the best self were led by "humane spirit," without which society lapses into anarchy:

> The great men of culture are those who have a passion for diffusing, for making prevail, for carrying from one end of society to

another, the best knowledge, the best ideas of their time; who have laboured to divest knowledge of all that was harsh, uncouth, difficult, abstract, professional, exclusive; to humanize it, to make it efficient outside the clique of the cultivated and learned, yet still remaining the *best* knowledge and thought of that time, and a true source, therefore, of sweetness and light.[280]

Arnold also acknowledged that each person embodied several phases of the self—worst, ordinary, and best. Partners or family members may witness our worst self, replete with vanities and depravities. The ordinary self is just that, dominated by ego, conscious of what others have and it lacks and eager to complain or covet at the hint of favoritism or unfairness. The best self knows that everyone has a higher purpose in life. The best self does not recognize icons with celebrity status or supermodel good looks. The best self sees its own reflection in others—so much so, says mythologist Joseph Campbell—that in moments of crisis, we do not distinguish "otherness" in neighbors. How else to fathom why people risk their lives running into burning buildings or leaping into flood waters to rescue complete strangers? The answer, says Campbell, invoking the philosophy of Arthur Schopenhauer, is that such crises represent breakthroughs "of a metaphysical realization, which is, that you and the other are one, that you are two aspects of the one life, and that your apparent separateness is but an effect of the way we experience forms under conditions of space and time."[281]

To live deeply, we must first learn to live linearly and horizontally, appreciating each encounter and acknowledging the best self in others of every race, creed, or culture. Doing so we do not predetermine which person is more appealing based on physical looks or social graces. We look people in the eyes, not to ascertain pigment but purpose. We see family, friends, neighbors, partners, peers, and strangers according to the content of their consciences rather than the inventory of their households. Accumulation of wealth does not define self-worth, as it does "net worth" according to the annual Forbes list of wealthiest moguls, financiers, tycoons, and power brokers. Anyone can live deeply with a compassionate or kind deed, a loving word, a timely gift, or a nurturing soul. Mother Teresa never sought icon status, but she became known through good works that set an example for everyone, even presidents and princes. "Let us not be satisfied with just giving money," Mother Teresa once said in an oft-cited quotation. "Money is not enough, money can be got but others need your heart to love them." The "heart" symbolizes conscience. When we act conscientiously toward others, we contribute to society every day, enriching communities in small but significant ways over time.

The wealth of the seven richest men in the world can obliterate poverty in our time, according to human rights advocates. That may be true. But soon the moral pandemics of greed and desire will take hold anew, reestablishing the old order of the ego and ordinary self. In his book, *Ethics for the New Millennium*, the Dalai Lama echoes that same sentiment, asking readers of conscience "to turn toward the wider community of beings with whom we are connected and for conduct which recognizes others' interests alongside our own."[282] He asserts that love and compassion will help heal many social concerns, including violence, addiction, and divorce, which are problems of conscience requiring moral solutions, without which there is no hope for lasting peace or peace of mind. Those who embrace that universal ideal enjoy moral rather than economic prosperity—the wherewithal to meet challenges and to foresee outcomes of actions compassionately. As a consequence, they will experience new levels of reciprocal affection and fellowship.

Before that can happen, however, those who seek balance and wellbeing must gauge the impact of media and technology on their values, interactions, and relationships. Otherwise too many individuals will continue to seek acceptance through the very vehicles that have deprived them of it, feeling disconnected in a wired world. In the final chapter of *Interpersonal Divide*, we will address this conundrum and repatriate to our villages—not by eschewing media and technology, but by integrating them conscientiously into our three-dimensional lives.

Journal Exercise

Discretion is defined in *the Oxford English Dictionary* (shorter edition) as "the power of deciding, or of acting according to one's own judgment." To do so, one must rely on individual perception. Perception concerns how you view a problem, person, or situation. Overconsumption of media and overuse of technology often skew perception. Because of that, perception is subject to change, especially when emotions are high during mediated crises or interpersonal confrontations at home or at work. As you develop discretion, you will make prudent "judgment calls" in your own, your group's or the community's interest, knowing which medium, if any, is correct for the message.

Keep a "discretion journal" for one week, recording how you responded during tense times—interpersonally or virtually. Note whether your response helped resolve or worsen the situation, again noting whether the interaction occurred interpersonally or virtually. Practice the tenets below and assess whether they proved effective in both interpersonal and mediated communication.

- Accept your gut instinct, but reject your first reaction.

  Learn to feel your *ethics* as well as your anger. Perception is often distorted when you feel tempted, manipulated, or deceived—standard media fare according to villain-victim motifs. Relearn physical feelings in physical place associated with your values so when questionable situations arise, you can practice discretion in any environment, real or virtual.

  Accepting your gut instinct is one thing, but acting on it is quite another. Gut instincts can bring back memories of past experience and thus can cloud the immediate situation, especially when the convenience of technology allows for impulsive use. Thus,

  1. *Don't speak before thinking.* When you "speak what's on" or "give a piece of" your mind, especially on-line, you also risk betraying yourself, creating more problems, and causing bleaker circumstances for yourself and others.
  2. *Don't phone, e-mail, or fax until your emotions subside.* If angry, determine if you are reacting because someone is using loaded language or an uncivil tone of voice. Remember to focus on the content, not on the tone, which may be altered by technology, to help ease the pressure so you can convey your viewpoint credibly.
  3. *Seek counsel with someone impartial.* Resist spreading rumors or gossip, especially on-line, to ease emotional stress. Rumors and gossip invite more of the same and typically worsen problems. If confused or troubled by interpersonal or mediated exchanges, consult with someone whose judgment you trust before responding.

- Focus on perception first, and then solve the problem.
  Try these methods:

  1. *Comprehend.* Do not interrupt discussions to express your views the way talking heads do on television. Instead your goal

should be to understand fully what the other party is saying before formulating your response—in virual or real habitat.

2. *Research*: What you don't understand, learn, contacting knowledgeable sources or using libraries or search engines. The more you know, the keener your perception and the wider your range of choices.

3. *Priorities*: Make your choices reflect your priorities as they pertain to treatment of others, remembering the Golden Rule, again in physical and virtual habitat.

- Solve problems without creating greater ones.

1. *Use appropriate but penetrating discourse*, even when others are inappropriate or uncivil, in both on-line and face-to-face exchanges.

2. *Do the necessary analysis* before judging others' work or person, realizing the long-term impact of interpersonal and/or mediated confrontations.

3. *Embrace a shared set of values* that analyzes or honors all viewpoints—even ones with which you disagree—in the interest of diversity and community in both physical and virtual habitat.

Discussion/Paper Ideas for Chapter Eight

- Discuss observations from the Journal Exercise above.
- Discuss the validity of these assertions:

1. Authentic role models are an endangered species not because Hollywood erodes family values but because media erode perception of community, depicting a flat and episodic world.

2. Of all the devices that mobilize society and flatten relationships, from data to dates, the mobile telephone leads the pack. Mobile phones not only blur place but obliterate it because the source of a disembodied voice can be anywhere, literally.

3. Children who learn how to negotiate disputes interpersonally in inclusive environments usually end up socially enriched, able to meet future challenges, especially ones created by media and technology.

- Discuss central theses and themes on ethics and community from Suggested Readings below.

Suggested Readings from Chapter Eight

Blackburn, Simon. *Being Good: A Short Introduction to Ethics*. New York: Oxford University Press, 2001.

Gardner, Howard, Csikszentmihalyi, Milhaly, and Damon, William. *Good Work: When Excellence and Ethics Meet*. New York: Basic Books, 2001.

Murray, David, Schwartz, Joel, and Lichter, S. Robert. *It Ain't Necessarily So: How Media Make and Unmake the Scientific Picture of Reality*. Lanham, MD: Rowman & Littlefield, 2001.

Repatriation to the Village

There is more than a verbal tie between the words common, community, and communication. . . . What they have in common in order to form a community or society are aims, beliefs, aspirations, knowledge—a common understanding. The communication which insures participation in a common understanding is one which secures similar emotional and intellectual dispositions—like ways of responding to expectations and requirements.

—JOHN DEWEY, *Democracy and Education*

Ethical Inventories

Those who seek acceptance must first accept their situation, examining the roles that media and technology play in their lives and then monitoring—and *tempering*—usage. That is the first bold step toward repatriation to the village, for when we temper use of technology and consumption of media, the first thing that we gain is time—for family, friends, neighbors, colleagues, and others. We do not waste time online or on couches; we do not misuse media and technology, complicating or neglecting key relationships. We streamline our lives, communicating clearly at the right moment through the proper medium, or none at all, and experience fewer misunderstandings at home and at work. With time comes opportunity: to enhance our well-being through exercise or education, to expand consciousness through interactions with others, and to deepen conscience through service to others. Those are requisites of the human condition, and we ignore them at our own risk.

The unexamined life is not worth living, Socrates observed. Throughout this book we have examined contemporary life, documenting the quest for fulfillment as frenetic now as ever in the annals of history.

Aristotle advised, *Seek moderation in all things*. Moderation is an ethical and a communal construct, restoring balance in individuals and preserving resources in communities. Repatriation to the village requires moderation, too, to mitigate the influence of mass media and electronic communication. Tim Berners-Lee, creator of the World Wide Web, states that moderation in all things, including technology, helps people attain higher levels of well-being and happiness. Berners-Lee believes that isolated individuals are inherently unhappy and have trouble making balanced decisions. Conversely, a person "who's worried about the environment and international diplomacy and spends no time sitting at home or in his local community also has trouble making balanced decisions and is also very unhappy," he states, concluding: "It seems a person's happiness depends on having a balance of connections at different levels"[283] in both virtual and physical place.

To attain such balance, we have to ask why we bought a piece of technology and determine if we are using it for that reason. Otherwise marketing provides the answer, suggesting alternate uses that may or may not be in line with priorities. The same holds true with media consumption. If we do not temper and analyze use of *any* electronic device, we may set into motion a domino effect that widens the interpersonal divide:

Dominoes of Media

1. The more media we consume, the less we interact with others in real habitat.
2. The less we interact, the more we misinterpret the actions and motives of others.
3. The more we misinterpret, the less rewarding our relationships.
4. The less rewarding those relationships, the more we indulge in programming.
5. The more programming we consume, the less sure we are of personal values.
6. The less sure we are of values, the more influence marketing has on our choices.
7. The more that marketing targets us, the less keen our perception becomes.
8. The less keen our perception, the more interpersonal problems we encounter.

9. The more problems we encounter, the less equipped we are to resolve them, precisely because we lack the necessary perception and interpersonal skills.
10. *The effect?* We seek self-help, exposing ourselves to more media and technology.

Dominoes of Technology

1. The more technology we use, the less we interact with others in real habitat.
2. The less we interact, the more we rely on technology to entertain ourselves and communicate with others.
3. The more we rely on technology, the less sure we are of boundaries involving space, time, and identity.
4. The less sure we are of boundaries, the more we intrude on others or misinterpret messages.
5. The more we intrude and misinterpret, the less stable our relationships.
6. The less stable those relationships, the more we replace them with virtual ones.
7. The more we fulfill our needs electronically, the less privacy we experience.
8. The less privacy we experience, the more influence marketing has on behavior.
9. The more such influence on behavior, the less sound our judgment becomes, intensifying our search for acceptance.
10. *The effect?* We seek self-help, exposing ourselves to more media and technology, beginning the cycle anew.

To break the cycle, we have to examine media consumption and technology use, analyzing their influence on our outlook and values. Media provide outtakes on life that condense and simplify complexities, generating flat perception of a round interpersonal world. Technology filters vital interpersonal cues—from eye contact to hand gesture—amplifying or deleting factors that change our perception of the world and each other. One such factor, seemingly minor when first mentioned, is the absence of facial expression in e- and voice mail and in typical phone and mobile phone communication. The deletion of facial cues—one factor out of many—illustrates why we may overreact or feel insulted in electronic exchanges when no affront or offense was intended at all. In truth, people have to develop exceptional oral skills to compensate for lack of facial expression. As psychologist Paul Ekman observes in *Telling Lies*, "The face can reveal the particulars of emotional experience that only the poet can capture in words."[284] Ekman notes that the face shows:

- Which emotion is felt—anger, fear, sadness, disgust, distress, happiness, contentment, excitement, surprise, and contempt can all be conveyed by distinctive expressions;
- Whether two emotions are blended together—often two emotions are felt and the face registers elements of each;
- The strength of the felt emotion—each emotion can vary in intensity, from annoyance to rage, apprehension to terror, etc.[285]

As covered in previous chapters, there are many more interpersonal cues besides facial expression—from body language and tone to pauses and space considerations—that inform us about motive in face-to-face interactions. When we deprive ourselves of such data, because of the convenience of technology, which invites contact on demand, we are apt to misinterpret intentions of others and respond inappropriately, complicating relationships. This book has documented that phenomenon over several chapters, noting the time that the average user spends in cyberspace and the habits that are likely to develop because of that. When place, time, and identity are blurred, conscience and consciousness, which should function harmoniously, also blur so that we cannot easily resolve everyday problems without creating greater ones. Relationships may falter at home or at work. As we attempt to mediate disputes using the same technology that may have spawned them—generally oblivious of that effect—we encounter the interpersonal divide, which we must cross to repatriate to the village, ascertaining:

- *Why* we bought a particular device, establishing whether it is advancing or subverting our goals and priorities.
- *When* to use that equipment to interact with others and, equally as important, when *not*.
- *Where* to use technology (especially mobile and monitoring equipment) and where *not*.
- *Who* should have access to media and technology in households with children.

- *What* we can do for others in real habitat, contributing to community.

- *How* to interact face-to-face with others to resolve problems and meet challenges, articulating our views and assessing contrary ones mindfully.

The time has come to self-assess—not psychologically, but programmatically and technically. Media and technology not only tend to isolate us from other human beings, they also generate an illusion that we truly are connected by wires. *Puppets, not people, are connected by wires.* The illusion, however, is narcotic because the graphics transfix, the disembodied voices resonate within us, and the videos stream like consciousness. So much so that we fail to ask basic questions and employ common sense to set us on the path again to peace and empowerment.

In the end we must evaluate the impact of media and technology on our priorities and estimate the time that we spend each day in virtual habitat. Those who do such assessments usually learn that little time is left at the end of the day to contribute to community. Community service used to be viewed as a career asset. Now it is just as apt to be deemed a nuisance if volunteerism is not integrated with corporate objectives. To be sure, companies invest millions of dollars in civic causes—otherwise known as "social marketing"—but often do so because of image rather than moral considerations. The practice dates back to the Ma Bell break up of 1984 when AT&T helped define the "new corporate citizen," believing that philanthropic initiatives should help advance business interests in a decidedly "Janus-faced" manner, with "one face serving the community, the other serving AT&T's business units."[286] As such, marketing infiltrated philanthropy—yet another indicator of our collective priorities. Our personal priorities are just as suspect. We can afford to wile away hours consuming programming or communicating electronically, without much regard for the cumulative impact of our high-tech habits. That impact is obvious during personal and professional crises, for that is when people need clear perception and keen interpersonal skills, which media skew and technology blurs.

Foci of Our Discontent
Crises bring out the best and worst in us, forcing us to act on instinct or principle. We confront the aftermath of our anger or discontent. We

experience harassment or are accused of it. We mismanage accounts, lose money or composure, or vent at colleagues, children, or partners. We rerun scenes and scenarios, wondering: *Did I do the right thing? Should I apologize? Did someone take advantage of me? Is my boss exploiting or entrusting me with this extra work? Should I stand ground on principle or overlook a snub at home or at work? Should I marry, sue, reconcile, divorce?* Answers to such life-altering questions rely on good judgment, naturally, the ability to apprehend the dynamics of a situation and to communicate effectively with others to reach an acceptable resolution or, barring that, to accept the situation or the consequences. Sound judgment is based on perception, how we see a problem, assess viewpoints, and foresee resolutions. We cannot focus sufficiently to resolve problems when our perception is faulty, usually because we are consumed by fear or because we fail to gauge the complexity or severity of problems.

Consequences can be dire when the stakes are high in the high-tech media age. For starters, many of us have lost our sense of timing from overexposure to virtual reality, where we spend so much of our day. Some of us also have lost a sense of occasion—when and where to confront an issue or a person—and end up complicating situations, even though we had intended to resolve them. Because we lack practice interacting with others face-to-face, or act on impulse using technology, we cannot always foresee how people might respond to our thoughts, words, and deeds. In fact, some of us spend years and thousands of dollars in legal fees untangling our many interpersonal snarls. People often wonder how this could have happened because they lead routine lives—routine, in that they spend most of their day consuming media and using technology. *Could that, perhaps, be the cause?*

The human condition is unique and contradictory. We are conscious enough to make incredible inventions to span the space that we should inhabit for peace and well-being. Those inventions divide us digitally and interpersonally. Our primary habitats have become our workstations and home entertainment centers, allowing us access to the virtual world but cutting us off from each other in the physical world. We communicate electronically out of convenience or on whim and misinterpret as much as we convey about intentions. We are, by turns, uncivil or submissive at work, creating a dicey symbiosis of aggressor and victim, both of whom are fear-driven. We consume media that reinforce optimum levels of fear and buy more gadgets to feel secure, only to discover that they bind us to the very workstations and entertainment centers that are the foci of our discontent. Life has become more stressful, despite the digital toys and tools at our fingertips. Even those with media careers who typically have favorable opinions about technology concede that it causes stress. A study at the Indiana University School of Journalism, involving some 450 journalism professors and administrators, measured attitudes toward technology. Of six categories included in the study, only "time constraints"—time to get things done—ranked higher than technological stress, which surpassed concerns about tenure and also contributed to job dissatisfaction and burnout.[287] Time to get things done may correlate to technology use, as we have hitherto observed.

That seems to be the case with most white-collar jobs utilizing media and technology. Jill Andresky Fraser, finance editor of *Inc.* magazine, covering the corporate world, believes that workplace technology was put in place because of its purported ability to lighten job tasks, lower costs, and boost performance—all of which are associated with overwork and stress levels. Technology, she writes, "has done more than simply *facilitate* the current trend of working longer and harder. It may, indeed, have exacerbated patterns of overwork and job stress by broadening many white-collar staffers' (and their employers') definitions of 'on the job' to include areas far beyond the traditional confines of their office space."[288]

Add to that stress the loss of privacy, again as we have documented repeatedly in *Interpersonal Divide*. A Denver-based research group notes that corporations routinely monitor more than one third of the 40 million-plus U.S. workforce with access to Internet and e-mail. Workplace surveillance is easy to put in place, relatively low-cost, and combines well with computer power and wireless and/or mobile technologies. Chief researcher Andrew Schulman notes, "One of the main lessons from this study is that today, more than any other factor, inexpensive technology is driving the growth of employee monitoring. It's cheap and easy to record and stores more and more office activities that once were ephemeral."[289] Schulman also notes that workplace monitoring to catch an occasional slacker or to uncover criminal behavior may lead to litigation against the surveilling company in addition to contributing to a hostile environment. The latter occurs when motive is misinterpreted by company or employee, because both share use of the same invasive technologies that alter content and influence outlook.

Virtual environment doesn't change when an employee leaves the workplace for home. As communication scholars Joseph Straubhaar and Robert LaRose observed in 1996, "The ultimate in work decentralization is telecommuting, in which the employee's home office is linked to the workplace via telephone, electronic mail, facsimile, and teleconferencing systems."[290] The equipment required for telecommuting in 1996 became standard home office fare for white-collar professionals by the end of the twentieth century. Many workers, especially those who have been "outsourced" by companies cutting health care benefits and retirement costs, are required to have the same office setups at home as they had at work. Boundaries between home and work blur. Activities homogenize. Typical homes contain computer stations in several rooms designed for interpersonal activities, from parlor to bedroom. Marketing has as much access to us as we have to each other communicating electronically. That only adds to the tension. Technology-induced job stress is so pronounced that many of us, eager to get home, typically have no idea what to do when we get there, to engage the mind or interact with partners and children. "Ironically, jobs are actually easier to enjoy than free time," writes Mihaly Csikszentmihalyi, a psychologist who believes that creativity, or "flow," provides a deep sense of satisfaction. Work, he adds, has "built-in goals, feedback, rites, and challenges, all of which encourage one to become involved in one's work, to concentrate and lose oneself in it. Free time, on the other hand, is unstructured, and requires much greater effort to be shaped into something that can be enjoyed."[291] Families used to enjoy both the effort to structure free time and the free time itself. However, like children unable to do complex LEGOs, we lack the patience and energy, consigning ourselves to the media and technological marvels whose primary functions, paradoxically, are meant to enhance communication and interaction.

Many of us feel anxious for good reason. Media and technology are not particularly effective in conveying the three requisites of conscience: the need to love and be loved, to have meaningful relationships, and to contribute to community. However, media and technology excel at titillating the urge for sex and simulating relationships with strangers in an environment that lacks touch and topography. Why shouldn't we feel isolated?

Esther M. Sternberg, a physician specializing in the central nervous system, writes in *The Balance Within: The Science Connecting Health and Emotions*: "Logic suggests that our increasing reliance on electronic communications might increase social isolation. Indeed, some studies suggest that unlimited access to e-mail actually increases people's sense of loneliness and isolation."[292] That may be true. With respect to health issues, however, electronic communication also can help patients become better-informed health consumers. E-mail, in particular, can be used to schedule medical appointments, consult with physicians on routine matters, and participate with other patients in discussion-board conversations about symptoms or therapies.[293] While these functions are empowering or illuminating, they cannot replace entirely the enduring bonds of interpersonal contact, especially at critical moments in one's life. During such times nearness to family and friends is vital. The farther the geographic distance, the greater the isolation.

Sternberg also addresses the concept of distance. In discussing telemedicine, she observes that technology delivers diagnosis and treatment via video to isolated communities. The irony again is in the appropriated word. In the earlier instance, concerning e-mail, Sternberg defined "isolation" as a lonely feeling within a person. However, in the second instance, she refers to isolation as a place on a map. Herein lies the lesson: Technology cannot resolve the *feeling* of isolation, no matter how sophisticated the software program or interactive the Web site; but technology can bridge *physical* distance between communities.

That has social and moral implications. The more we try to bridge the physical divide, relying on electronic communication, the wider the interpersonal one becomes. The objective, then, concerning health care, is to use technology wisely, gaining access to data or doctors and discussing that information or receiving treatment at a later date in person. Likewise electronic communication also can establish new contacts and relationships that should be nurtured interpersonally when time and occasion warrant. In the end, virtual and physical realities must work harmoniously to advance goals and priorities. Otherwise attempts to repatriate to the village, locally or globally, will falter.

Mis-Mediated Messages

Typical users receive so many messages through so many media and high-tech gadgetry that it is difficult to reconcile:

- *Content.* What is the message telling us? How is the particular medium—e-mail, mobile phone, television—altering perception?

Where (from what place) are we receiving or sending that message and how, if at all, does *that* alter content?

- *Motive.* What is the marketing motive of the particular medium? How does that motive mesh with my personal and professional priorities? How does it serve or erode my fundamental relationships?
- *Displacement.* To what extent does the medium "displace" me, transporting me out of real habitat to a virtual one? How does using the medium occupy my time or alter my sense of time? Does the medium, along with the customer service associated with it, (a) reaffirm, (b) have no effect on, (c) or devalue my sense of self-worth and/or identity?

We should consider each of these issues separately—a key step, because content, motive, and displacement occur simultaneously and subtly. Many of us do not assess how content of our messages is going to be altered by the medium used to convey it. That effect usually disguises intent, so much so at times, that our motives may be questioned and, by extension, our values, too. Perhaps future generations will overcome feelings of displacement and master communication in real and virtual habitats. But the fact is, current generations have yet to achieve that goal, primarily because relatively few educators, supervisors, information officers, consultants, and even mentors have brought the issue to the forefront of their agendas. The matter has been tabled interminably. In 1985, communication professor Joshua Meyrowitz published with Oxford University Press a discussion-starter book reminiscent of this one, titled *No Sense of Place: The Impact of Electronic Media on Social Behavior.* Although Meyrowitz dealt primarily with television, his assessment of blurring of identity and place was ahead of its time and on target. More important, he admonished educators to focus on the interpersonal ramifications of electronic media:

> Those readers who are accustomed to studies of media effects that discuss primarily the characteristics or content of *media* may be surprised at how much this book describes the structure of *interpersonal* behavior. The analysis of the dynamics of face-to-face interaction grows out of my belief that much media research has been limited to looking at narrowly defined responses to media content (such as imitation or persuasion) because researchers have largely ignored those aspects of everyday social behavior. . .[294]

We cannot afford to ignore such aspects any longer. Indeed, understanding and adjusting for effects of mediated communication may prove to be the most important habits that each of us must develop to maintain relationships at home and at work.

Relationships are varied and diverse. The intrinsic nature of any relationship—trusting, competitive, loving, controlling, or kind—also influences content of messages, mediated or interpersonal. In other words, a kind person is apt to send kind messages via e-mail and do so without prompting or premeditation, especially if a bond exists with the receiver. But all of us are not kind. And that same caring individual may be ineffective in more complicated e-mail exchanges requiring discretion or data. Moreover, relationships in virtual space benefit or suffer on account of actions occurring in physical place. In all likelihood, those who compliment or condemn each other face-to-face will continue to do so electronically. There are countless other factors in addition to technology that affect how we view, treat, and communicate with each other. However, the question at hand concerns:

- *Impact.* To what extent has electronic communication played a part in enhancing or deteriorating a particular relationship?
- *Discernment.* Do we wish to continue dialogue through a particular medium or through another or none at all, opting for face-to-face interaction or none whatsoever?
- *Practice.* How can we alter the content of our electronic messages so that our intent is more easily discerned?

Psychologist Paul Ekman notes that people routinely misinterpret each other even in face-to-face encounters, with body language and facial expressions signaling emotions, "especially the meaning of other people's actions and the motives that lead people to act one way or another."[295] Simply put, misinterpretation is only human. But that all-too-human trait is exacerbated when we communicate electronically because of the absence of interpersonal cues. Worse, overuse and consumption of television and Internet complicate typical symptoms, further undermining relationships, writes Marie Winn in *The Plug-In Drug: Television, Computers, and Family Life.* "Studies show the importance of eye-to-eye contact, for instance, in real-life relationships, and indicate that the nature of one's eye contact patterns, whether one looks another squarely in the eye or looks to the side of shifts one's gaze from side to side, may play a significant role in one's success or failure in human relationships."[296] Effective eye contact, like anything else, requires practice. No eye contact occurs when individuals gaze at television and computer screens several hours per day, affecting development of trust in the company of others. The consequence is twofold: We are apt to misinterpret messages and motives because technology filters or alters them; we are prone to keep making those misinterpretations because we lack practice interacting in real community. To compensate, we should give others the benefit of the doubt when communicating electronically and develop interpersonal intelligence, learning social and physical cues in our daily interactions. That is the price tag of instantaneous communication, and if we do not want to pay it, because we react angrily to anyone questioning our character, capability, or authority, we had better develop other means to maintain relationships . . . or accept consequences of social detachment, which include:

- *Overreaction.* We will invest more time, energy, and money in the reaction mode, answering people according to perceived rather than real intent and following up with memos, grievances, and reports and/or pursuing other legal, personal, and institutional remedies.
- *Depreciation.* We will feel devalued by the response-reaction process and seek acceptance more urgently, pursuing others or ambitions obsessively and/or questioning our self-esteem when we fail to find acceptance in sufficient quantity to make us feel worthy again.
- *Isolation.* We will dwell increasingly in solitary home offices or lonely cubicles, looking to media to entertain us and technology to connect us, further eroding conscience and consciousness and ensuring that we will continue to misinterpret others in both real and virtual habitats.

Because so many of us suffer similar symptoms, entire relationships can change overnight on the basis of a single mismediated message. That phenomenon concerns Howard Rheingold and other technology analysts. Writes Rheingold, "Anyone who has experienced a misunderstanding via e-mail or witnessed a flame war in an on-line discussion knows that mediated communications, lacking the nuances carried by eye contact, facial expression, or tone of voice, increase the possibility of conflicts erupting from misunderstandings."[297] The contention in

Interpersonal Divide is that such misunderstandings, far from being exceptions, are fast becoming the norm in virtual habitat. The spillover occurs in physical habitat, too, continuing an unfortunate cycle, when electronic adversaries who live or work in the same location encounter each other face-to-face and then escalate differences, ignoring or offending each other, all because of a misconstrued mediated message. That being the case, we must repatriate to villages without taking with us the digital baggage of simplistic misinterpretation and summary judgment, learning to be mindful of others in *any* environment.

A Place in the Village

To use technology appropriately, we have to evaluate such aspects as viewpoint, place, and occasion and employ civility, patience, and tact. We must safeguard privacy, too, remembering that virtual messages can go *public*. Private messages, especially e-mail and voice mail text, may appear in tomorrow's newspapers—in theory or in fact. So a community-based value system has never been more vital. In less mediated eras, people had two value systems—one at home and another at work. That era has ended. Technology has blurred interpersonal boundaries, requiring people of conscience to adopt values that not only suit lifestyles or cultures but that also transcend and apply to physical and virtual space.

Because technology is mobile, our ethics should be, too. In the end each individual must develop values to live three-dimensionally in an inclusive but mediated society. There are only a few ground rules. In general, personal ethics should acknowledge the requirements of conscience and consciousness—that we love and are loved by others, cultivate meaningful relationships, and contribute to community, foreseeing consequences of our actions before taking them and appreciating the blessings of each phase of biological life.

Values also should be:

- *Socially beneficial.* Without a social benefit, a value can be misused or misapplied. Loyalty, for instance, may be essential for organized crime; however, such crime doesn't serve community.
- *Morally focused.* Without a sense of right and wrong, we would not understand what is or is not beneficial.
- *Personally edifying.* Without enlightenment, we would not readily acknowledge the best self and the human condition.

- *Culturally inclusive.* Without inclusivity, we limit contributions to community, undermining social benefits, morality, and enlightenment.

Those tenets also apply to media and technology, which should be beneficial and educational, advancing inclusive priorities that serve society. Otherwise current social ills and mediated effects may worsen over time, afflicting future generations. Indeed, children weaned on the high-tech commercialism of the twenty-first century will have to overcome digital addictions, which threaten perception of community as never before. According to Marie Winn, "The invention of the electric light, the automobile, or the telephone changed most adults' lives significantly, but not the lives of the youngest children. They continued to spend their days in pretty much the same way small children have spent their days throughout history. They slept, they ate, and the rest of their time they engaged in the enormously varied complex of activities that falls in to the category of *play*."[298] That has changed, perhaps forever, writes Winn, noting that new electronic technologies—specifically home computers, video and game consoles—isolate children in front of screens and "displace outdoor play, schoolwork, practice of musical instruments, hobbies, and leisure-time reading."[299] Consumer technology consumes children, a fact of life with which educators increasingly must contend, along with the commercialism that has a firm foothold now in wired schoolrooms across the country.[300] As more districts address digital divides, providing access and computers, adding hours of screen time to television viewing at home, children will continue to exhibit behaviors associated with lack of interaction and interest in real community. Asks Winn, "How might such a distortion affect a child's development of trust, of openness, of an ability to relate well to *real* people?"[301]

Throughout this book we have seen how media and technology harm relationships—guardian/child, spouse/partner, neighbor/neighbor, boss/employee, employee/client, and so forth. Relationships suffer when participants cannot communicate effectively. They suffer when people misperceive reality or misinterpret motives. Any type of mismediated message—a sender intending one thing and a receiver inferring another—complicates relationships, especially when a person's senses are deprived of stimulation (sight, voice tone, facial expression, body language) and participants, a sense of place, time, occasion, and identity. Marketing further affects relationships when it automates and depersonalizes service, determining how people use media and technology—whether or not that use actually enhances our lives and well-being or advances our goals and priorities.

We confront a triptych of challenges:

- Overconsumption of media, eroding perception about community.
- Overuse of technology, eroding communication in community.
- Marketing, eroding both.

To appreciate those factors, we should examine how technology and media affect us as individuals. That will vary, of course. However, once we take a personal inventory, as recommended earlier in this chapter and as detailed in the Journal Exercise at the end of this chapter, answers will be more obvious. To conceive them, we need a quiet place to reflect, devoid of background media noise (no stereos, televisions, voice mail, mobile phones, telephones, or laptops left on or operational) and a pencil and sheet of paper. Those medieval handheld implements do not caution you in mid-epiphany that "You've got mail!" or that you made a spelling or grammatical error. We can also invite a group of family members, friends, colleagues, or neighbors to discuss community-building issues face-to-face, enjoying their company in a welcoming environment—again, devoid of background media noise. In truth, nothing can be more self-affirming than people of conscience discussing substantive matters in homes, churches, cafés, cafeterias, schools, libraries, meeting halls, parks, backyards, front porches, and other hospitable milieus.

Media and technology can pave the way to the global village that many of us envision. However, we should not rely on them to help us attain enduring states of fulfillment, which interaction in and contributions to community consistently provide. We cannot possibly learn about world cultures fully without media and technology, which can inspire us to embrace inclusivity and to visit other countries. When we do, we will greet each other on the crossroads of life rather than on the exit ramps of Web, understanding that our own insatiable need for acceptance also is expressed elsewhere in a diversity of ways, but always through and with other people.

Media and technology can be links through which we engage and befriend such people. To establish true relationships with them, however, we will have to repatriate to our own villages before visiting theirs.

We will have to meet them on their own turf, too, unencumbered by the consumerism promoting travel in real and virtual environs. How else will we feel the collective conscience so that we do not misinterpret overtures of others according to our own high-tech conventions, which we transmit worldwide? How else will we love our neighbors as ourselves and leave a legacy for future generations so that offspring can resolve global issues by considering viewpoints other than their own? How else will we foresee the consequences of our actions at home or at work if those actions are mediated according to the dictates of marketing and circuitry? How else can our awareness grow into the wisdom that reverberates through the ages, acknowledging that our search for acceptance can never truly be attained because it is, precisely, that quest that binds us to each other while we exist on this plane and planet?

Journal Exercise

In the first journal assignment, you took an inventory of media appliances and technology devices in your home and workplace/school. Over the course of the book how, if at all, has your perception changed about media and technology effects?

To determine that, take a more detailed inventory:

At Home

- *Hours spent using high-tech media equipment, not using it, interacting in public.* How many hours per day do you consume media and use technology, including watching television or VHS/DVD movies, listening to radio or CD players and stereos, playing video or computer games, browsing the Internet, reading and sending e-mail, using mobile phones and telephones, Palm Pilots, handhelds, digital cameras, and other electronic gadgets and appliances? Compare that total to hours spent in the home on activities not associated with media and technology. Finally, count hours spent each day outside the home on activities not associated with media and technology. *Compare lists.*
- *Number of times per day spent multitasking.* How many times during the day do you multitask with two or more media on simultaneously, such as television, stereo, and radio, and/or two or more software applications or pieces of technology operating si-

multaneously, such as mobile phone, laptop, and desktop? *How, if at all, does such use affect the tasks at hand? How does it affect your attention to other people or activities in the household?*

- *The number of operational high-tech media appliances at peak periods.* Count the number of high-tech media appliances turned on at the height of activity in the household, including televisions, VCRs, DVD players, stereos, game consoles, computers, answering and fax machines, cell phones, and telephones. *Which ones are being used and which, ignored or idle? Which ones typically bring us joy, affirmation, stress, health worries, or additional work?*

Now do a similar inventory:

At Work

- *Hours spent consuming or using media and technology.* How many hours per day do you consume media and use technology at your place of employment, including television, Internet, and e-mail? *How many of those hours do you spend interacting face to face with colleagues, clients, or others? Which approach—interacting with others via media and technology, or interpersonally— results in more success or effectiveness?*
- *Number of commercials and promotions at the height of activity.* How many advertisements and marketing ploys are you exposed to during a peak hour at work using media and technology? The workplace used to be relatively free of media and marketing. Now, even in academic or government settings, it is full of advertisements, spam, streaming audio/video, promotions, pop-up messages, and more. *How many such ads and promotions engage or distract you? What is the impact on your effectiveness, focus, and work load?*
- *Inventory of equipment and programs.* Count the appliances and applications at the workplace, including cell phones, pagers, electronic schedulers, e-mail, voice mail, answering machines, faxes, computers, recording and monitoring devices, scanners, listservs, news groups, databases, closed circuit televisions, computer and cable networks, and so on. These devices and applications were supposed to make work easier or tasks more efficient so that we could go home on time to enjoy family, friends, and neighbors. *Which ones are efficient, and which inefficient? Which complicate*

relationships and which nurture them? Which can you eliminate or use less frequently to become more effective?

Discussion/Paper Ideas for Chapter Nine

- Discuss observations from the Journal Exercise above.
- Discuss the validity of these assertions:
  1. If we do not temper and analyze use of any electronic device, we may set into motion a domino effect that widens the interpersonal divide.
  2. Media and technology are not particularly effective in conveying the three requisites of conscience: the need to love and be loved, to have meaningful relationships, and to contribute to community. Conversely, media and technology excel at titillating the urge for sex and simulating relationships with strangers in an environment that lacks both touch and topography.
  3. Media and technology, when used appropriately, may help in the search for acceptance. But we should not rely on them as much as we do to attain an enduring state of fulfillment, which only interaction in and contributions to community can provide.
- Discuss central theses and themes on interpersonal versus mediated communication from the Suggested Readings below.

Suggested Readings from Chapter Nine

Berners-Lee, Tim. *Weaving the Web*. New York: HarperCollins, 1999.

Meyrowitz, Joshua. *No Sense of Place: The Impact of Electronic Media on Social Behavior*. New York: Oxford University Press, 1985.

Winn, Marie. *The Plug-in Drug: Television, Computers, and Family Life*. New York: Penguin, 2002.

NOTES

Preface

1. Pippa Norris, *Digital Divide* (Cambridge, England: Cambridge University Press, 2001), p. 4.

2. Manuel Castells, *The Power of Identity* (Oxford, England: Blackwell, 1997), p. 2.

3. James Howard Kunstler, *Home from Nowhere: Remaking Our Everyday World for the 21st Century* (New York: Simon & Schuster, 1996), pp. 299–300.

4. Robert D. Putnam, *Bowling Alone: The Collapse and Revival of American Community* (New York: Simon & Schuster, 2000), p. 26.

5. Ben H. Bagdikian, *The Information Machines* (New York: Harper & Row, 1971), p. 1.

6. Marie Winn, *The Plug-in Drug: Television, Computers, and Family Life* (New York: Penguin, 2002), p. x.

7. Lelia Green, *Communication, Technology and Society* (Thousand Oaks, CA: Sage, 2002), p. 150.

8. Fair use involves the purpose and character of the use (commercial vs. educational), the nature of the copyrighted work (published vs. unpublished), the amount and substantiality of the portion used in relation to the copyrighted work as a whole (qualitative vs. quantitative), and the effect of the use on the potential market or value of the copyrighted work (adverse vs. no effect). See *The First Amendment Handbook*, 6th ed. (Arlington, VA: The Reporters Committee for Freedom of the Press, 2003), p. 91.

9. Laura J. Gurak, *Cyberliteracy: Navigating the Internet with Awareness* (New Haven, CT: Yale University Press, 2001), p. 162.

10. Ibid., p. 162.

Introduction

11. Parker J. Palmer, *The Company of Strangers* (New York: Crossroad, 1981), p. 39.

12. Ibid., p. 48.

13. Ibid., p. 21.

14. Palmer noted a disturbing trend in physical habitat to shield one's self from contact with others, driving alone in cars to work, parking in underground garages and working in cubicles apart from the public, returning home in isolation and then watching television alone in an empty house. See Ibid., p. 21.

15. According to Robert D. Putnam, author of *Bowling Alone: The Collapse and Revival of American Community* (New York: Simon & Schuster, 2000), civic virtue is closely related to "social capital," whose vitality requires a dense network of reciprocal social relations: "A society of many virtuous but isolated individuals is not necessarily rich in social capital," p. 19.

16. Trust is a key component of community involvement. The "civically disengaged," according to Robert D. Putnam, tend to be less open and honest with others, believing themselves to be surrounded by adversaries. (See Putnam, p. 137.)

17. Everette E. Dennis and John C. Merrill, *Media Debates: Great Issues for the Digital Age* (Belmont, CA: Wadsworth, 2002), p. 34.

18. Ibid., p. 34.

19. "What some news organizations promise," AOL Time Warner Mission Statement; retrieved October 24, 2003, from the World Wide Web http://www.journalism.org/resources/tools/citizens/promises.asp?from=citizens.

20. Microsoft: Living Our Values; retrieved December 4, 2001, from the World Web http://www.microsoft.com/mscorp/values.htm. As of October 2003, Microsoft had changed its mission statement, relegating "community" to this statement: "showing leadership in supporting the communities in which we work and live." In explaining the change in its value system, Microsoft noted the following: "Over the last three decades, technology has transformed the way we work, play, and communicate. Today, we access information and people from around the world in an instant. Groundbreaking technologies have opened the door to innovations in every field of human endeavor, delivering new opportunity, convenience, and value to our lives. Since its founding in 1975, Microsoft has been a leader in this transformation. As a reflection of that role—and to help us focus on the opportunities that lie ahead—we have established and embraced a new corporate mission." The updated values and mission statement were retrieved from the Web at this URL: http://www.microsoft.com/mscorp/mission/. Curiously, one of the few remaining archives of the older mission statement could be found in an Australian telecommunications site, Span, at this URL: http://www.span.net.au/s04p41m18.htm.

21. Theodore Roszak, *The Cult of Information* (Berkeley, CA: University of California Press, 1994), p. 11.

22. "New industries spring up to help us balance our lives," *Sacramento Bee*, reprinted in (NY) *Times Herald-Record*, May 15, 2004, p. 37.

23. Ibid., p. xiv.

24. Paschal Preston, *Reshaping Communications* (Thousand Oaks, CA: Sage, 2001), p. 243.

25. James W. Chesebro and Dale A. Bertelsen, *Analyzing Media: Communication Technologies as Symbolic and Cognitive Systems* (New York: Guilford Press, 1996), p. 7.

26. Andrew Feenberg, *Questioning Technology* (London: Routledge and Kegan Paul, 1999), p. 220.

Chapter One

27. James Howard Kunstler, *The Geography of Nowhere* (New York: Simon & Schuster, 1994), p. 114.

28. "81 Million TV Sets in America Receive Programming Exclusively from Free, Over-the-Air Television," National Association of Broadcasters news release; retrieved October 16, 2003, from the World Wide Web http://www.nab.org/Newsroom/PressRel/Releases/5401.htm.

29. "What digital divide?" by Sonia Arrison, Pacific Research Insitute; retrieved October 18, 2003, from the World Wide Web http://www.pacific research.org/pub/ecp/2002/epolicy03–13.html.

30. "Disposition and End-of-Life Options for Personal Computers," H. Scott Matthews et al., Carnegie Mellon University; retrieved October 16, 2003, from the World Wide Web: http://www.ce.cmu.edu/GreenDesign/comprec/NEWREPORT.PDF.

31. Howard Rheingold writes in the 2000 edition of *The Virtual Community: Homesteading on the Electronic Frontier*: "I must therefore reconsider and retract the words I originally published here in 1993. I owe it to my critics . . . [for noting] that I clearly proclaimed nostalgia for community" p. 362. He poses questions about virtual community on p. 363.

32. Laura J. Gurak, *Cyberliteracy: Navigating the Internet with Awareness* (New Haven, CT: Yale University Press, 2001), p. 146.

33. Ibid., p. 147.

34. Juliet B. Schor, *The Overworked American: The Unexpected Decline of Leisure* (New York: Basic Books, 1992), p. 1.

35. Ibid., p. 23.

36. Robert D. Putnam, *Bowling Alone: The Collapse and Revival of American Community* (New York: Simon & Schuster, 2000), p. 223.

37. Schor, *The Overworked American*, p. 119.

38. John O'Shaughnessy and Nicholas Jackson O'Shaughnessy, *The Marketing Power of Emotion* (New York: Oxford University Press, 2003), p. 108.

39. Ibid., p. 86.

40. Kunstler, *The Geography of Nowhere*, p. 167.

41. Herbert Jack Rotfeld, *Adventures in Misplaced Marketing* (Westport, CT: Quorum, 2001), p. 200.

42. James Howard Kunstler, *Home from Nowhere*, p. 22.

43. "About Sprawl-Busters"; retrieved November 23, 2001, from the World Wide Web http://www.sprawl-busters.com/aboutsb.html.

44. See http://www.sprawl-busters.com/slamdunk.html; retrieved December 26, 2002, from the World Wide Web.

45. Telephone interview conducted April 14, 2003.

46. Ibid.

47. "The Media and Entertainment World of Online Consumers," Arbitron; retrieved January 15, 2003, from the World Wide Web http://www.arbitron.com/downloads/I9Presentation.pdf.

48. Putnam, *Bowling Alone*, p. 63.

49. Gene I. Rochlin, *Trapped in the Net: The Unanticipated Consequences of Computerization* (Princeton, N. J: University of Princeton Press, 1997), p. 88.

50. "The Deserted Library: As Students Work Online, Reading Rooms Empty Out—Leading Some Campuses to Add Starbucks," by Scott Carlson, *The Chronicle of Higher Education*, November 16, 2001, p. A35. Also available on-line; retrieved October 29, 2003, from the World Wide Web http://chronicle.com/prm/weekly/v48/i12/12a03501.htm.

51. "Amazon.com: Forget Being Earth's Superstore. Can It Turn a Profit?" by Lee Barney, December 18, 2000, TheStreet.com; retrieved December 5, 2002, from the World Wide Web http://www.thestreet.com/funds/gutcheck/1215763.html.

52. "Amazon halts expansion, eyes subletting space," by Dan Richman, July 13, 2001, *Seattle Post Intelligencer*; retrieved November 20, 2001, from the World Wide Web http://seattlepi.nwsource.com/business/31107_amazon13.shtml.

53. This is particularly true in the bookstore business, especially when books and journals are digitized, requiring databanks—information *about* information—which a bookstore owner also must pay to tap. Moreover, most people assume that digitized resources are more cost-effective than books and journals—a fallacy that causes problems in state and college libraries. In "The Deserted Library," Scott Carlson quotes Mark Y. Herring, dean of library services at Winthrop University, who notes that electronic resources are far more expensive than most people believe. Only some 6 percent of academic journals are available online, Herring observes; however, many state boards and officials seem to believe students can get anything online. "We have someone on the state commission on higher education in South Carolina who says, We don't need any more libraries—we're going to buy one book and start beaming it out to all universities," Mr. Herring says. "Well, that shows a fundamental lack of understanding about how this works. . . . If we digitized our collection, it would reach half-a-billion dollars." From "The Deserted Library: As Students Work Online, Reading Rooms Empty Out—Leading Some Campuses to Add Starbucks"

by Scott Carlson, *The Chronicle of Higher Education*, 16 November 2001, p. A35.

54. Herbert Jack Rotfeld, *Adventures in Misplaced Marketing*, p. 31.

55. Theodore Roszak, *The Cult of Information* (Berkeley, CA: University of California Press, 1994), p. 207.

56. John O'Shaughnessy and Nicholas Jackson O'Shaughnessy, *The Marketing Power of Emotion*, p. 5.

57. Dinesh D'Souza, *The Virtue of Prosperity: Finding Values in an Age of Techno-Affluence* (New York: The Free Press, 2000), p. 189.

58. Lelia Green, *Communication, Technology and Society* (Thousand Oaks, CA: Sage, 2002), p. 75.

59. Ibid., p. 75.

60. Nicholas Negroponte, *Being Digital* (New York: Vintage, 1996), p. 154.

61 Haynes Johnson, "News and the 21st Century: A Winding Road Leads to Training" in *Newsroom Training: Where's the Investment: A Study for the Council of Presidents of National Journalism Organizations* (Miami: Knight Foundation, 2002), p. 59.

62. Ibid.

63. See "Professor George Smoot" biography, *Current Biography* (Vol. 55, No. 4 April 1994); retrieved December 26, 2002 from the World Wide Web http://aether.lbl.gov/www/personnel/Smoot-bio.html.

64. Rheingold, *The virtual community*, p. 313.

65. "Scott McNealy: Privacy Advocate," by Richard Smith, June 18, 2001; retrieved September 12, 2001, from the World Wide Web http://www.privacyfoundation.org/commentary/tipsheet.asp.

66. Tim Berners-Lee, *Weaving the Web* (San Francisco: HarperSanFrancisco, 1999), pp. 143–44.

67. Jill Andresky Fraser, *White-Collar Sweatshop: The Deterioration of Work and Its Rewards in Corporate America* (New York: Norton, 2001), p. 10.

Chapter Two

68. James Howard Kunstler, *The Geography of Nowhere* (New York: Simon & Schuster, 1994), p. 167.

69. Dalai Lama, *Ethics for the New Millennium* (New York: Riverhead Books, 1999), p. 8.

70. Dietrich Bonhoeffer, *Writings Selected*, ed. by Robert Coles (Maryknoll, NY: Orbis, 1998), p. 100.

71. Ibid, p. 118.

72. Matt Ridley, *The Origins of Virtue: Human Instincts and the Evolution of Cooperation* (New York: Penguin, 1996), p. 6.

73. Ibid.

74. Simon Blackburn, *Being Good: A Short Introduction to Ethics* (Oxford: Oxford University Press, 2001), p. 43.

75. Ram Dass, *Still Here: Embracing Aging, Changing, and Dying* (New York: Riverhead, 2000), p. 108.

76. John O'Shaughnessy and Nicholas Jackson O'Shaughnessy, *The Marketing Power of Emotion* (New York: Oxford University Press, 2003), p. 1.

77. Jill Andresky Fraser, *White-Collar Sweatshop: The Deterioration of Work and Its Rewards in Corporate America* (New York: Norton, 2001), p. 13.

78. James Howard Kunstler, *Home from Nowhere: Remaking Our Everyday World for the 21st Century* (New York: Simon & Schuster, 1996), p. 21.

79. Albert Einstein, *Ideas and Opinions* (New York: Wings Books, 1954), pp. 53–54.

80. "Jen," by Richard Hooker, Washington State University's *World Civilization China Glossary*; retrieved August 19, 2000, from the World Wide Web http://www.wsu.edu:8000/~dee/GLOSSARY/JEN.HTM.

81. Ram Dass, *Still Here*, p. 81.

82. Paul Davies, *The Mind of God* (New York: Simon & Schuster, 1992), p. 16.

83. The Universal Declaration of Human Rights, adopted and proclaimed by General Assembly resolution 217 A (III) of 10 December 1948; retrieved December 26, 2002, from the World Wide Web http://www.un.org/Overview/rights.html.

84. "A Contarian Future for Minds and Machines" by Selmer Bringsjord, *The Chronicle Review*, 3 November 2000, p. B5. Also see Theodore Roszak's *The Cult of Information* (Berkeley, CA: University of California Press, 1994), pp 120–121, in which he demystifies technological intelligence by reducing them to their primitive logical building blocks:

> *This* is the same as *that*; put these together.
> *This* is not the same as *that*; put *this* someplace else.
> If *this* is so, then *that* is so; move right along.
> If *this* is so, then *that* is not so; *that* can be eliminated.
> Either *this* or *that*; make a choice.

85. Nielsen Media Research. (1999, May). *TV Viewing in Internet Households* [Report]; retrieved August 19, 2000 from the World Wide Web http://www.nielsenmedia.com/reports/tvandinternet.html. Note: While each viewer typically only watches 13 channels, those channels vary from viewer to viewer.

86. "Television Viewing Patterns—1999," a report by Myers Research, p. 1: Myers Research (1999, September); retrieved August 19, 2000, from the World Wide Web http://www.myersreport.com/tvp.html.

87. Ibid.

88. Nielsen Media Research (1999, May).

89. Ibid.

90. Howard Gardner, *Leading Minds* (New York: Basic Books, 1995), pp. 298–99.

91. Such popular media as *First for Women*, a leading newsstand magazine, quote self-help experts regularly on handling office stress. In "Handle Difficult Co-workers," in the 19 November 2001 issue, readers are told to "be direct," "see the other side," "find common ground," and "then let go" (p. 80), counseling readers to visit "stresscure.com" for more information—an all too common remedy that is part of the disease in the wired workplace.

92. Mihaly Csikszentmihalyi, *Flow: The Psychology of Optimal Experience* (New York: Harper Perennial, 1990), p. 21.

Chapter Three

93. New York Community Trust; retrieved December 11, 2002, from the World Wide Web: http://www.nycommunitytrust.org. An example of the importance of such trusts is "The September 11th Fund," which received $510 million and granted $341 million for cash assistance and services, recovery efforts, and support to rebuild communities in New York City and Washington, DC. The trust used the remaining $170 million to provide "mental health counseling, employment assistance, health care, legal and financial advice, cash assistance, and help for school children, small businesses and nonprofits."

94. Robert D. Putnam, *Bowling Alone: The Collapse and Revival of American Community* (New York: Simon & Schuster, 2000), p. 176.

95. Gerry Lange and Todd Domke, *Cain & Abel at Work* (New York: Broadway Books, 2001), p. 151.

96. Iyanla Vanzant, *Yesterday, I Cried: Celebrating the Lessons of Living and Loving* (New York: Fireside, 2000), p. 21.

97. Kenneth Burke, *A Grammar of Motives* (Berkeley, CA: University of California Press, 1969), p. 113.

98. Steven A. Beebe, Susan J. Beebe, and Mark Redmond, *Interpersonal Communication: Relating to Others* (Boston: Allyn and Bacon, 2002), pp. 382–83.

99. James Howard Kunstler, *The Geography of Nowhere* (New York: Simon & Schuster, 1994), p. 275.

100. Putnam, *Bowling Alone*, p. 62.

101. Ibid., p. 91.

102. "Please turn off our radio before you read this," by Jeff Sallot, *The Globe and Mail*, 6 August 2001, p. 1.

103. "Work Incivility Rises," CBS News; retrieved June 1, 2001, from the World Wide Web http://www.cbsnews.com/stories/1999/08/12/national/main57921.shtml.

104. "Well, Excuse Me! ABCNEWS Poll Shows Many Think Manners Are Poor," by Gary Langer, ABC News; retrieved June 1, 2001, from the

World Wide Web http://more.abcnews.go.com/sections/living/DailyNews/manners_poll990517.html.

105. "Trouble Next Door," by Bryan Burrough, *Vanity Fair*, August 2001, p. 138.

106. "Technology versus Journalistic Responsibility," by Judith Marlane, *Media Ethics*, Fall 2000, p. 5.

107. *Newsroom Training: Where's the Investment: A Study for the Council of Presidents of National Journalism Organizations* (Miami: Knight Foundation, 2002), p. 47.

108. Manuel Castells, *The Power of Identity* (Oxford, England: Blackwell, 1997), p. 321.

109. James W. Chesebro and Dale A Bertelsen, *Analyzing Media: Communication Technologies as Symbolic and Cognitive Systems* (New York: Guilford Press, 1996), pp. 87–90.

110. Marie Winn, *The Plug-in Drug: Television, Computers, and Family Life* (New York: Penguin, 2002), p. 5.

111. Andrew F. Wood and Matthew J. Smith, *Online Communication: Linking Technology, Identity, & Culture* (Mahwah, NJ: Lawrence Erlbaum, 2001), p. xvii.

112. Ibid., p. 19.

113. James Howard Kunstler, *Home from Nowhere: Remaking Our Everyday World for the 21st Century* (New York: Simon & Schuster, 1996), p. 85.

114. Esther M. Sternberg, *The Balance Within: The Science Connecting Health and Emotions* (New York: W.H. Freeman, 2001), p. 149.

Chapter Four

115. James W Chesebro and Dale A Bertelsen note that the first oral language was formulated some 7,000 years ago and the first principles of phonetic alphabetic some 4,000 years ago in the Sinai and Canaan in 2000 B.C. See *Analyzing Media: Communication Technologies as Symbolic and Cognitive Systems* (New York: Guilford Press, 1996), p. 14.

116. Ibid., p. 17.

117. Andrew Feenberg, *Questioning Technology* (London: Routledge. 1999), pp. 183–84.

118. Manuel Castells, *The Power of Identity* (Oxford, England: Blackwell, 1997), p. 243.

119. Tom Standage, *The Victorian Internet* (New York: Berkeley, 1999), p. 211.

120. *The Associated Press—The First 50 Years*; retrieved September 26, 2000, from the World Wide Web http://www.ap.org/anniversary/nhistory/first.html.

121. Ibid.

122. Donald Shaw, Bradley J. Hamm, and Diana L. Knott, "Technologi-

cal Change, Agenda Challenge and Social Melding: Mass Media Studies and the Four Ages of Place, Class, Mass and Space," *Journalism Studies*, Vol. 1. No. 1, 2000, p. 57.

123. Martin Lindstrom, *Clicks, Bricks & Brands* (London: Kogan Page, 2001), p. 5.

124. "Westclox History"; retrieved October 26, 2003, from the World Wide Web http://clockhistory.com/westclox/company/ads/benseries/bigintro.htm.

125. Juliet B. Schor, *The Overworked American: The Unexpected Decline of Leisure* (New York: Basic Books, 1992), p. 119.

126. Ben H. Bagdikian, *The Information Machines* (New York: Harper & Row, 1971), p. 161.

127. "A Slice of History," *Academic Computing Newsletter*, Fall 1998, Penn State University; retrieved October 29, 2003, from the World Wide Web http://www.psu.edu/cac/news/nlfa98/slice.html.

128. "Captain Midnight: The Premiums," Old Time Radio; retrieved September 20, 2000, from the World Wide Web http://www.otr.com/cm_premiums.html.

129. *Philadelphia Inquirer*, 1 November 1938, as cited in *Popular Writing in America*, Donald McQuade and Robert Atwan (New York: Oxford University Press), p. 127.

130. E.L. Boyer, *Ready to Learn: A Mandate for the Nation* (Princeton, NJ: The Carnegie Foundation for the Advancement of Teaching), p. 79.

131. "Children and Television Violence," by John P. Murray, *Kansas Journal of Law & Public Policy*, 1995, Vol. 4, No. 3, p. 7; retrieved September 20, 2000, from the World Wide Web http://www.nisbett.com/child-ent/children_and_television_violence.htm.

132. Robert D. Putnam, *Bowling Alone: The Collapse and Revival of American Community* (New York: Simon & Schuster, 2000), p. 221.

133. Pippa Norris, *Digital Divide* (Cambridge, England: Cambridge University Press, 2001), p. 28.

134. Bagdikian, *The Information Machines*, p. 229.

135. "Highlights of 1960," The Boomer Initiative; retrieved September 14, 2000, from the World Wide Web http://www.babyboomers.com/years/1960.htm.

136. David Halberstam, *The Fifties* (New York: Villard Books, 1993), p. 195.

137. For a retrospective of Congressional hearings on the impact of television, see "The Forgotten Battles: Congressional Hearings on Television Violence in the 1950s," by Keisha L. Hoerrner, *Web Journal of Mass Communication Research*, 2:3 June 1999; retrieved September 14, 2000, from the World Wide Web http://www.scripps.ohiou.edu/wjmcr/vol02/2–3a-B.htm.

138. "The Effects of Media Violence on Children," Jane Ledingham, C. Anne Ledingham, and John E. Richardson; retrieved October 29, 2003 from

the World Wide Web http://www.hc-sc.gc.ca/hppb/familyviolence/html/ nfntseffemediarech_e.html.

139. Herbert J. Gans, *Popular Culture & High Culture: An Analysis and Evaluation of Taste* (New York: Basic Books, 1999), p. 49.

140. Putnam, *Bowling Alone*, p. 62.

141. John Seabrook, *Nobrow: The Culture of Marketing, the Marketing of Culture* (New York: Vintage, 2001), pp. 152–53.

142. Manuel Castells, *The Power of Identity*, p. 356.

143. Hodding Carter III, Ohio University speech, 3 May 2002.

144. Ibid.

145. Brand Report, Ashton Brand Group, "Branding in the Technological Era," Volume X–Spring 2000; retrieved November 1, 2001, from the World Wide Web http://www.ashtonbg.com/brandreports/branding_tech_era1.html#Special.

Chapter Five

146. Theodore Roszak, *The Cult of Information* (Berkeley, CA: University of California Press, 1994), p. 8.

147. *Newsroom Training: Where's the Investment: A Study for the Council of Presidents of National Journalism Organizations* (Miami: Knight Foundation, 2002), p. 47.

148. Helen Thomas, *Front Row at the White House* (New York: Scribner, 1999), p. 381.

149. "The Third Kennedy–Nixon Debate," 13 October 1960; retrieved August 19, 2001, from the World Wide Web http://www.jfklibrary.org/60–3rd.htm.

150. Manuel Castells, *The Power of Identity* (Oxford, England: Blackwell, 1997), p. 318.

151. "The Third Kennedy–Nixon Debate," 13 October 1960.

152. Everette E. Dennis and John C. Merrill, *Media Debates: Great Issues for the Digital Age* (Belmont, CA: Wadsworth, 2002), p. 100.

153. Gene I. Rochlin writes in *Trapped in the Net: The Unanticipated Consequences of Computerization* (Princeton, NJ: Princeton University Press, 1997): "Like the computer, the automobile continues to nurture the mythic dimensions of autonomy and personal freedom. But that freedom lives mostly in the world of advertising, where vehicles are pictured on mountaintops instead of in traffic jams. What is not advertised are the costs and demands of the network of roads, highways, and the other elements needed to make the automobile useful," p. 48.

154. Pippa Norris, *Digital Divide* (Cambridge, England: Cambridge University Press, 2001), p. 11.

155. James Howard Kunstler, *The Geography of Nowhere* (New York: Simon & Schuster, 1994), p. 165.

156. Ibid.

157. Herbert J. Gans, *Popular Culture & High Culture: An Analysis and Evaluation of Taste* (New York: Basic Books, 1999), p. 43.

158. "Focus on the Household," by Jock Bickert, *Marketing Tools*, November/December 1995, p. 1; retrieved September 20, 2000, from the World Wide Web http://www.marketingtools.com/publications/mt/95_mt/9511_mt/mt389.htm.

159. Kenneth Burke, *A Rhetoric of Motives* (Berkeley, CA: University of California Press, 1969), p. 55.

160. See Martin Lindstrom, *Clicks, Bricks & Brands* (London: Kogan Page, 2001), p. 7.

161. Joseph Turow and Lilach Nir, *The Internet and the Family 2000*, Annenberg Public Policy Center report, p. 27.

162. "Captain Midnight: The Premiums," Old Time Radio; retrieved September 20, 2001, from the World Wide Web http://www.otr.com/cm_premiums.html.

163. Gerry Lange and Todd Domke, *Cain & Abel at Work* (New York: Broadway Books, 2001), p. 158.

164. Ibid., p. 3.

165. Ibid., p. 4.

166. "Is your TV set watching you?" by Jane Weaver, CNBC News; retrieved August 19, 2001, from the World Wide Web http://stacks.msnbc.com/news/592190.asp.

167. "Goodbye, bar codes; hello, transmitters within packages," by Emily Gersema, Associated Press, in the Des Moines Register, 20 July 2003, p. 2D. Also available on-line at the Prepaid Press; retrieved October 29, 2003, from the World Wide Web http://www.prepaidpress.com/archive/07-18-03/xtras03.htm.

168. "Scott McNealy: Privacy Advocate," by Richard Smith, Privacy Foundation; retrieved August 19, 2001, from the World Wide Web http://www.privacyfoundation.org/commentary/tipsheet.asp?id=44&action=0.

169. Howard Rheingold, *The Virtual Community: Homesteading on the Electronic Frontier* (Cambridge, MA: MIT Press, 2000), pp. 314–15.

170. "Sun on Privacy: 'Get Over It'" by Polly Sprenger; retrieved April 10, 2001, from the World Wide Web http://www.wired.com/news/politics/0,1283,17538,00.html.

171. Susan B. Barnes, *Computer-Mediated Communication: Human-to-Human Communication Across the Internet* (Boston: Allyn & Bacon, 2003), pp. 30–31.

172. Andrew Feenberg, *Questioning Technology* (London: Routledge. 1999), p. 99.

173. "The Mission and the Medium," The Knight Higher Education Collaborative, in *Perspectives*, July 2000, p. 3.

174. Dinesh D'Souza, *The Virtue of Prosperity: Finding Values in an Age of Techno-Affluence* (New York: The Free Press, 2000), p. 92.

175. "What parents should do if their children are on drugs"; retrieved October 29, 2003, from the World Wide Web http://www.antidrugs.8k.com/parents3.htm. Symptoms are taken from "For parents: Warning signs of substance abuse," by Michael Petracca, February 7, 2000, as reported on about.com.

176. Marie Winn, *The Plug-In Drug* (New York: Penguin, 1977), p. 25.

177. Theodore Roszak, *The Cult of Information*, p. xxxv.

178. "In the Lecture Hall, a Geek Chorus," by Lisa Guernsey, *New York Times*, 7 July 2003, p. E1. Also available online; retrieved October 29, 2003, from the World Wide Web http://www.nytimes.com/2003/07/24/technology/circuits/24mess.html?ex=1374379200&en=433abe96f0ff152c&ei=5007&partner=USERLAND

179. "The Culture of Technology on Campus," by Parker Snyder, *Journal of College and Character*; retrieved August 19, 2001, from the World Wide Web http://www.CollegeValues.org/reflections.cfm?id=77&a=1.

180. Ibid.

181. Ibid.

182. Mihaly Csikszentmihalyi, *Flow: The Psychology of Optimal Experience* (New York: Harper Perennial, 1990), p. 18.

183. "A Researcher Says That Professors Should Be Attentive to Students' Approaches to Learning," by Dan Carnevale, *The Chronicle of Higher Education*, 29 June 2001; retrieved October 24, 2001, from the World Wide Web http://www.chronicle.com/free/2001/06/2001062901u.htm.

184. Ibid.

185. Huston Smith, *Why Religion Matters* (San Francisco: HarperCollins, 2001), p. 82.

186. "Healing without the Human Touch," by Wallace Immen, *The Globe and Mail*, 7 August 2001, p. R5.

187. "Telemedicine Is Emerging As a Cost-Effective Healthcare Alternative," by Ernest D. Plock, U.S. Department of Commerce; retrieved November 28, 2001, from the World Wide Web http://www.technology.gov/digeconomy/30.htm.

188. "Next Frontiers," *Newsweek*, 25 June 2001, p. 50.

189. Statement for the Record of Louis J. Freeh, Director Federal Bureau of Investigation Before the Senate Committee on Judiciary Subcommittee for the Technology, Terrorism, and Government Information; retrieved October 24, 2001, from the World Wide Web: http://www.fbi.gov/congress/congress00/cyber032800.htm.

190. Ibid.

191. Ibid.

192. Tim Berners-Lee, *Weaving the Web* (San Francisco: HarperSanFrancisco, 1999), p. 144.

193. E-mail interview conducted October 31, 2000.

Chapter Six

194. Marshall McLuhan and Quentin Fiore, *The Medium Is the Massage: An Inventory of Effects* (San Francisco: HardWired, 1996 reprint), p. 67.

195. Theodore Roszak, *The Cult of Information* (Berkeley, CA: University of California Press, 1994), p. 149.

196. Ibid., 161.

197. Phillip Marchand, *Marshall McLuhan: The Medium and the Messenger* (New York: Ticknor & Fields, 1989), p. 57.

198. David F. Noble, *The Religion of Technology: The Divinity of Man and the Spirit of Invention* (New York: Penguin, 1997), p. 49.

199. Dinesh D'Souza, *The Virtue of Prosperity: Finding Values in an Age of Techno-Affluence* (New York: The Free Press, 2000), p. 178.

200. Ibid., p. 125.

201. Personal interview conducted May 3, 2001.

202. Neil Postman, *Technopoly: The Surrender of Culture to Technology* (New York: Vintage, 1993), pp. 14–15.

203. Ibid., p. 15.

204. Marshall McLuhan, *Understanding Media: The Extensions of Man* (Cambridge, MA: The MIT Press, 2002), p. 57.

205. Ibid., p. 61.

206. "The Playboy Interview: Marshall McLuhan," *Playboy*, March 1969, p. 61.

207. James W Chesebro and Dale A. Bertelsen, *Analyzing Media: Communication Technologies as Symbolic and Cognitive Systems* (New York: Guilford Press, 1996), p. 5.

208. Robert D. Putnam, *Bowling Alone: The Collapse and Revival of American Community* (New York: Simon & Schuster, 2000), p. 175.

209. "New Media Initiative" advertisement, *The Chronicle of Higher Education*, 23 March 2001, p. C34.

210. McLuhan and Fiore, *The Medium Is the Massage*, p. 14

211. Marchand, *Marshall McLuhan: The Medium and the Messenger*, p. 237.

212. "The Playboy Interview: Marshall McLuhan," p. 64.

213. Howard Rheingold, *Smart Mobs: The Next Social Revolution* (Cambridge, MA: Perseus, 2002), p. 71.

214. Gene I. Rochlin, *Trapped in the Net: The Unanticipated Consequences of Computerization* (Princeton, NJ: Princeton University Press, 1997), p. 37.

215. Personal interview September 17, 2002.

216. Tim Berners-Lee, *Weaving the Web* (San Francisco: Harper San Francisco, 1999), p. 133.

217. "AOL executive chides content developers," by John Motavalli, *Yahoo! Internet Life*, 19 June 1997; retrieved February 22, 2001, from the World Wide Web http://www.zdnet.com/zdnn/content/ylio/0619/ylio0001.html.

218. James Howard Kunstler, *Home from Nowhere: Remaking Our Everyday World for the 21st Century* (New York: Simon & Schuster, 1996), p. 23.

219. Marshall McLuhan and Quentin Fiore, *The Medium Is the Massage*, p. 68.

220. "AOL executive chides content developers."

221. Chesebro and Bertelsen, *Analyzing Media*, pp. 87–90.

222. Berners-Lee, *Weaving the Web*, p. 130.

223. "Back to the Future of Education: Real Teaching, Real Learning," by James Perley, *Commentary*, September/October 1999; retrieved February 22, 2001, from the World Wide Web http://horizon.unc.edu/TS/commentary/1999–09.asp.

224. "The Playboy Interview: Marshall McLuhan," p. 61.

225. Joseph Straubhaar and Robert LaRose, *Communications Media in the Information Society* (Belmont, CA: 1996), p. 290.

226. Ray Tomlinson is credited with inventing e-mail in 1971 on the ARPANET, the precursor to the Internet, whose roots date back to 1957, when the Soviet Union launched Sputnik. The U.S. Defense Department, in response, created the Advanced Research Projects Agency to establish military supremacy in science and technology. For more information, see "Pioneers of the Internet," by Margaret M. Knight, *Rensselaer Magazine*, September 2000; retrieved October 30, 2003, from the World Wide Web http://www.rpi.edu/dept/NewsComm/Magazine/Sep00/Pioneers.html.

227. Rochlin, *Trapped in the Net*, p. 17.

228. Noble, *The Religion of Technology*, p. 205.

229. Ibid., p. 206.

230. "The Playboy Interview: Marshall McLuhan," p. 72.

231. McLuhan and Fiore, *The Medium Is the Massage*, p. 16.

232. See Michel Crozier, Samuel P. Huntington and Joji Watanuki, *The Crisis of Democracy* (New York: New York University Press, 1975), p. 98.

233. According to a recent ABC News poll, Midwesterners, "renowned for their mild manners, in fact have the nation's highest rate of swearing in public, narrowly edging out Westerners. It's Southerners who're most apt to keep a civil tongue." See "Well, Excuse Me! ABCNEWS Poll Shows Many Think Manners Are Poor," by Gary Langer, ABC News; retrieved May 18, 2001, from the World Wide Web http://204.202.137.115/sections/living/DailyNews/manners_poll990517.html.

234. Personal interview Nov. 4, 2001.

235. "Wasted Time," ABCNews.com, August 7, 2001; retrieved October 30, 2003, from the World Wide Web http://more.abcnews.go.com/sections/living/dailynews/multitask010807.html.

236. Thomas Paine, *Common Sense*, 1776 (Mineola, NY: Dover, 1997), p. 25.

Chapter Seven

237. Theodore Roszak, *The Cult of Information* (Berkeley, CA: University of California Press, 1994), p. 13.

238. Kenneth Burke, *A Rhetoric of Motives* (Berkeley, CA: University of California Press, 1969), p. 261.

239. Howard Rheingold, *Smart Mobs: The Next Social Revolution* (Cambridge, MA Perseus, 2002), p. xxi.

240. Parker J. Palmer, *The Active Life: A Spirituality of Work, Creativity, and Caring* (San Francisco: Jossey-Bass, 1990), pp. 66–67.

241. Rheingold, *Smart Mobs*, p. 120.

242. John Seabrook, Nobrow: *The Culture of Marketing, the Marketing of Culture* (New York: Vintage, 2001), pp. 92–93.

243. Huston Smith, *Why Religion Matters* (San Francisco: HarperCollins, 2001), p. 19.

244. Joshua Meyrowitz, *No Sense of Place: The Impact of Electronic Media on Social Behavior* (New York: Oxford University Press, 1985), p. 104.

245. "Media Violence," American Academy of Pediatrics, policy statement, November 2001; retrieved October 30, 2003, from the World Wide Web http://www.aap.org/policy/re0109.html.

246. "Suicide and Suicide Attempts in Adolescents," American Academy of Pediatrics, April 2000; retrieved March 15, 2001, from the World Wide Web http://www.aap.org/policy/re9928.html.

247. "Media Violence," op. cit.

248. Jean M. Twenge, "College Students and the Web of Anxiety," *The Chronicle of Higher Education*, 13 July 2001, p. B14.

249. Ibid., p. B14.

250. Ibid., p. B14.

251. "Marketing to Children Harmful: Experts Urge Candidates to Lead Nation in Setting Limits," press release, Center for Media Education, 18 October 2000; retrieved March 15, 2001, from the World Wide Web http://www.cme.org/press/001018pr.html.

252. Hayden Carruth, "Poetry in a Discouraging Time: A Symposium," *The Georgia Review*, Winter 1981, p. 739.

253. Michael Real, *Exploring Media Culture* (Thousand Oaks, CA: Sage, 1996), pp. 79–80.

254. Martin Lindstrom, *Clicks, Bricks & Brands* (London: Kogan Page, 2001), p. 260.

255. "College students and computer, video and Internet games," Pew Internet & American Life, 6 July 2003; retrieved July 22, 2003, from the World Wide Web http://www.pewinternet.org/releases/release.asp?id=6.

256. "College students and computer, video and Internet games," Pew Internet & American Life.

257. Rheingold, *Smart Mobs*, p. 158.

258. "OU combats riots with education," by Matt Neznanski, *Ames Tribune*, April 24, 2004, p.1.

259. "Ames police continue to investigate Veishea riot," by Jason Kristufek, *Ames* (Iowa) *Tribune*, April 20, 2004, p. 1.

260. "Sex, Lies: What to Tell the Kids," by Putsata Reang and Susan Gilmore, *The Seattle Times*, 27 January 1998; retrieved March 15, 2001, from the World Wide Web http://seattletimes.nwsource.com/news/nation-world/html98/kids_012798.html.

261. "The Little Clintons," by Peggy Noonan, *Wall Street Journal*, 12 February 1999; retrieved October 30, 2003, from the World Wide Web http://www.peggynoonan.com/article.php?article=59.

262. Howard Gardner, Milhaly Csikszentmihalyi, and William Damon, *Good Work: When Excellence and Ethics Meet* (New York: Basic Books, 2001), p. 5.

263. Howard Rheingold, *Smart Mobs*, p. 184.

Chapter Eight

264. David Murray, Joel Schwartz, and S. Robert Lichter, *It Ain't Necessarily So: How Media Make and Unmake the Scientific Picture of Reality* (Lanham, Maryland: Rowman & Littlefield, 2001), p. 7.

265. Ibid., p. 188.

266. Clifford G. Christians, John P. Ferre, P. Mark Fackler. *Good News: Social Ethics & The Press* (New York: Oxford University Press, 1993), p. 14.

267. See Christina Hoff Sommers, "Teaching the Virtues," *Chicago Tribune Magazine* reprint, 12 September 1993, p. 16.

268. Howard Gardner, Milhaly Csikszentmihalyi, and William Damon, *Good Work: When Excellence and Ethics Meet* (New York: Basic Books, 2001), p. 125.

269. Ram Dass, *Still Here: Embracing Aging, Changing, and Dying* (New York: Riverhead, 2000), p. 18.

270. Esther M. Sternberg, *The Balance Within: The Science Connecting Health and Emotions* (New York: W.H. Freeman, 2001), p. 149.

271. Martin Lindstrom, *Clicks, Bricks & Brands* (London: Kogan Page, 2001), p. 149.

272. Parker J. Palmer, *The Active Life: A Spirituality of Work, Creativity, and Caring* (San Francisco: Jossey-Bass, 1990), p. 136.

273. "The Next Ruling Class," by David Brooks, *Atlantic Monthly*, April 2001, p. 45.

274. See Benjamin M. Compaine, Ed., *The Digital Divide: Facing a Crisis or Creating a Myth* (Cambridge, MA: MIT Press, 2001), p. 40: "Given the great advantages accruing to those who have access, it is not economically or socially prudent to idly await the day when most, if not all, homes can claim connectivity. Part of the short-term answer lies in providing Internet access at community access centers. . . ."

275. Pippa Norris, *Digital Divide* (Cambridge, England: Cambridge University Press, 2001), p. 26.

276. Donald W. Shriver, Jr., *An Ethic for Enemies* (New York: Oxford University Press, 1995), p. 36.

277. Albert Einstein, "Society and Personality," in *Ideas and Opinions* (New York: Crown, 1954) Wings Books reprint, p. 12.

278. Albert Einstein, "The World as I See It," in *Ideas and Opinions*, p. 8.

279. Ibid., p. 9.

280. Matthew Arnold, "Culture and Anarchy," *Selected Prose*, ed. P.J. Keating (New York: Penguin, 1982), p. 226.

281. Bill Moyers and Joseph Campbell, "Following Your Bliss," *Parabola*, Vol. 13, No. 2, p. 29.

282. Dalai Lama, *Ethics for the New Millennium* (New York: Riverhead Books, 1999), pp. 23–24.

Chapter Nine

283. Tim Berners-Lee, *Weaving the Web* (New York: HarperCollins, 1999), p. 206.

284. Paul Ekman, *Telling Lies* (New York: Norton, 2001), p. 125.

285. Ibid., p. 125.

286. Craig Smith, "The New Corporate Philanthropy," *Harvard Business Review*, May–June 1994, p. 108.

287. "Technology Causes Stress for Journalism Professors, Report Says," by Susannah Dainow, *The Chronicle of Higher Education*, 10 August 2001; retrieved August 19, 2001 from the World Wide Web http://www.chronicle.com/free/2001/08/2001081003t.htm.

288. Jill Andresky Fraser, *White-Collar Sweatshop: The Deterioration of Work and Its Rewards in Corporate America* (New York: Norton, 2001), p. 75.

289. "The Extent of Systematic Monitoring of Employee E-mail and Internet Use," by Andrew Schulman, Workplace Surveillance Project, 9 July 2001; retrieved October 30, 2003, from the World Wide Web http://www.sonic.net/~undoc/extent.htm.

290. Joseph Straubhaar and Robert LaRose, *Communications Media in the Information Society* (Belmont, CA: Wadsworth, 1996), p. 452.

291. Mihaly Csikszentmihalyi, *Flow: The Psychology of Optimal Experience* (New York: Harper Perennial, 1990), p. 162.

292. Esther M. Sternberg, *The Balance Within: The Science Connecting Health and Emotions* (New York: W.H. Freeman, 2001), p. 150.

293. The American Cancer Society operates an e-mail center allowing cancer patients and their families to receive quick, objective information from an information specialist or oncology nurse. The Society also hosts several discussion boards so that visitors can ask questions, exchange ideas and share stories. See: http://www.cancer.org/docroot/home/index.asp.

294. Joshua Meyrowitz, *No Sense of Place: The Impact of Electronic Media on Social Behavior* (New York: Oxford University Press, 1985), p. 9.

295. Paul Ekman, *Telling Lies*, p. 327.

296. Marie Winn, *The Plug-in Drug* (New York: Penguin, 2002), p. 158.

297. Howard Rheingold, *Smart Mobs: The Next Social Revolution* (Cambridge, MA: Perseus, 2002) p. 192.

298. Winn, *The Plug-in Drug*, p. 283.

299. Ibid., p. xii.

300. Marie Winn notes in *The Plug-In Drug* (2002) that a company named Channel One struck a Faustian bargain with a number of school districts in 1989, providing high-tech equipment to pump television into schools. The catch was, the class had to sit through two minutes of commercials. "It was a notable first in American education, the first breach in the educational stronghold by commercial interests," p. 117.

301. Ibid., p. 158.

BIBLIOGRAPHY

Arnold, Matthew. "Culture and Anarchy" in *Selected Prose*, ed. P.J. Keating. New York: Penguin, 1982.

Bagdikian, Ben H. *The Information Machines*. New York: Harper & Row, 1971.

Barnes, Susan B. *Computer-Mediated Communication: Human-to-Human Communication Across the Internet*. Boston: Allyn & Bacon, 2003.

Beebe, Steven A., Beebe, Susan J., and Redmond, Mark. *Interpersonal Communication: Relating to Others*. Boston: Allyn and Bacon, 2002.

Berners-Lee, Tim. *Weaving the Web*. San Francisco: HarperSanFrancisco, 1999.

Blackburn, Simon. *Being Good: A Short Introduction to Ethics*. Oxford: Oxford University Press, 2001.

Bonhoeffer, Dietrich. *Writings Selected*, ed. by Robert Coles. Maryknoll, NY: Orbis, 1998.

Boyer, E.L. *Ready to Learn: A Mandate for the Nation*. Princeton, NJ: The Carnegie Foundation for the Advancement of Teaching.

Burke, Kenneth. *A Grammar of Motives*. Berekley, CA: University of California Press, 1969.

———. *A Rhetoric of Motives*. Berkeley, CA: University of California Press, 1969.

Castells, Manuel. *The Power of Identity*. Oxford, England: Blackwell, 1997.

Chesebro, James W. and Bertelsen, Dale A. *Analyzing Media: Communication Technologies as Symbolic and Cognitive Systems*. New York: Guilford Press, 1996.

Christians, Clifford G., Ferre, John P., Fackler, P. Mark. *Good News: Social Ethics & The Press*. New York: Oxford University Press, 1993.

Compaine, Benjamin M., Ed. *The Digital Divide: Facing a Crisis or Creating a Myth*. Cambridge, MA: MIT Press, 2001.

Crozier, Michel, Huntington, Samuel P., and Watanuki, Joji. *The Crisis of Democracy*. New York: New York University Press, 1975.

Csikszentmihalyi, Mihaly. *Flow: The Psychology of Optimal Experience*. New York: Harper Perennial, 1990.

D'Souza, Dinesh. *The Virtue of Prosperity: Finding Values in an Age of Techno-affluence.* New York: The Free Press, 2000.

Dalai Lama. *Ethics for the New Millennium.* New York: Riverhead Books, 1999.

Dass, Ram. *Still Here: Embracing Aging, Changing, and Dying.* New York: Riverhead, 2000.

Davies, Paul. *The Mind of God.* New York: Simon & Schuster, 1992.

Dennis, Everette E. and Merrill, John C. *Media Debates: Great Issues for the Digital Age.* Belmont, CA: Wadsworth, 2002.

Einstein, Albert. *Ideas and Opinions.* New York: Wings Books, 1954.

Ekman, Paul. *Telling Lies.* New York: Norton, 2001.

Feenberg, Andrew. *Questioning Technology.* London: Routledge and Kegan Paul, 1999.

Fraser, Jill Andresky. *White-Collar Sweatshop: The Deterioration of Work and Its Rewards in Corporate America.* New York: Norton, 2001.

Gans, Herbert J. *Popular Culture & High Culture: An Analysis and Evaluation of Taste.* New York: Basic Books, 1999.

Gardner, Howard. *Leading Minds.* New York: Basic Books, 1995.

Gardner, Howard, Csikszentmihalyi, Mihaly, and Damon, William. *Good Work: When Excellence and Ethics Meet.* New York: Basic Books, 2001.

Green, Lelia. *Communication, Technology and Society.* Thousand Oaks, CA: Sage, 2002.

Gurak, Laura J. *Cyberliteracy: Navigating the Internet with Awareness.* New Haven, CT: Yale University Press, 2001.

Halberstam, David. *The Fifties.* New York: Villard Books, 1993.

Kunstler, James Howard. *Home from Nowhere: Remaking Our Everyday World for the 21st Century.* New York: Simon & Schuster, 1996.

———. *The Geography of Nowhere.* New York: Simon & Schuster, 1994.

Lange, Gerry and Domke, Todd. *Cain & Abel at Work.* New York: Broadway Books, 2001.

Lindstrom, Martin. *Clicks, Bricks & Brands.* London: Kogan Page, 2001.

Marchand, Phillip. *Marshall McLuhan: The Medium and the Messenger.* New York: Ticknor & Fields, 1989.

McLuhan, Marshall and Fiore, Quentin. *The Medium Is the Massage: An Inventory of Effects.* San Francisco: HardWired, 1996 reprint.

McLuhan, Marshall. *Understanding Media: The Extensions of Man.* Cambridge, MA: MIT Press, 2002.

Meyrowitz, Joshua. *No Sense of Place: The Impact of Electronic Media on Social Behavior.* New York: Oxford University Press, 1985.

Murray, David, Schwartz, Joel, and Lichter, S. Robert. *It Ain't Necessarily So: How Media Make and Unmake the Scientific Picture of Reality.* Lanham, MD: Rowman & Littlefield, 2002.

Negroponte, Nicholas. *Being Digital.* New York: Vintage, 1996.

Noble, David F. *The Religion of Technology: The Divinity of Man and the Spirit of Invention.* New York: Penguin, 1997.

Norris, Pippa. *Digital Divide.* Cambridge, England: Cambridge University Press. 2001.

O'Shaughnessy, John and O'Shaughnessy, Nicholas Jackson. *The Marketing Power of Emotion.* New York: Oxford University Press, 2003.

Paine, Thomas. *Common Sense,* 1776. Mineola, NY: Dover, 1997.

Palmer, Parker J. *The Active Life: A Spirituality of Work, Creativity, and Caring.* San Francisco: Jossey-Bass, 1990.

———. *The Company of Strangers.* New York: Crossroad, 1981.

Postman, Neil. *Technopoly: The Surrender of Culture to Technology.* New York: Vintage, 1993.

Preston, Paschal. *Reshaping Communications.* Thousand Oaks, CA: Sage, 2001.

Putnam, Robert D. *Bowling Alone: The Collapse and Revival of American Community.* New York: Simon & Schuster, 2000.

Real, Michael. *Exploring Media Culture.* Thousand Oaks, CA: Sage, 1996.

Rheingold, Howard. *Smart Mobs: The Next Social Revolution.* Cambridge, MA: Perseus, 2002.

———. *The Virtual Community: Homesteading on the Electronic Frontier.* Cambridge, MA: MIT Press, 2000.

Ridley, Matt. *The Origins of Virtue: Human Instincts and the Evolution of Cooperation.* New York: Penguin, 1996.

Rochlin, Gene I. *Trapped in the Net: The Unanticipated Consequences of Computerization.* Princeton, NJ: University of Princeton Press, 1997.

Roszak , Theodore. *The Cult of Information.* Berkeley, CA: University of California Press, 1994.

Rotfeld, Herbert Jack. *Adventures in Misplaced Marketing.* Westport, CT: Quorum, 2001.

Schor, Juliet B. *The Overworked American: The Unexpected Decline of Leisure.* New York: Basic Books, 1992.

Seabrook, John. *Nobrow: The Culture of Marketing, the Marketing of Culture.* New York: Vintage, 2001.

Shriver, Donald W., Jr. *An Ethic for Enemies.* New York: Oxford, 1995.

Smith, Huston. *Why Religion Matters.* San Francisco: HarperCollins, 2001.

Standage, Tom. *The Victorian Internet.* New York: Berkeley, 1999.

Sternberg, Esther M. *The Balance Within: The Science Connecting Health and Emotions.* New York: W.H. Freeman, 2001.

Straubhaar, Joseph and LaRose, Robert. *Communications Media in the Information Society* Belmont, CA: Wadsworth, 1996.

Thomas, Helen. *Front Row at the White House.* New York: Scribner, 1999.

Vanzant, Iyanla. *Yesterday, I Cried: Celebrating the Lessons of Living and Loving.* New York: Fireside, 2000.

Williams, Tannis MacBeth. *The Impact of Television: A Natural Experiment in Three Communities*. New York: Academic Press, 1986.

Winn, Marie. *The Plug-In Drug*. New York: Penguin, 1977.

———. *The Plug-In Drug*. New York: Penguin, 2002.

Wood, Andrew F. and Smith, Matthew. *Online Communication: Linking Technology, Identity, & Culture*. Mahwah, NJ: Lawrence Erlbaum, 2001.

INDEX